THE LONGEST DRIVE

Circle City, Alaska
to Ushuaia, Argentina

The Longest Drive

David A. Humphries

Victoria, British Columbia, Canada
2020

ISBN 978-1-77835-368-0 (paperback)
ISBN 978-1-77835-369-7 (e-book)

Author & Publisher: David A. Humphries
Book Design: Arifin Graham, Alaris Design
Copy Editor: David Greer
Photography: Margarita Humphries

Dedications

And o'er the hills, and far away
Beyond their utmost purple rim,
Beyond the night, across the day,
Thro' all the world she follow'd him.
—Tennyson

This book is dedicated to my wife Margaret (Margarita) who has been everything to me since we married. Without her, this epic journey would never have been attempted, would never have succeeded, and this book would never have been written. Simple as that.

It is also dedicated to our three children Lisa, Martin, and Rick, and to their children. I hope it inspires someone, someday, somewhere, to tackle something that initially appears unachievable, or perhaps something a little out of step with the norm.

continued ...

This book is also dedicated to the older reader. For you, I give two things. First, a quote from Tennyson's poem *Ulysses*:

Come, my friends,
'Tis not too late to seek a newer world.
Push off, and sitting well in order smite
The sounding furrows; for my purpose holds
To sail beyond the sunset, and the baths
Of all the western stars, until I die.
It may be that the gulfs will wash us down:
It may be we shall touch the Happy Isles,
And see the great Achilles, whom we knew.
Though much is taken, much abides; and though
We are not now that strength which in old days
Moved earth and heaven; that which we are, we are;
One equal temper of heroic hearts,
Made weak by time and fate, but strong in will
To strive, to seek, to find, and not to yield.

And second, I give you my father-in-law, Dick Moreno, a man both positive and encouraging and a man who personifies that Spanish expression "nunca te rindas" (don't ever give up).

Dick Moreno: Parasailing in Mexico, age 99 and 49 weeks. "He was just a speck in the sky." As I write, Dick is 102 and counting.

Table of Contents

Glossary

adobe: Bricks made of mud and straw

aduana: Customs

asado: Social event; meats on a grill: chorizo, ribs, steak, intestine, flank steak, and more

B.A.: Buenos Aires

boliche: Little general store selling dry goods, bottles of wine, sometimes a post office

bucks: Canadian dollars

caldo: Hot

calle: Street

cerrado: Closed

chacra: Small ranch or farm

claro: Of course, clearly

cojones: Balls, testicles

cordillera: Andean mountain range, often parallel ranges with intervening plateau region

dollars: American

estancia: Large ranch raising sheep and cattle.

far out: Great, cool

gaucho: Farmhand, horse-breaker, expert horseman, Argentine cowboy

groovy: Excellent, amazing

lago: Lake

lamb: A sheep less than a year old

league: English measurement, 4.83 kilometres (three miles)

Mauser: Repeating rifle

moula: Money

peones: People who do menial tasks; unskilled labourers

rio: River

SWAT: Special weapons and tactics law enforcement unit using specialized military equipment and tactics in the U.S.A.

viejo: Old

FEDERACION INTERAMERICANA DE
TOURING Y AUTOMOVIL CLUBES

CARNET DE PRESENTACION
INTRODUCTION CARD

Emitido a: Mr. David Albert
Issued to: HUMPHRIES

Socio del: CAA-British Columbia
Member of: Auto. Assoc.-Victoria

Emitido por: Canadian Automobile
Issued by: Association

Fecha: 17 June 1976
Date:

GENERAL MANAGER

Sello y firma del Club emisor
Seal and signature of issuing Club

CANADIAN AUTOMOBILE ASSOCIATION

PART I

VICTORIA, B.C. TO CIRCLE CITY, ALASKA

Circle City
Fairbanks
Dawson City
Whitehorse
Haines
Dawson Creek
Prince Rupert
CANADA
Victoria
San Francisco
USA
San Diego
Tucson
San Carlos
Mazatlan
Mexico City
MEXICO
PANAMA
San Salvador
EL SALVADOR
Colón
Panama City
Buenaventura
Bogota
COLOMBIA
Cali
ECUADOR
Quito
Tumbes
PERU
Cuzco
Lima
La Paz
Nazca
Arequipa
Tacna
BOLIVIA
Santiago
CHILE
ARGENTINA
Orsorno
Bariloche
Perito Moreno
El Calafate
Punta Delgada
Ushuaia

WHEN I WAS IN MAQUINCHAO

"Dick," I said to my future Argentine father-in-law, "I think my landlord may be a Nazi."

"You mean that guy Kruger I saw outside your place yesterday?" Dick replied.

"Yes," I answered, "but how'd you know his name?"

"Well," Dick explained, "it's been over twenty years, but I remember him. He's ten years younger than me and was a porter and waiter at the Hotel Tunquelen in Bariloche, where we lived. I didn't know him well but understood he came from Switzerland. Well, of course, all local Germans seemed to be from there, if you know what I mean. Anyway, he disappeared sometime in the early to mid-fifties."

"Dick," I said, "last month I went to his main floor apartment with Margaret to pay my rent and asked if he could get me a better bed. He said he'd get one from another place he had down the road. He had an accent so I asked where he was from and he said 'Bariloche, a little town in Argentina.' Well, Margaret spoke up immediately and said that's where she grew up. Now Kruger and his wife Gerta, who was standing right there, were clearly stunned to find Margaret was from the same town. I mean, there are few Argentines here, and certainly none from Bariloche. But the usual follow-up questions expected like 'Where did you live in Bariloche?' or 'When did you come to Victoria?' never came. Instead, he took my cheque, said he'd get the bed later that day, and then closed his door. I found that very strange.

"Anyway, now kind of curious, I searched the title to where I'm renting on Rockland at the Land Title Office. The title showed they bought it back in 1967 so they were the owners and not just caretakers. Then, as I was already there, I thought I may as well do a name search to see what else Helmut and Gerta owned. Sure enough, they owned another house closer to town on Rockland and where he was getting that bed. I drove past it the next day on the way to work. It's another huge old mansion that's been converted to probably a dozen suites. The lot looks about one hundred metres deep. They bought that one back in 1957."

"Well, there you go," said Dick. "I couldn't believe my eyes seeing him at your place. Now how can a forty-five or so year old German porter from little Bariloche come to Victoria and in two or three years buy an enormous mansion? And if that isn't ridiculous enough, you're telling me that he also owns that converted mansion where you're renting? That place must have another nine or more rental units. You're probably right. Their money must have come from connections from the war, or maybe from a Swiss bank account, or maybe money from the sale of confiscated Jewish treasures, something like that."

"Dick," I asked, "If he was a Nazi, exactly how would he have escaped and reached Argentina in the first place?"

"Well," Dick replied, "I think one of three ways. The first is a well-known story. In 1940, the German pocket battleship, *Graf Spee*, was sinking merchant ships in the South Atlantic. The British figured it would soon attack South American shipping lines needed for the war effort, so they put three cruisers off Buenos Aires and waited. Sure enough, the *Graf Spee* appeared, and a terrific battle took place. The British had the smaller guns but still managed to inflict some hull damage, so the *Spee's* captain headed for the port of Montevideo in Uruguay for repairs.

"Now the captain, Langsdorm or Lang something, yeh, Langsdorff, that's who it was, Kapitän Langsdorff. Anyway, he cabled

Hitler and Hitler told him to scuttle the *Spee* if trapped. So on December 17th, and I remember the date exactly because that's Uncle Herbert's birthday, the *Graf Spee* left Montevideo and joined up with two Argentine tugs. Langsdorff then transferred his crew to the tugs and blew up his ship. Then he went back to Montevideo and sat around for a few days and probably getting quite depressed. So what does he do? He pulls out a large German flag and lays it on the floor. Then he lies down, puts a Luger to his head, and blows his brains all over the room. Same as Hitler did five years later. Many of the ship's crew remained in Argentina. They would have been just regular Germans though and not the higher-ups, so wouldn't have been able to do much looting. I think that possibility is out.

"The second way he could have reached Argentina was on one of the two German subs that landed at Mar del Plata after the war ended. And there were always rumours of other subs secretly landing, and then being scuttled farther south in the province of Santa Cruz. People always talked about Hitler coming to Argentina in one of those subs. That's probably nonsense but makes a good story. Subs are a possibility, though.

"The best possibility for Nazis with stolen money and Jewish valuables and all that, and escaping to Argentina, were on routes set up through the Vatican and with President Perón's assistance. Perón was a big Nazi supporter until he changed sides just before World War II ended. I read that thousands of Nazis got to South America that way at the end of the war. No, he sounds like he was a Nazi, that's for sure. You should follow this up."

Dick had a lot of good stories of life in the Argentine, and I listened to them all. I also kept taking out his daughter. Margaret and I married four months later and life began its predictable course–house, mortgage, child, life insurance, followed by larger house, larger mortgage, second child, and more life insurance. The sequence was unpredictable, but there was no denying the predictability of the events themselves. Life was becoming very secure. It was also becoming very boring. My late twenties were soon my mid-thirties. More and more my secretary found me staring vacantly out my fifth-floor window of my one-man law office at the corner of Douglas and Fort. At home, Margaret listened in stony silence to endless talk of travelling somewhere, anywhere.

Now, under normal circumstances, this restlessness would have disappeared. Another midlife crisis dissolved into reality. My father-in-law and his storytelling did not, however, appear under the definition of normal circumstances.

Sunday family dinners were his time to reminisce. At one moment, a young Dick would be wandering the Patagonia on horseback with his father and two brothers. "We would take two twelve-gauge shotguns, a Mauser, a little meat, a sack of bread, and nothing else. We'd be gone a month at a time," he'd recall. And if the conversation turned to fishing, he'd tell of fighting twelve-pound rainbows at Lago General Pass. "For a lure," he'd say, "we'd use just a piece of red wool. The trout would almost kill each other to get at it."

And he would sometimes recount, "Did I ever tell you about my Seabee running out of gas? Well, Jean was seven months pregnant at the time with Margaret. We were heading for the town of Neuquén. I glanced at the gas gauge and, you know, I still can't explain it. It showed empty. I spotted the Rio Negro through the cloud cover and we hit that river fifty kilometres from any living soul. The next thing I knew...."

His favourite stories, however, revolved around his days at a large estancia [ranch] in the heart of the Patagonia, Estancia Maquinchao. Owned by the Rio Negro Land Company, and with its board of directors in England, this sheep ranch comprised in total 100 square leagues, so 2,330 square kilometres. He loved his idle days as a youth in Maquinchao and returned there at every available storytelling opportunity.

That's Maquinchao as in, "David, you bringing up those two boxing fights reminds me when I was in Maquinchao. We were having a small asado of one sheep, or barbecue as you call it here, when after too much vino, two gauchos suddenly pulled their facóns [belt knives] from their belts. It was a serious knife fight and ended with one getting slashed across his face."

Or that's Maquinchao as in, "Margaret, that sheepskin jacket you have on reminds me of when I was in Maquinchao during the spring shearing season. You can't imagine. Why, in one paddock alone there would be two thousand sheep. First the ewes were separated from the lambs. Then the lambs were processed on a long narrow table. The first catcher would clip an ear to mark the company. The next catcher would clip an ear in another spot to show the year of birth. There were six catchers. I can't remember what the next two did. The fifth would lop off the tail. And if it was a male, he would then yell 'macho' to signal the final catcher. He was the castrator. All the male lambs of course had to be castrated."

"Oh, Dick," his Scottish wife Jean would say after this story had started up again, "not again, not at the dinner table." But there was never any stopping Dick.

On he would go. "The castrator would take a little knife and slit the sack. Then he'd grab the testicles with his teeth and pull. Well, how can I say it, he would bite them off. Why, in no time, there would be a pile of pelotas a metre high. And don't think they were wasted. The paisanos [Italian workers] would have a little asado. Delicious!"

Well, I had absolutely no idea how many lambs' balls it took to reach a metre, and quite frankly had no intention of ever finding out. I also had no desire to eat lamb's balls, track down old Nazis, force land planes in the rivers of Patagonia, fish with woollen lures, or go hunting with a Mauser. In fact, I didn't know whether a Mauser had four legs or you pulled its trigger. Yet as the years passed and his stories streamed endlessly forth, I slowly became drawn by the adventure and the romance and the old Wild West of it all, that is Patagonia.

On Christmas Eve, 1975, Dick produced an old yellowed clipping from the Buenos Aires newspaper, *La Nación*. It recounted the adventures of a young Ricardo Moreno, and how in 1939 he'd become the first person to travel the sixteen hundred kilometres from Bariloche to Buenos Aires by motorcycle. Thirty-six years later Dick had something else in mind, and something else far more grand.

"Canada to Argentina by motorcycle," he announced. "I wouldn't have my old Norton, but if Jean would leave the shop I'd go tomorrow. I'd use a Harley-Davidson, and with a little sidecar for mum. What a fantastic trip it would be. You should go," he had said, "You should go," his voice trailing off and his fifty-eight-year-old eyes glistening with excitement.

The 'why' of such a journey was as clear and personal to Dick as it was clear and personal to me and to all travellers. The 'when' of the trip was a non-issue. Our daughter Lisa would be five in August, and in first grade a year later. The 'when' was early this summer or not at all. Whatever remaining hesitation I had crumbled that Christmas Eve, and I started secretly planning for an early departure.

Now the 'where.' There's a beginning and an end to every journey, and then there's what lies in-between. With a trip by plane, the beginning and the in-between are unimportant and uninteresting. It's only the end that matters. A journey on foot, under sail, or by vehicle, is different. Now it's the in-between, the journey itself that matters, and such a journey demands a good beginning and a good ending. It requires definition.

Cycling across North America from the Pacific Coast to the Atlantic Coast. That's defined. A canoe trip from the source of the Amazon to its mouth. That's defined. Contrast that with a bike ride from Pittsburgh, Pennsylvania to Gila Bend, Arizona. No definition. Is it two thousand five hundred or six thousand kilometres? What exactly does this guy know about Gila Bend that's so interesting? Is he riding a bike just to save bus fare?

British Columbia, Canada, to Argentina also lacked definition, but a map provided the answer. The Pan-American Highway ended at Circle City, Alaska, 250 kilometres north of Fairbanks, and eighty short of the Arctic Circle. You couldn't drive any farther north. That would be the beginning. The old Argentine penal colony of Ushuaia on the Island of Tierra del Fuego was the southernmost town in the world. There would be the end. Circle City, Alaska, to Ushuaia, Argentina. It didn't have the ring of Cape to Cairo but it didn't sound too bad, not bad at all.

I now had the 'where,' the 'when,' and the 'why.' All that was left was the 'how.'

FRANK LLOYD WRIGHT

All dreamers can handle the 'when,' the 'where' and the 'why' of travel. It's the 'how' that stumps them. How can I leave my job? How can I leave my studies? How can I leave my girlfriend? In our case, it was how can we travel for a year with four-year-old Lisa and son Martin, barely eight months old.

Volkswagen vans initially looked promising. They were economical and easy to manoeuvre and could fit into a ship's container to avoid the impassable roadless stretch between Panama and Colombia called the Darién Gap. Yet they raised questions. When fully loaded, could they climb 4,000 metres into the heartland of Peru? How many mechanics in Ecuador and Bolivia had even seen a Volkswagen engine, let alone fixed one? Were spare parts available? What about ground clearance? What about the lack of upfront protection if we were in an accident? In the end, it was obvious really. Four in a van for a year would be ridiculous.

Next considered were motor homes. They were comfortable and spacious but somehow just too comfortable, too spacious. This wasn't going to be Jimmy and Susan off to the lakeside and camping cheek by jowl with Barney and Madge. Nor was it going to be Steinbeck, ambling across the U.S. of A. for what turned out to be an uneventful three or so months with his little dog Charley. This was going to be thirty thousand to forty thousand kilometres of paved roads, gravel roads, stone roads, mud roads, flooded roads, and no roads. We needed something customized, not the usual sterile blend of fibreboard and plaid upholstery whipped off an assembly line.

The nail in the coffin for motor homes was the Darién Gap. This 160-kilometre stretch of jungle and swamp between Panama and Colombia was impassable by vehicle. Whatever was chosen had to be shipped around it. Now what if shipping by container, instead of on a ship's deck or in a hold, was the only available option, and the motor home didn't fit inside? That would be the end. David had a dream. David closed his office. David sold the house. David screwed up. And considering the journey planned and who was going, that was undoubtedly the popular prediction.

When Margaret discovered Ford agencies existed in South America, everything fell into place. The question of 'how' now had a two-part answer. To resolve concerns of necessary power to climb the Andes, ground clearance, safety, parts availability, and knowledgeable mechanics, we decided on a three-quarter ton Ford SuperCab pickup with a rear bench seat. Being mechanically challenged, a used truck was not an option. Detroit received an order for a May 1st delivery date.

That took care of part one of the 'how.' The other part was living accommodation. I designed a three-metre long camper to slip into the truck's 2.4-metre-long box. It had a toilet, a small hidden compartment to keep stuff hidden, a fake wall to hide larger items, and a stove, fridge, and heater, and all running on propane.

When it came to sleeping, however, I outdid myself. With all cab-over campers, the rear dining table and seating area had to be adjusted every night to allow sleeping for children. At night, and with nowhere to sit, we would either have to sit outside until bedtime or go to bed when the kids went. To solve this dilemma, I designed the cab-over campers' bed portion that overhangs the truck's cab to be twenty centimetres higher than normal. Then, instead of just using these extra twenty centimetres as extra headroom for us, I designed two twenty-centimetre high drawers that could be pulled out from under our bed area. At night, one drawer would be pulled out over the stove and the other drawer over the sink. The kids would sleep in the two drawers. (And in case you're wondering, both drawers would remain open!) Our seemingly impossible sleeping dilemma was solved. I considered this innovative design nothing short of brilliant.

"Yes, dear," Margaret had said, "you're the Frank Lloyd Wright of campers. There're few men alive who could spend thirty straight nights locked up in their den and come up with such a stroke of genius."

The camper plans were completed, and off they went to a small local camper manufacturer and with a request for a May 1st completion date.

Next to come was the paperwork. Lists detailing the location of Canadian embassies, YMCAs, campsites, automobile clubs, and Ford agencies were filed away. They were followed by notarized copies of our four birth certificates, four passports, medical insurance, two international driver's licences, the vehicle ownership and insurance, our vaccination books showing shots received, blood type information, and marriage certificate. Finally, eighty passport photos possibly needed for visas were included. All original documents would be eventually tucked away inside the camper's especially designed hidden compartment. Its discovery, I claimed, could only be accomplished by a stroke of luck equal to winning the lottery or by a complete dismantling of the camper.

Next considered was the problem of taking a truck and camper through Central and South America. Countries like Argentina that manufactured motor vehicles protected their industries by imposing import duties reaching to 300 per cent. Then, and as further protection to their industries, and to prevent travellers from simply selling their desirable foreign-made vehicles for a nice profit and leaving the country, something *The South American Handbook* called a Carnet de Passages en Douane had to be acquired before departure. It was acquired by first putting down a healthy deposit and then by posting a bond equivalent to 150 per cent of the truck's value. The carnet was to be presented at border crossings as assurance we exited with, and not without, our vehicle. And to get the deposit back and bond cancelled, the carnet had to be returned to the local automobile club with all appropriate border stamps. The local British Columbia Automobile Club staff was initially stumped, and understandably so, because nobody had ever attempted such a journey from Victoria. After two days, however, everything was sorted out and our carnet was added to our pile of documents.

May 1st came and went. No truck and no camper. Finally, on May 15th, and a mere two weeks short of our departure date, our truck dealer called. The truck had arrived. White with dark blue trim, our truck had two bench seats, two batteries, two spares with winter treads, dual gas tanks and gas cap locks, air conditioning, a sliding rear window, and a host of must-have extras that considerably bumped up the base price. The engine was a 460 cu. in., the most powerful gas guzzling motor Ford produced. Surely, I thought, this beauty would propel us with ease and safety high into the Andes.

We then proceeded to customize. Off came the tires, on went Michelins. Off came the headlights, on went Bosch lights. Out came the radio, in went a Blaupunkt radio and cassette player. Off came the front bumper and on went a personally designed and more sturdy bumper and complete with a cage-like iron grill guard and bug screen that would definitely make us the clear winner in a head-on car crash with anything. A Warn winch was then installed up front to get out of any predicaments.

Two four-inch-long posts with a small hole drilled through the top of each post were welded to the engine block, and two holes were then drilled into the hood. When the hood was closed, the posts protruded through the holes. Two padlocks were then attached through the holes in the posts to secure the hood. That setup would surely prevent theft of the battery, and other car parts under the hood. Locking lug nuts secured the wheels, and the propane tank storage area was secured by a large padlock. Our truck cum tank was now ready to rumble.

A scant two days before departure, camper builder Verne called. "Camper's ready," he announced. "Followed your drawings right to the letter. Didn't change anything. It's a beauty."

Upon arrival, we found our new home precariously balanced on four stilts.

"Those are your hydraulic jacks," said Verne. "You use them to get the camper on and off the truck."

Very gently, Verne slipped our truck under the camper. The hydraulics were eased off, and the camper was slowly edged downward towards the truck bed.

"It's a bit heavy," Verne commented, seconds before a jack snapped.

Verne's plump wife wandered over to offer her two bits' worth.

"Verne, who designed this thing?"

"Goddamn it, Sylvia," muttered Verne, "just get me another jack from the red cabinet." Verne's neck veins were bulging, and for good reason. The camper lay draped over the truck like a fat giraffe with a broken leg. Even worse, we still owed him the bulk of his account.

Finally, and with the jack replaced, the camper was lowered into the truck box. The truck sank lower and lower. Surely, I thought, the rear bumper was going to hit the ground. Finally it sank no lower. Ground clearance, I thought, where's our ground clearance? Bloody hell, we're leaving in two days.

Sensing my concern, Verne offered a rather unconvincing solution.

"Keep your tires pumped," he said. "You'll be fine."

Final payment was made and we drove home to make last-minute preparations. Camping supplies, food, and clothing for every climate, and all previously stockpiled, were packed away as were all documents. Piled into one cupboard was every conceivable necessity for now ten-month-old Martin. Also stashed away were first aid, cleaning, repair, and tool kits.

A little library had a travel section containing *The South American Handbook* and Gunther's *Inside South America.* Next was a 'how to' section including how to play poker, play bridge, play guitar, and a few other bucket list items. The final section included the two volume H.G. Wells classic *The Outline of History*, Brierly's *The Law of Nations*, and a book written in 1909 called *The Two Great Questions; The Existence of God, and the Immortality of the Soul.* I had acquired these last three books thirteen years before in England and stuck them at the bottom of my too small olive-coloured parachute jumper's backpack purchased for five pounds at an army surplus store. I had then proceeded to pack them around Europe for nine months without reading a single page. I had no idea why I thought that they would at long last be read, but in they went anyway.

As for truck parts and repair supplies, I was at a bit of a loss. I mean, what could possibly go wrong with a truck showing sixteen kilometres on the odometer?

"Take the basics like plugs, belts, hoses, hose clamps, pressure gauge, oil, and brake fluid," advised my father-in-law. "Also take a gas funnel with a filter. You don't want bad gas in your truck. And take pliers, a wrench, and a regular screwdriver and a Phillips. That should do it. Oh, and buy a spare water pump. And take some electrical tape and fourteen-gauge wire. South American mechanics can work wonders with wire. And maybe get one of those spotlights you can buy that plug into your cigarette lighter. You could use it for reading street signs and for checking people out. And, of course, jumper cables. And that reminds me, have you got a gun?"

A gun, I thought. All these months of inspirational Sunday family dinner stories, and now two days before leaving, he gives me the gun speech?

"What do you mean a gun?" I said. "I've never shot one let alone owned one. I could hide it in my secret compartment alright but if I got caught crossing a border with a gun I'd be in serious trouble."

"I guess you're right," Dick said, "but you should have something. Los Angeles is dangerous, and Mexico, you always read about tourists being hijacked. And once into Peru, and Bolivia, well the people high in the Andes are quite uneducated, muy primitivo, as we Argentines say. You can't reason with them even if you could speak Spanish, and of course, you can't speak a word."

We spent the last two days collecting truck parts and trying to convince ourselves that protection wasn't an issue. Finally, on the morning of June 2, 1976, we filled up with water, gas, and propane, said goodbye to both families, and slowly lumbered out of Victoria, British Columbia. We were heading up island to take a ferry from Port Hardy to Prince Rupert, and then a second ferry from Rupert to Haines, Alaska. A drive to Fairbanks, Alaska, would be next, and then north from there to Circle City, located just short of the Arctic Circle. We would then turn around and head south in an attempt to complete what would become history's longest north to south overland journey through the Americas, if, and it was a big if, we made it.

3

NORTH TO ALASKA

It was raining hard when the ferry from Port Hardy, Vancouver Island, neared Prince Rupert.

"Where you headed?" asked an old deckhand.

"Haines," I answered. "It's in Alaska, kind of tucked into a corner, near Skagway. We take a ferry from here tomorrow morning. Then we head farther north, up Fairbanks way."

"Yeh, I know where Haines is," he said. "Overloads?"

"Yeh, camper's too heavy," I said, "probably twelve hundred pounds over the truck's warranty."

"Overloads," he repeated, "you got overloads?" as he glanced down at the rear bumper.

"Oh, overloads," I said, having absolutely no idea what he was talking about. "Not sure. Only had this thing three days."

"Well, you better get 'em," he said, shaking his head as he walked away, "you better get 'em."

It was raining even harder by the time we docked, and twenty-five kilometres of torrential rain later we pulled into a quiet campsite on a small lake. I had harboured a vision of our first campsite for a long, long time. Huddled near a crackling fire while sipping a mug of coffee spiked with maybe a shot of rum. Periodically poking at a rainbow trout sizzling in the frying pan. A stack of dry firewood at the ready. Out in the solitude of the wilderness, and experiencing life as it was meant to be lived.

Here there was no crackling fire and no sizzling rainbow trout. And there certainly wasn't a stack of dry firewood. Rain pounded down relentlessly. Everything was soaked. The camper floor was soon covered in mud. Martin was crying for his bottle. Lisa was crying because it probably seemed like what a four-year-old should be doing when soaked and hungry.

"This is ridiculous," said Margaret furiously. I said nothing. After all, it was ridiculous.

It was still raining early the next morning as Lisa and I picked our way through the underbrush to the lakeshore. On our return trip, she spied a yellow and green plant in a marshy area near the trail. Then and there we had our first father and daughter moment.

"What's that, daddy?" she asked.

"Why, that's a skunk cabbage dear," I replied.

"Daddy," she said, "is that where skunks come from?"

"No, honey," I said smiling, "we'll have to talk about that a little later."

After breakfast, we drove back to Rupert, cleared customs, and then boarded the ferry for Alaska. It was still raining.

About eighty kilometres out, we crossed into the United States. The ferry slowly snaked through the little islands, which along with a narrow strip of coast, comprise southeastern Alaska. Up the Inside Passage we sailed, briefly stopping at Ketchikan, Wrangell, and Juneau. Finally, and twenty-two hours and 650 kilometres from Rupert later, we docked at Haines, Alaska.

We then headed north through stands of hemlock and spruce on the gravel and potholed Haines Highway for about fifteen kilometres. And here continued America's 'world's largest' fixation. First it had been the Alaska State Ferry System, the world's largest ferry route. Then it had been Ketchikan, home to the world's largest collection of totem poles. Now we had reached the Chilkat River with the world's largest known congregation of bald eagles. Three world's largest and we had just started! It was stunning to think what lay ahead!

After forty-five minutes we reached a campsite on Mosquito

Lake. The truck and camper were cleaned, things re-organized, and a couple of days of camping later, we were on our way. Being on the road now just less than a week, and with supplies running low, we pulled up in front of a small log cabin, and which appeared to be a general store. A corrugated tin roof extended over its front porch. Stacked to the right side of the front door was a cord of firewood, and leaning against the wood was an old mattress. The cabin was maybe two metres at most from the gravel road. It appeared the cabin had been built first, and then the road, a clear case of the cart before the horse.

Out front, and right on the road's edge, was an old blue gas pump with a clear glass ball on top. To operate it, the sign said you first figured how much gas you wanted, gas was then pumped to the desired level in the glass ball, a valve was opened, and then by gravity feed your tank was filled. I couldn't tell if it ran off a generator or had a hand pump. Maybe it didn't even work. As Margaret opened the screen door, I noticed a "For Sale" sign nailed to the outside wall.

Inside, the floor was tongue-and-groove, unstained and pitted with grit from years of use. The shelves were faded one-by-ten boards displaying for sale a few rows of packages and cans. It looked very bleak and very empty. A person could probably pack up the store's entire contents in an hour and be gone.

"Good morning," said Margaret.

"Morning, dear," answered an elderly lady in a green apron behind the counter.

"Any fresh or frozen meat?" I asked.

"No meat," she replied, "but we have Spam and some canned corned beef."

"What about milk and eggs?" I inquired.

"No delivery this week," she replied, "but we do have powdered milk and even some powdered eggs."

"Don't suppose you have any bread." I asked hopefully.

"No, afraid not," she said smiling, "but got lots of crackers."

By now I had surveyed the entire room. There was no meat section, no frozen food section, no dairy section, and no produce section. There was also no cash register. And all for a very good reason. There was no electricity.

"Nice place you have here," I ventured, as Margaret started piling cans of Spam, corned beef, and crackers on the counter.

"Yes," she said, "we've had a happy life here. Forty-five years in all. It's up for sale now. Fact is, it's been up for sale for over a year. My Harry isn't well and I'm pushing seventy-five. There's a young hippie fellow and his lady friend interested. Put down five hundred dollars as a deposit."

"Where you going when you sell?" Margaret asked.

"Well, dear, we're on the waiting list for a home in Prince George, the Golden Gates or Golden Heaven. Something like that. Harry knows the name. It sounds wonderful. We should be there by the fall."

"Well good luck," I said, "hope the deal closes."

As we walked back to the truck, Margaret glanced at the mound of corned beef cans I was carrying.

"Well, look at that," she said.

I glanced down."Look at what?" I asked.

"The corned beef dear, the corned beef. See, look at the label."

And there they were, words I had never seen before:

Hecho en Argentina
Made in Argentina

We left the roadhouse, and after a sixty-five-kilometre drive, and with no direct road access to Alaska, we crossed into British Columbia. Then, and after another short drive of sixty kilometres, we reached Canada's Yukon. We were now on the Yukon Highway, and on the final stretch to reach the Alaska Highway. Now to keep the road's surface out of marshy areas, the road builders had raised it about two metres. The road was riddled with potholes, and very slippery. Progress was painfully slow. As my impatience grew, I pushed harder. Our speed was upped to fifty-five or so kilometres an hour, and I settled into a trance playing what I was mindlessly considering a game of 'racing car driver dodging the potholes.'

"Slow down," said Margaret, "what's the hurry?"

We had just covered a straight stretch of maybe ten kilometres and I guess that's where the pickup had caught up. The driver pulled out to pass at the very instant I turned left to dodge another pothole. The driver had no choice. Off the road his pickup flew and down the two-metre embankment.

Suddenly, Margaret screamed. "My God, look to your left!"

I glanced left, and two metres below, and hurtling over rocks and small stumps and underbrush, was the roof of a pickup, racing us neck and neck.

We continued side by side for another fifty metres. What is this, I thought, some kind of a macho Yukon drag race? Then I understood. It was for me to slow down, not him. I slowed to twenty, he gunned to sixty, and the pickup shot up the embankment. In seconds, it had disappeared around a curve.

And therein, you see, lies the difference between city man and Yukon man. City man, having been cut off by some idiot not watching what was coming hard from behind and merrily racing along dodging potholes, would have stopped, fired off a list of obscenities, and then checked for damage to his pickup. Only then would city man have confronted his predicament. Could he now get up enough speed to climb up the steep gravel embankment? And if not, it could mean a long, lonely wait to be rescued, and if winter time, that could be the ball game. Only a fool would have stopped, and fools don't last long in the Yukon.

At Haines Junction, the Yukon Highway met up with the Alaska

Highway, and soon we reached the United States Border Inspection Station. We were now back in the State of Alaska, the chunk of land the U. S. of A. had picked up from Russia in 1867 for, and wait for this, less than two cents an acre. Now that's inflation!

The truck was performing well, the only visible damage being a cracked windshield. The camper was another story. The water tank had just split at its seam. Water was continuously leaking all over the floor, and re-creating the mud nightmare of Prince Rupert. Attempts at repairing the tank with glue proved fruitless. Disgusted, we drained the tank, abandoned the water system, and resorted to our two plastic water containers. A bigger problem, however, was my architectural masterpiece, the cab-over bed portion of the camper that extended over the truck's roof. The extra weight of the two sleeping drawers for the kids was creating too much stress. As we closed in on Fairbanks, the cab-over started bouncing off the truck's roof. After a short stop at North Pole, we proceeded to Fairbanks where I purchased a seven-centimetre-thick sheet of foam rubber and jammed it between the truck's roof and camper. The noise was muffled but the bouncing continued.

I guess I should point out that when I wrote 'North Pole' I meant North Pole, Alaska, population about a thousand, and fifty kilometres shy of Fairbanks. Our guidebook said that in 1944, the owners of the area, the Dahl and Gaske Development Company, had named the settlement North Pole. They were hoping to attract a toy maker who could then claim its toys were, yes, made at the North Pole. It must have seemed at the time a stroke of capitalistic genius. Even now, it sounds, to me at least, positively brilliant. Then again, I was the proud inventor of the cab-over-two-drawer-for-children sleeping centre. Looking back, I guess before naming it North Pole, somebody should have talked to a four-year-old.

"Daddy," Lisa had said, "I don't want a teddy bear made here. I want one made by the elves at the real North Pole, the one with the post from the barber shop."

A four-year-old could have saved them a lot of time and money. No toy maker ever did come to North Pole.

After our attempt to fix the bouncing camper, we headed to the Fairbanks Golf & Country Club, advertising itself as, yes, you guessed it, the most northerly golf course in the world. Now, instead of the 'world's largest' we had moved into the 'most northerly' territory. They probably have the most northerly of a lot of things I thought–the 'most northerly bowling alley,' the 'most northerly McDonald's,' probably even the most northerly brothel.

I went to the first tee as a single and teed up. Instantly, the attack of the Alaskan mosquitoes began. Seven or eight landed on each hand as I lashed away. We hurried down the short par four looking for my snap hook, and four more mosquito attacks later, was on in five. The 'green' consisted of sand and a smidgen of oil. It was an actual sand green, common in the days of wooden-shafted clubs, and found in areas where growing and maintaining grass proved difficult.

Margaret used the nearby lawn roller to flatten my line. And just how fast were those sand greens back in the day? Your answer is not very fast. (Maybe a four on the stimp if you're a golfer.) Three putts later it was an eight. A quadruple bogey, an Alaskan snowman. I quit after one hole and we started our final 250-kilometre push to Circle City on the banks of the Yukon River. The mosquitoes won ten and eight.

4

CIRCLE CITY, TEX RICKARD, AND WYATT EARP

In 1887, Jack McQuesten constructed a two-storey trading post on the south bank of the Yukon River, and, calculating it rested on the Arctic Circle, named his trading post Circle. Jack was wrong. The Arctic Circle was eighty kilometres farther north. In the early years, business was confined to Athabaskan Indians and white fur traders and the selling of a few supplies to the odd prospector in the region. All this changed in 1893 when two Russian half-breeds struck gold on nearby Birch Creek. The news spread quickly and after reaching the Bering Sea, hopeful prospectors headed up the Yukon by steamship, loaded up with supplies at Jack's trading post, and then tackled the remaining ten-kilometre portage to Birch Creek.

Three years later, and in the spring of 1896, a twenty-six-year-old named George Lewis "Tex" Rickard arrived at Circle City. By this time, Circle City, as it was now called, was a bustling village with four hundred low built-to-the-ground log buildings. The logs were chinked with moss, mud, paper, cardboard, old clothes, and whatever else was handy. Roofs were covered with moss and topped off with a foot-thick layer of dirt. It's said that every summer each house had a nice roof garden. By the time Rickard arrived, twenty-eight saloons had sprung up along with two variety theatres, eight dance halls, a hospital, a church, and a library. The population had swelled to around seven hundred. Circle City had temporarily earned the somewhat dubious title 'Paris of the North.'

Young Rickard staked a claim in the Birch Creek area but it

proved to be worthless. Then in December, news reached Circle City. Back in August, there had been a gold strike on a tributary of the Klondike. Rickard immediately set out in the dead of winter and pulling his supply-laden sled. Rickard struggled four hundred kilometres up the now frozen Yukon River to its confluence with the Klondike, and to what soon became Dawson City. Other prospectors followed Rickard in that long trek from Circle City to Dawson, and still more followed in the spring of 1897 by steamship, and after the Yukon had thawed. The prospectors were soon followed by the shopkeepers, the saloonkeepers, and what the prospectors wished as much as their food and drink, the prostitutes. Everybody was racing to Dawson City and the Klondike. The exodus virtually wiped Circle City from the map. Young Rickard staked claims, bought interests in existing claims, and then sold out to large mining syndicates. In a year, he had amassed upwards of $60,000. By the summer of 1898, he had lost it all at cards.

Then, within weeks, his fortunes changed again. News reached Dawson City of yet another gold strike, this time down on the coast near Anvil City. Off Rickard headed back down river by riverboat. Winter, however, was closing in fast. After about eight hundred kilometres, and with the Yukon River quickly freezing up, the riverboat Tex had booked passage on was forced to stop at the tiny settlement of Rampart to wait for the spring thaw.

Meanwhile, news of the Klondike had also reached Yuma, Arizona, and one Wyatt Earp. Almost twenty years had passed since his days as a lawman in Dodge City and Tombstone. Almost twenty years since Earp, brothers Virgil and Morgan, and their friend Doc Holliday had faced down Ike and Billy Clanton and the McLaury brothers at the O.K. Corral. Rumours of picking nuggets off bushes were just too much to resist for Earp, and by the fall of 1898, a now fifty-year-old Earp and wife Josie were heading up the Yukon River by riverboat for Dawson City. Like Rickard, however, Earp had started too late and, caught by the gathering river ice, his riverboat was also forced to pull ashore, and also at Rampart for the winter.

At ice break-up, Rickard and Earp headed off together downriver four hundred or so kilometres to the coast to Anvil City, shortly to change its name to Nome. Both opened up saloons, both raked in the gold dust from the prospectors, and soon became fast friends.

Earp spent the final days of his life prospecting in Nevada and California, and on January 13, 1929, at age eighty, died in Los Angeles.

Meanwhile, as modest as were the final twenty-five years of Earp's life, the remaining twenty-five years of young Tex Rickard bordered on the unbelievable. In 1903, and now thirty-three, he promoted his first boxing fight. This adventurer, prospector, hustler, gambler, and saloonkeeper had finally discovered his true calling. Fight promoter.

On July 4, 1910, in Reno, Nevada, Rickard forever changed the world of boxing. He pitted former world heavyweight champion, James J. Jeffries, by now retired for five years, against the terrifying black man that nobody could beat, Jack Johnson. Jeffries, the original great white hope, was destroyed in fifteen rounds. Promotion followed promotion over the next ten years. Dempsey vs. Carpentier attracted eighty thousand fans and was boxing's first million-dollar gate. Dempsey vs. Firpo, the Wild Bull of the Pampas, followed and drew ninety thousand. Jack Dempsey vs. Gene Tunney drew one hundred and twenty thousand. Their rematch was the first two-million-dollar gate for boxing. Then, and still in the Roaring Twenties, Tex raised $5,000,000 to build Madison Square Garden in New York. He installed an ice rink and a hockey team and called the team the New York Tex's Rangers. 'Tex's' was later dropped. Rickard died January 6, 1929, at age 59, seven days before his old friend Wyatt Earp. Earp died a Wild West legend and Rickard a sporting legend, and both a long, long way from their days in the Yukon and Alaska. As for Circle City, it didn't fare as well as Earp or Rickard, and by their death, and the onset of the Great Depression in 1929, its population had dwindled to fifty.

Today, and eighty years after its heyday, all that remained of Circle City was a dusty road running about a hundred metres alongside the Yukon River, a small trading post, maybe two dozen ramshackle houses in total, and that's about it. Wooden fish traps, five to seven metres long, lay resting in the side yards of the nearest two houses fronting the river. Across the road from the traps was a three-room clapboard shack surrounded by oil drums, lumber, and plywood. In front were a green and red children's swing set and a decades-old white wringer washing machine. A black German shepherd lay asleep in the middle of the road. It was about twenty-five degrees Celsius. Nobody was in sight.

We wandered down to the Yukon and to a red barge pulled up and cabled to shore. Its stern jutted out twenty-five or so metres into the fast-flowing Yukon. A battered outboard was tied to it down current. After a few minutes, a man popped out of the barge's white wheelhouse and slowly walked the length of the barge to shore.

"You the owner of that camper?" he asked.

"Yeh, Dave," I replied.

"Wally, Wally Jorgensen. I saw you wandering around. Not much to do up here except some hunting and fishing. Maybe a visit to the old cemetery upriver if you like that sort of thing."

"Yeh, that's about what I figured," I said. "Thought I'd try a little casting but the river looks pretty muddy."

"Nope, can't fish here," Wally replied. "All that glacial silt and mud, the fish couldn't see your lure. Don't waste your time. Say, I bet your daughter would like a boat ride. How 'bout we go upriver a ways in the outboard?"

"Well, thanks," I said, "that'd be nice."

Wally's deckhand appeared and the six of us piled into the flat-bottomed outboard and headed out. The surface was flat as we pushed slowly along against the current.

"Now see over there," said Wally, "that looks like the other bank but it's not, it's an island. The Yukon here's maybe five kilometres wide in all. This here is just the south channel, runs maybe seven or eight knots."

"So Wally," I asked, "what do you do up here all year?"

"Well just ply the river mainly," he replied. "We go upriver to Eagle and Dawson City regular-like. Take most anything: heavy equipment, trucks, lumber, food supplies, animals sometimes. 'Course that's only in the summer from say mid-June to early September. After that, the Yukon's ice-bound from its mouth to the headwaters. Me and Joe, we go to Fairbanks from freeze-up 'til the following spring. It's pretty quiet up here nowadays. Hard to believe. I read where back around 1896 there were thousands here. In fact, one book I read said Circle City was the largest place north of Seattle. Yup, hard to believe."

"So, uh, Dave," Wally continued, "I noticed your British Columbia plates. What're you and your wife doing way up here with two kids?"

"Well, Wally," I said, "we're planning to take a long drive. I call it my mid-thirties drop out. We're heading south from here early tomorrow."

"How far?" asked Joe the deckhand.

"Oh, maybe to a river we saw just near Fairbanks. Maybe do a little fishing."

"No," said Joe, "how far you going in all? Like California?"

"Well, to the bottom of South America," I replied.

"South America, why that's, that's what, ten thousand miles?" asked Joe.

"Closer to twenty thousand," I replied.

"Why you doing it?" Wally asked. "You rich or something?

Get fired? You don't look like one of them hippie types I seen in Fairbanks."

"No", I said, "just thought we should see more of the world before the kids go to school, kind of see what's over the next hill, check out that girl from Ipanema, know what I mean?"

"Yeah, sort of," Wally mumbled. "Went to Seattle in '71 just after my wife up and left me. Don't know really why I went. Guess I went to find another woman, or find, you know, myself, sort of. That bloody woman and her prick of a lawyer cleaned me right out. You know, she left me with my 68 pickup and that's it. Took every goddamn thing that wasn't nailed down. Anyway, I came back from Seattle in two weeks. Nothing down there for me. It's all up here. What I mean is, have a look at our car licence plates. "North to the Future" they say, and that's my point. Alaska is the future. It's not just a bunch of old gold rush stories. We got the biggest State by a mile and Alaska probably has no more people than Seattle. Probably less."

"Yeh, that reminds me of something somebody told me years ago," I said. "I was hitchhiking in Italy and this guy in a Mercedes, a Canadian, picks me up. Said he'd been working in Milan for a couple of years as a chartered accountant. That's like a CPA in the States. Anyway, he talked about how he loved the theatre, the opera in Milan, art galleries in Florence, jazz, that sort of stuff. In fact, he said he'd recently seen Chet Baker. I told him that when I was in Paris, I'd stopped for a late dinner at a little café on Rue de la Huchette called Le Chat Qui Pêche. I think that means the cat that fishes or something like that. Anyway, I told him I'd heard someone playing the trumpet. So, after dinner, I got up and went through this beaded curtain, and then down a flight of stone stairs. And there in this century's old smoke-filled underground dungeon, and right under the café, was Chet Baker himself.

"So I said to him, his life in Milan sounded pretty interesting, especially seeing Chet Baker, but he was Canadian, and Canada, was after all, the country of the future. And if Canada was the country of the future, why would he want to live and work in Italy? You know what he said? He said, 'Canada may be the country of the future, but I like to live in the present.'"

Wally stared straight ahead and said nothing for about two minutes. God, I thought, maybe he's now second-guessing his entire life up here in futureville. Or maybe he's just concluded I'm a prick lawyer like his ex-wife's. Finally, he raised his head and spoke.

"Chet Baker," he said, "Chet Baker. Who the hell's Chet Baker?"

A few minutes later, Wally signalled Joe to head back. Circle City shortly reappeared in the distance, and now being pushed by the strong current, we soon were back on shore. We thanked Wally and Joe, left them to their daily routines, and walked over to the trading post for a few supplies.

After dinner, and by ten o'clock, both kids were fast asleep. Margaret and I walked down the few metres to the river's edge. The sun had sunk to its lowest and remained there just above the Yukon River. A red glow filled the sky. It was June 20th. Tomorrow was summer solstice. It was somehow fitting our long journey south would begin on the longest day of the year.

The next day after breakfast I went through what soon became my daily routine. Water, oil, brake, power steering, and gas fluid levels were all checked. Anything low was topped up. Any tire looking low was pressure tested. The padlocks securing the propane and water tank compartments were double checked. Finally, the two padlocks on the hood were snapped shut and the camper door locked. It was a daily ten-point check I was to follow for the next year.

Wally wandered over to say good-bye.

"Dave," he said, "I remember you said your camper's been

bouncing off the truck's roof. You got to buy some shocks to hold the camper's cab-over up. Otherwise it's gonna snap in half and there goes your bed. Looks to me like somebody buggered up the design. And your rear end's dragging. Your camper's way too heavy. You need to get overload springs and soon."

"Well, thanks Wally," I said, "I'll look into it."

Margaret asked if he'd take a picture of us and camper. We stood next to the ten-foot high sign marking the end of the Steese Highway and that would mark the beginning of our journey south.

WELCOME TO CIRCLE CITY
Established in 1893
Interior Alaska's Oldest Major Gold Camp
Population 68
The End of the Road
Most Northerly Point on Connected American Highway System

I stared at the sign for a few moments, pondering the enormity of what lay ahead. Finally, Wally snapped the picture, we piled into the truck, and off we headed back down the Steese Highway to Fairbanks. After our four-thousand-kilometre journey north, and at long last, we were heading south.

THE JOURNEY OF SEBASTIAN SNOW

{SOUTH TO NORTH THROUGH THE AMERICAS}

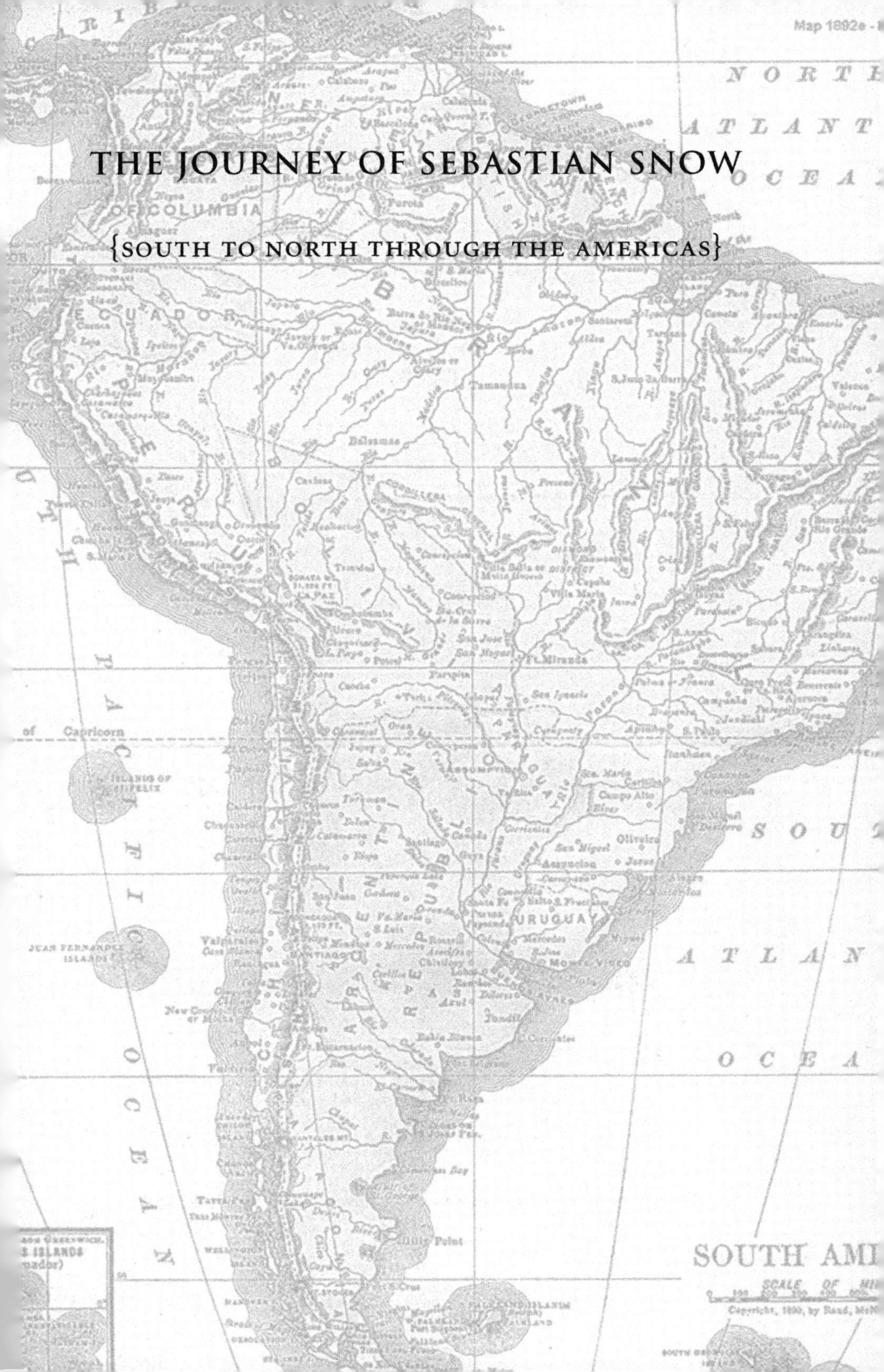

FOUND AMAZON'S SOURCE

'Bash on, regardless' motto of gentleman adventurer

Sebastian Snow, who has died aged 72, was one of the last amateur gentlemen adventurers.

Mr. Snow carried out his explorations and wanderings in the jungles of South America with a minimum of support and the smallest of parties. Mildly eccentric in the manner of the traditional Victorian explorer, Mr. Snow had a wonderful sense of humour and was charmingly impractical – content to leave such mysteries as the kerosene stove and elementary cooking to his Indian helpers.

As a result, all his travels had a flavour of Evelyn Waugh, but this did nothing to diminish his achievements. His trip down the Amazon at the age of 22 was described by his great friend, mountaineer Chris Bonington, as one of the great solo adventures of the post-war years.

Before he set off, the Peruvian geographical society washed its hands of his venture. "I paid a friendly call on them," Mr. Snow recalled. "They made it obvious that my aromatic presence was not required and laughed me to scorn."

But, braving ferocious rapids, snakes, head-hunters and pirates, Mr. Snow navigated the 5,641 kilometres from the source in the Peruvian Andes to the Atlantic on canoes and balsa log rafts.

Excerpt from Sebastian Snow's obituary, *National Post*, May 9, 2001

5

THE RUCKSACK MAN

Ah, but a man's reach should exceed his grasp,
Or, what's a heaven for?
—ROBERT BROWNING, "ANDREA DEL SARTO"

On February 3, 1973, and thirteen days after his forty-fifth birthday, a balding, Eton-educated, and eccentric Englishman named Sebastian Snow left the former penal colony of Ushuaia, Argentina, at the southernmost tip of Tierra del Fuego, and headed for Alaska. Snow planned to walk. Not walk and hitchhike. Not walk, but bus or boat the more difficult stretches. Walk. Walk the entire length of South America, and then through Central America, and then the U.S. of A, and then Canada, and then continue right up into Alaska. Quite simply, Snow was planning to complete the longest walk in history.

Snow moved along at a thirty-seven-kilometre-a-day clip with a sixty-pound knapsack on his back, day after day, week after week, and month after month. Seven months alone just to cross Argentina, and one solitary bath in those seven months. He walked through La Paz, Bolivia, at a shade under four thousand metres, passed by Lake Titicaca, the highest navigable lake in the world, hiked to Machu Picchu, the Lost City of the Incas, and then through Ecuador. There Snow had been offered a compass. The offer was refused. Snow's response was apparently that as he would be going north all the way, it wouldn't be needed. Eventually, he reached the settlement of Barranquillita, a cluster of buildings in northern Colombia, and the beginning of the Darién Gap. He entered this 160-odd kilometre roadless stretch of swamp and tropical rain forest separating Colombia and Panama, in the rainy season, and with a twenty-year-old Canadian named Wade Davis in tow.

Why undertake the journey at all, I thought, and why in God's name walk? Walking put him touch with the people, Snow had written. A rapport could be established. Yet any man intending to walk for three or four years is clearly an introspective man, a loner, probably with no family, and surely with little need to be 'in touch' with anyone. For such a man, the desire to establish some sort of a rapport with mankind seemed a bit off, as did his other reasons given, the self-sufficiency of it all, the travelling at man's natural pace, and the chance to reflect.

What else then. Fame? Guinness Book of Records? Material for a book? All could come if he was successful, all three could motivate. Perhaps, however, it was something deeper. Perhaps, like everyone, he was just searching for some meaning, or a place, or for somebody to love, or for someone to love him.

Through his mother Gwen, who I amazingly found was living right here in Victoria, B.C., I located Wade Davis in Washington, D.C. It was now twenty-six years since Davis and Snow had tackled the Darién. An ethnobotanist and author of numerous books, including the Governor General's Award-winning *One River*, and *The Serpent and the Rainbow*, Davis was comfortably ensconced as an explorer-in-residence at The National Geographic Society headquarters. Davis was one of its first seven named explorers-in-residence, which group also included well-known Jane Goodall.

It quickly became clear in our phone conversation that it had been Snow in tow, and not Davis. It was Davis who was the outdoorsman, the compass user, the Spanish speaker, and the one with the personal skills to procure and retain the necessary guides and carriers.

"Sebastian," related Davis, "was the type of Englishman who thought if he spoke the Queen's English loud enough he would be understood."

"What was he like?" I asked. "Was he married? Was he easy to deal with? I mean, the walk was an unusual thing to attempt."

"No," Davis replied, "I don't think Sebastian ever married.[1] He was basically a professional adventurer. Back in the fifties, and in his early twenties, he had discovered the origin of the Amazon. In fact, he went from its source to its mouth in about ten months. He once described his journey from Ushuaia as an 'ongoingness' into a 'neverendingness.' Really, he was quite extraordinary. Very courageous, almost proud of his clumsiness, and extremely neurotic. He seemed to deliberately be underprepared so he could write a good story. By the way, parts of the book he wrote, called *The Rucksack Man*, he plagiarized from my journal."

"So did he ever say why he was doing it?" I asked. "What pushed him?"

"Well," said Davis, "he was earning a little money writing columns for the London *Observer*."

"No," I said, "I meant more philosophically."

"Philosophy had little to do with it. Maybe psychology," replied Davis. "It, of course, all stemmed from a serious thigh injury he received playing football or rugby at Eton. The doctor told him he'd never walk again. And I guess in a way he's been walking ever since. He's done some incredible things."

So there it was, not fame and fortune at all, nor a book, nor some deep-seated search in life for something. Underlying it all was just a doctor's blunt statement to a young man. Challenge met. Obstacle overcome. Very English. To Snow, however, it had become more than a challenge. It had evolved into an obsession.

Five pairs of boots, five missing teeth, and a year and half from Ushuaia later, Snow crossed into Panama. He arrived in poor health. A hornet sting, a scorpion bite, leeches, ticks, foot

1 Snow had, in fact married in 1957 and had four children, but divorced in 1970, so before he met Wade Davis. He died on April 20th, 2001, at age 72.

rot, trench mouth, and over twenty-two kilos lost had ground him down. As he related in his book, *The Rucksack Man*:

> I had to decide whether to return to England to recuperate or whether to continue my walk up North America to Alaska. Or should I walk across to Washington?
>
> But could I go on? I wanted to go on, to accomplish the longest walk in the world and indeed I knew I could. My legs would keep me going, my brain would accept it but what about the rest of me?
>
> They told me I was in bad shape and that if I continued I would become a wizened old crock. Toothless, bald, emaciated, permanently broken in health. All my teeth would fall out and maybe my liver would pack up.

Wade Davis put it to me a little differently.

"Sebastian basically went mad," he said. "I mean, he must have lost at least fifty pounds. Apparently Sebastian got as far as Costa Rica before ending up in hospital. Then one evening he got out of bed, left the hospital in his pajamas, and started his walk all over again. I heard he was arrested and jailed for a few days. Finally, someone from the British Embassy got him out and shipped him home. You can read about Sebastian and myself in my book, *One River*, which is at Munro's book store. All my books are there."

"What happened to him in the end?" I asked.

"Well, I don't know really," said Davis. "I last saw him in 1983 in Devon in a pub. He seemed rather down on his luck and he smelled. Maybe he's still alive."

Sebastian Edward Farquharson Snow never returned to complete the second half of his remarkable trek. But fail? Well, no, Snow didn't fail. Certainly he didn't hit a home run, but he did bounce a solid double off the outfield fence. Many in life never even step up to the plate.

PART II

CIRCLE CITY, ALASKA TO VICTORIA, B.C.

Circle City
Fairbanks
Dawson City
Whitehorse
Haines
Dawson Creek
Prince Rupert
Victoria
CANADA
San Francisco
USA
San Diego
Tucson
San Carlos
Mazatlan
Mexico City
MEXICO
San Salvador
EL SALVADOR
PANAMA
Colón
Panama City
Buenaventura
Bogota
COLOMBIA
Cali
ECUADOR
Quito
Tumbes
PERU
Cuzco
Lima
La Paz
Nazca
Arequipa
Tacna
BOLIVIA
Santiago
CHILE
ARGENTINA
Orsorno
Bariloche
Perito Moreno
El Calafate
Punta Delgada
Ushuaia

6

LAND OF THE MIDNIGHT SUN

The Steese Highway back to Fairbanks was in excellent condition, devoid of the potholes and washboard we'd encountered in the Yukon, and a few kilometres out of Circle City later, we pulled up alongside an abandoned green and white Chev van. Its driver had somehow managed to drive it over the embankment, and it was now head-first in a ditch. I noticed a sticker on the left-rear door window announcing "THE KING IS COMING." Who could that be, I pondered. Elvis? Arnie? Margaret spotted an orange bumper sticker partially hidden by the underbrush and jumped out to read it.

"Jesus saves," she said it read.

"Well," I replied, "he didn't save him."

The road wound its way through rolling hills covered with scrub bush and a few stubby trees. This far north, and due to a thick layer of sphagnum moss that prevents penetration of the sun's warmth, the first two or so metres are almost permanently frozen. On the south-facing slopes where the sun had partly thawed this permanent frost, or permafrost, small stands of white spruce and poplar had taken root. On the north-facing slopes, however, little thawing had taken place except the top half metre or so. Out of this thin layer of mush, or muskeg, little was growing other than little shrubs, some Arctic bell heather, Arctic forget-me-nots, and a profusion of unknown wildflowers. A few stunted and spindly black spruce, requiring little in the way of root systems, could also be seen. Soon, trees disappeared completely and the vast, flat, and treeless tundra of the Arctic ran to the horizon.

A short time later, the Chatanika River came into view and we followed it for about fifty kilometres. Among the stands of birch and white spruce along the river, and where little sunlight could reach, we could see small patches of snow. As we approached Fairbanks, huge tailings heaps filled the valley floor, courtesy of the bucket-line dredges brought into the area after prospectors had taken the easy gold. And if dredges hadn't been used by the mining companies, they had brought in water cannons. Under terrific pressure, water hoses had blasted away the hillsides in search for gold. It was quite a mess.

By late afternoon, we had reached Fairbanks with its population of thirty thousand. Small plain homes, flat-roofed warehouses, and numerous parking lots lined the grid of streets. Founded back in 1901 on the heels of a gold discovery by an Italian named Felice Pedroni (the locals changed his name to Felix Pedro), Fairbanks looked to be, like Alaska itself, a city of no frills. It looked very utilitarian and, quite frankly, rather forgettable. We passed through quickly, stopping only for gas and supplies.

I was still getting used to twenty-four-hour contact with an eleven-month sometimes crying, sometimes smelling, always demanding, and now a walking Martin. I grabbed two bottles of bourbon.

The Richardson Highway leaving Fairbanks was paved and we covered the 150-kilometre run to Delta Junction, and the official beginning of the unpaved Alaska Highway, in two hours.

"Let's try for Tok," I said. "The map says it's only 160 kilometres."

"Dear, it's eight o'clock," Margaret replied. "We should have stayed in Fairbanks. Lisa and Martin won't last until ten."

"Well, let's see how it goes," I said. After about sixty kilometres I had my answer.

"Mar-tinnn!" screamed Lisa. Margaret turned to find Lisa's hair sticking out of Martin's clamped fist.

Lisa started sobbing in her quiet way, while Martin started flinging his toys everywhere.

"See," said Margaret. "You're just like my dad. You men always want to drive just a little farther to find just a little better place to stay. Well, you just can't do that with two little children."

"OK, for Christ's sake, we'll stop," I said, turning up my offence as I quite obviously had no defence.

I hadn't seen it on the map, but by a stroke of luck we had reached Lisa Lake. Lisa thought that was quite exciting and, once assured her hair was still there, was soon back to her normal happy self. Martin was another story.

No amount of food or milk would settle him down. By ten o'clock, I had finished my third bourbon and had run out of bedtime stories that I was on-the-spot creating about three mythical travellers I called Rocky Raccoon, Porky Pig, and Gordy Gordo. In desperation, I started talking in soothing tones about my golf swing and my decision to switch from a fade to a draw, and on and on and on. This put Lisa to sleep immediately. Martin struggled to keep awake, but it was a useless struggle, and by ten fifteen he was also out cold.

"I'll have to use this golf talk sleep strategy more often," I said to Margaret.

"Well, it's always worked for me," she replied.

It still being daylight, and nicely fortified by Mr. Jim Beam, I grabbed my brand-new casting rod and Mitchell Garcia reel and headed to the lake. After a quick–as it turned out, too quick–rod assembly, I was ready to cast.

"I got one," I yelled, and in ten seconds a ten-inch grayling was flapping on shore. I cast a second time. Another strike, another ten-second battle, and this time a nine-inch trout. Two casts. Twenty seconds of 'battle.' Two fish!

"Nothing to this," I said smugly.

"David, what about playing the fish?" said Margaret. "You're not supposed to just reel it in at a hundred K's an hour and then bash it."

"Yeh, well they're too small to fool around with. One more cast. Maybe they're bigger farther out."

With that, I whipped the two-piece rod back and then violently hurled it forward. The violence of the hurl worked beautifully, and my lure landed a good thirty metres out with a huge splash.

Immediately, I sensed something wrong. Why the big splash? And why was my rod shorter? The answer was floating in the lake. The rod had separated and along the fishing line had shot the rod's top half.

"My rod," I yelled. "Look at my rod. Son of a bitch. I've lost my bloody rod. Christ, I just bought the bloody thing."

After she stopped laughing, Margaret, as usual, had the answer.

"Just reel it in," she said. "Just reel in your rod."

Just reel in my rod. Reel in my rod. Frantically, I power reeled, and in short order a tangled mess of line, lure, and rod lay at my feet.

"David," she said, "it's probably the wrong time to say it, but you can't just have a couple of drinks every time the kids get on your nerves."

"Margaret," I replied, "it is the wrong time, so please just leave me alone to fix this bloody mess."

Now, to date you've probably noticed virtually nothing has been written about our children, four-year-old Lisa and not quite one-year-old Martin. If you, the reader, do not have children, then clearly you'll have no interest in reading about kids in a camper. And if you do have children, well, there's little to explain, is there? That being said, all the above business about kids and storytelling and crying and parental frustration will not appear again in this book. In fact, as you continue reading, you're going to start wondering if our kids still even exist.

By eleven, I had untangled everything, cleaned my catch, tossed heads and guts into the lake, and was now safely inside the camper and free from those Alaska blood-sucking mosquitoes. Even at eleven, it was still daylight, for here it's daylight twenty-two hours a day for the three summer months. In fact, farther north in Barrow, it's daylight all twenty-four hours. On this first day south, we had covered 380 kilometres, our longest drive to date. For me, sleep came quickly. For Margaret, not so quick. She claimed I snored. What? Me snore?

The next morning, after eggs and trout, I doused our morning fire, Lisa said goodbye to Lisa Lake, and off we headed along the Alaska Highway. At Tok, we turned north, and an hour and a half later reached Chicken, population twenty, and named Chicken, they say, because nobody could spell ptarmigan, the local wild bird. I have no difficulty with that story.

Just past Chicken, we headed east along the 125-kilometre Top of the World Highway towards a ferry that would take us across the Yukon River to Dawson City. Potholes were virtually everywhere and everywhere they weren't, there was washboard. I thought the camper was going to fall apart. Progress was slow. We passed through Poker Creek and the U.S.A.–Canada Customs border crossing, so now were back again in Canada, and another 110 kilometres of lousy road later, reached the end of the Top of the World Highway.

Its dirt track ended at the edge of the Yukon River. No ferry terminal. No ramp. No sign. No people. No vehicles. Nothing. Nothing across on the other side of the Yukon River either, except a little white shack. What is this, I thought. Had the ferry service across to Dawson City been moved elsewhere? Had we taken a wrong road? We stared across the fast-flowing muddy Yukon for a few moments with absolutely no idea what to do.

"It's moving, there, over there," said Margaret, pointing at the white shack.

Sure enough, the little shack had left shore, and soon, the smallest ferry I had ever seen was fighting its way across the eight or so knot current. Seven minutes later, the little ferry that could slammed into shore in front of our camper. Down came a red ramp onto the dirt road, and off rumbled two identical Silver Bullet motor homes, both towing black Volkswagens, both occupied by retired couples, and both with California plates. This was to be the first of many times we would see elderly Americans travelling in pairs in northern Canada.

"Well, safety in numbers," I said. "Probably just been married too long and afraid if left alone they'd have nothing to say to each other."

"Sometimes you're such a cynic," said Margaret. "Not everybody's like you."

"I'm not cynical," I lied, before leading our lineup of three aboard the ferry, and minutes later, we were parked in the centre of the Klondike gold rush town of Dawson City.

7

THE KLONDIKE LOTTERY

Remember how you loved searching for candies in those Easter egg hunts as a kid? Well, if searching for gold, and the possibility of striking it rich sounds even better, then please read on. Or, if you're feeling your job's lousy, and life hasn't treated you fairly, and it's all been a rather tough slog, then this chapter should put more bounce in your step and make you realize that the life you have is just fine, thank you very much.

We usually split the driving but today I had done it all. Margaret went off with the kids to find a cafe. Tired now, I lay down with a small book about the Klondike. Now reaching Dawson City and the Klondike was no easy task. With what would eventually be a hundred thousand prospectors heading north from San Francisco and Seattle to the Klondike, it was crystal clear that all shelves in the trading posts would be stripped of goods in very short order. And once stripped, no more supplies by sternwheeler could reach Dawson until spring thaw the following May. As a prospector needed to remain for a year to make the trek worthwhile, empty shelves meant he had to pack in a year's food supply or risk starvation. And interested in making sure that a prospector didn't starve and become a burden was the Canadian government. It insisted that if a prospector came north he must, not just suggested to him, he must, pack in a year's supply of food. The government figured three pounds of food per day so that's half a ton. And this was a law that was enforced.

Here now is what the writer in that book I was reading suggested was needed for a year, and over double the governments half-a-ton calculation. (Either that government calculation was way off or this writer was a big eater.)

FOOD

flour – 250 pounds
2 cases canned tomatoes – 144 pounds
salt – 20 pounds
2 cases canned cabbage – 128 pounds
well cured bacon – 150 pounds
2 cases canned corn – 90 pounds
ham – 50 pounds
split peas – 50 pounds
coffee – 20 pounds
evaporated onions – 10 pounds
tea – 15 pounds
desiccated potatoes – 50 pounds
sugar – 150 pounds
pilot bread – 50 pounds
dried fruit – 200 pounds
black beans – 100 pounds
rice – 100 pounds
baking powder – 10 pounds
butter – 100 pounds
beet extract – 2 pounds
lard – 60 pounds
pepper – 1 pound
cereals – 100 pounds
mustard – 1 pound
case condensed milk – 60 pounds
two cases corned beef – 112 pounds
misc – matches, string, coal oil in tin cans – 122 pounds
candles, 20 bars soap – 10 pounds, 2 cases roast beef – 132 pounds, 2 cases beef tongue – 138 pounds, 2 cases canned fruit – 110 pounds

TOTAL: 2,535 pounds (1,150 kilos)

HARDWARE

1 long-handled shovel	whetstone
1 pick	hand ax
1 ax, duplicate handles	shaving outfit
5 pounds wire nails	frying pan
5 pounds pitch	kettle
2 large files	Yukon sheet-iron stove
hammer	bean pot
jack plane	utensils
brace and bits	2 buckets
large whipsaw	2 miner's gold pans
hand saw	150 feet, 5/8 inch tape
draw knife	chisel
jack knife	

Add clothing, a tent, fishing tackle, toss in a repeating rifle and cartridges, and you're closing in on one and a half tons. (No toilet paper?)

Now once all their supplies were collected and piled dockside in Seattle, prospectors had two options to reach Dawson City and the Klondike. Those leaving early enough could go by ship to the Bering Sea, and then by one of eight sternwheelers up the Yukon River to Dawson City, and a total of almost seven thousand kilometres. Expensive but doable.

Those leaving later in the year, and who couldn't go up the Yukon before the sternwheelers stopped running in September at freeze-up, were left with the second option. They headed by ship to Juneau and then to Skagway. From there, they had two options.

The least popular was the White Pass Trail. A prospector taking this option packed his gear by horse up and over the snow-covered treacherous trail, and a trail so narrow that in some parts it was less than a metre wide. Then he returned to the trailhead for a second load, and then a third, and then a fourth, and until all his supplies were piled at Lake Bennett near the headwaters of the Yukon River. His horse, of course, did the heavy lifting if, and a big if, it survived. Unfortunately, at least three thousand didn't. The trail became known as the Dead Horse Trail. If a prospector ran short of food, he ate his dead horse. Then, once that hundred kilometres had been completed and Lake Bennett reached, the prospector built a raft, piled on board his huge stack of supplies, abandoned his horse to starvation (if it hadn't been eaten), and then, and hopefully avoiding capsizing, floated a further four hundred or so kilometres along the fast-flowing, and dangerous in parts, Yukon River to Dawson City.

A prospector's second option, and the preferred route, was through nearby Chilkoot Pass. Although the Chilkoot Trail was somewhat shorter than the White Pass Trail, it was far more treacherous. Being too steep, and therefore impassable for horses, the trail forced a prospector to haul his ton or more of supplies on his back and sled, and up and over rugged rocks and glaciers. Then, and just like the White Pass Trail users, he had to retrace his steps again and again and again until all his enormous pile of supplies reached Lake Bennett. Finally, and like option one, he would build a raft and head downriver to the Klondike. On arrival, the lucky ones staked their claim, built a log cabin, and chopped up a winter's supply of firewood. Two chapters later, Margaret had returned.

"What a quiet place," she said. "I got a good picture of this cute little yellow church. Most of the buildings, though, are in bad shape. Some are barely standing. You should see the old two-storey hardware store down the road. It's collapsing sideways. They've got it propped up by four big logs. It reminds me of our poor camper when we picked it up."

"Yeh, there's not much going on up here, is there," I said. "They'll probably eventually get it all restored for the tourists, but doubt I'll be one of them. Anyway, listen to this. Picture yourself in a four-by-six-metre cabin with no windows and a dirt floor.

Imagine living like that for a year. No toilet, melted ice for water, a few sticks of furniture, and a little sheet-iron stove. Okay? Now picture your one-room cabin in the middle of nowhere, no phone, no road, no neighbours, no horse, nothing. And for food, you get nothing fresh for a year, just bacon, canned goods, rice, beans, stuff like that."

"Well," replied Margaret, "I wouldn't want to live like that, but I can certainly picture it. That's how many people in Peru and Bolivia live high up in the Andes, except their houses are just made of stones or adobe bricks and with a grass roof. And far worse food. Even in Argentina, I've seen peones [unskilled labourers] live like that."

"That does sound depressing," she continued, "but at least those people had the hope of finding gold. The poor people in the Andes have no hope of anything. Anyway, what's your point? That we were well off in Victoria and shouldn't have thrown it all away, or what?"

"No, no," I said, "I just didn't realize how difficult things were up here back then and perhaps still are today."

It was tough enough to get to the Klondike in 1898, and probably even tougher to stay. It was, however, the search for gold that was the most unbelievable.

The first step in prospecting was to dig a test hole maybe five to six metres down to bedrock. Here was where the gold bearing gravel, if found at all, would be found. Unfortunately, the ground was frozen solid all winter. So what a prospector had to do was start using up his precious firewood supply, light a fire, and then keep it burning for twenty-four hours. That would soften about twenty centimetres of ground. Then he'd remove that twenty centimetres by pick and shovel, light another fire, and remove another twenty or so centimetres of ground. This would go on day after day until bedrock was reached. By my math, that's twenty-five or so days of twenty-four-hour-a-day fires. And if the hole didn't look promising, it was simply abandoned. Then, to keep from freezing to death, he would have to replenish his firewood supply. And after all that, away he would go and tackle test hole number two.

Now if he was one of the lucky ones and colour showed, he would start tunnelling along the gold-bearing layer, and lighting fire after fire. Very slowly, he would pile up tons of gravel, and what instantly became a series of frozen piles. Then when spring arrived, these piles were all thawed out using even more fires. And finally, when the streams started running, water was run through sluice boxes, all those tons of gravel were shoveled in, and with luck, the prospector struck it rich. A few claims paid $15,000 a day. A few men arrived in Dawson with hundred-pound sacks of gold dust. Some even sold their claims to mining syndicates for hundreds of thousands of dollars.

Most weren't so lucky. It's been estimated that perhaps only thirty thousand or so of the estimated one hundred thousand that headed for the Klondike ever got there. The remaining seventy thousand eventually gave up the struggle and headed back home, or starved to death on the way, or perished in the Yukon rapids.

And of those thirty thousand who did manage to reach the Klondike, many arrived too late and found everything staked out. Others who managed to stake a claim dug test hole after test hole through the winter, but found nothing. It was a lottery up here with mostly losers and very, very few winners. Wyatt Earp and Tex Rickard had the right idea. Just build a saloon, stock it full of high-priced booze, throw in a few hookers, and then go sit your butt near your warm stove. The prospectors would do the rest.

After our look-see around Dawson City, we headed south-east along the unpaved 325-kilometre Klondike Highway, and reached Whitehorse by late evening. Then, after a couple of days exploring the nearby Atlin Lake area, we reached the Alaska Highway.

Now the December 7, 1941, Japanese attack on Pearl Harbor had highlighted a serious concern to the Americans. The concern was the Japanese gaining control of the North Pacific shipping lanes. If that happened, and the supply chain was cut off to their military and air force bases in Alaska, then Alaska would be vulnerable to attack, and if Alaska fell, then Canada and the continental United States would have a serious problem. An overland supply route as a backup for shipping supplies was needed, a route was selected, and construction of the Alaska Highway began on May 3, 1942.

Exactly one month later, Japan attacked Alaska's Aleutian Islands of Attu and Kiska. In May of 1943, the Americans retook Attu. Then in August of 1943, and with the muddy and mosquito-infested and unpaved 2,237-kilometre Alaska Highway now completed, thirty-four thousand American and Canadian troops, supported by a hundred ships, tackled the retaking of Kiska. The troops landed unopposed. Incredibly, the Japanese force of five thousand had, under fog cover, evacuated. The Allies searched Kiska for five days and found nothing. Fifty-six American and Canadian troops were killed or wounded as friendly patrols fought each other in the fog and mist.

Thirty-three years after construction, the Alaska Highway was still all mud and mosquitoes and still unpaved. It was also seemingly misnamed, as only 357 of its 2,237 kilometres are in Alaska. We drove fourteen hundred kilometres on the muddy Alaska Highway, passing through Watson Lake, Fort Nelson, and Fort St. John, and finally reached pavement just outside of Dawson Creek. From there, it was a quick few days south through Prince George, Williams Lake, Cache Creek, and Vancouver, and a final short ferry ride later, we were back on Vancouver Island.

"Well, that's it," said Margaret as we drove off the ferry.

"Yeh, it's only an hour and three-quarters but the ferry ride this time seemed like forever," I replied.

"No," said Margaret. "That's it, period."

"What do you mean?" I answered. "You mean stop the trip

now? We've hardly started and I've closed my office, and we've got this camper, and we've rented our house out for a year!"

"Look dear," said Margaret, "Martin is one tomorrow. It's me who changes the diapers, and handles the crying, and all the mud. And Lisa, she's just four. We've got friends who won't drive two hours with their kids. This is very difficult, you know. It's very difficult."

I stared straight ahead, seeing tears coming in Margaret's eyes, but not knowing what to say. It proved a long thirty-minute drive to Victoria. It was completed in total silence.

North of Fairbanks: Margaret, Lisa, and Martin

North of Fairbanks: Log Cabin (sod roof)

Steese Highway: Fairbanks to Circle City

Circle City, Alaska: Pop. 68, Est. 1893

Circle City: "The End of the Road" – Most Northerly Point on Highway System

Ferry across Yukon River to Dawson City

Dawson City, Yukon Territory: built 1899
Original Palace Grand Theatre

Dawson City, Yukon Territory: built 1899

Alaska Highway

The 1970s: "Far out"

The 1970s: "Groovy"

8

REGROUPING IN THE TEABAG CITY

Long ago, I discovered a simple truth about travel. Simply put, as time passes by, the rough edges of your travels are worn smooth. You can easily tell when this smoothing-out process is complete. That's when your most often repeated travel stories to those 'listening' were yesterday's nightmare moments. They are also, by the way, the best received. For example, nobody ever cared about my good-time travel stories like being in a French movie with Jean Paul Belmondo, Catherine Deneuve, and her sister Françoise Dorléac. The unspoken responses I sensed were always "you're boring" or "you're bragging." And if the 'listener' was under fifty, the spoken reply was often "who are Belmondo and those sisters?" What my listeners liked were the tales of travel's rough moments, the bad and the very ugly. The ones they loved best, however, were the humiliating.

Like at age twenty-one going into a Swiss pharmacy with thirty-two-year-old Fred from Alberta, and a case of crabs. (I am not discussing seafood here.) The French word for crabs wasn't taught when j'entre dans la salle de classe. And Fred! The closest redneck Fred had gotten in school to French was a kiss, a safe, and some salad dressing. Nothing, however, bothered Fred. Extending his right arm, and to the obvious delight of the four cute fräuleins behind the counter, Fred proceeded to open and close his hand in, depending on how one looked at it, a very successful attempt to imitate a crab. (Readers, please always remember that advice your mother gave you. Put toilet paper on those public toilet seats.)

Or like my walking into an alley off the Champs Élysées with a black marketer promising me an excellent exchange rate, with dollars for three months' travel, and then emerging five minutes later with a bundle of old francs worth just slightly more than bugger all. (Old and new francs were both in circulation at that time with a hundred old equalling one new.) The stack of new francs flashed before me had been, by sleight of hand, switched for old ones. The switched stack of golden oldies I received for my dollars just covered my train ticket out of France, and to where, I might add, I never returned for five decades.

For Margaret, the smoothing-out process took all of two weeks. By then, the stress of dealing with the mud and the mosquitoes and the black flies and the crying, and possibly, although surely just a remote possibility, twenty-four-hour close quarter living with me, were all forgotten. She was now describing Alaska and the Yukon in tones she normally reserved for the Patagonia. We were back in quaint English wannabe Victoria, or the Teabag City as my deceased friend John once called it, but it was now quite clear. We were now only just passing through.

Having narrowly escaped hometown humiliation of an early failure, I set about doing some necessary pruning. I remembered reading about Charles Lindbergh and his preparations for his solo flight across the Atlantic back in 1927. Charlie had taken a pair of scissors and clipped away all the unnecessary edges of the flight charts he was going to carry to save some weight. Now ours was not a weight problem. (That certainly turned out to be wrong!) It was a space problem. First to go were books. Out went all those 'self-improvement' and all those 'how to' books I had never cracked. They were joined by those three unread books from long ago that still remained unread. Next to go were most of those to-be-used-once-only items, the ski clothes (what were we thinking), the collapsible chairs, my fishing rod and reel, and our little rubber raft. Also left behind was the metal detector which was to be used to locate all that gold plundered from the Incas by Pizarro and his gang and that any sloppy Spaniards had dropped.

Repairs came next. Those needed overload springs, as suggested on the ferry to Haines, and repeated by Wally in Circle City, were installed to boost the camper's sagging rear end. Shocks were attached above the front of each door and their other ends secured to the cab-over to hopefully prevent further cab-over bounce on the truck's roof. In human terms, I guess sort of a little bum and breast lift. With camper cosmetic surgery now completed, we drove to builder Verne's shop where he installed a new water tank. Verne assured us this one would last the entire journey. (Verne, buy a copy of this book and see if that was B.S.)

Two days before leaving, my father-in-law Dick again brought up the matter of protection.

"I have something for you," he said. "I cut it out of the newspaper while you were up north. Somebody off Yates Street is selling what they're calling a Protectstik that delivers a five-thousand-volt shock. Why don't you check it out before leaving tomorrow?"

Early the next morning I drove to town, walked up an alley off Yates Street on the west side of the Odeon Theatre, up two flights of stairs, and finally into a small office. Here I was greeted by a puffy-faced man of around fifty.

"So you're here about my ad," he said. "Here, I'll show you how it works."

With that, he produced a normal looking umbrella, unscrewed the silver tipped end, and dropped in five batteries.

"Now all you do now is flick the umbrella opening switch with your thumb. Somebody attacks, just poke 'em. They get five thousand of the best. Here, I'll show you."

Before I could answer, he reached out and touched my left pant leg.

"Well that's just a little shock," he said. "You don't get the full effect on the pant leg. Wait 'til somebody grabs it. They're on their ass. It's from South Africa. Don't know why you want it, but white women down there use it for protection. It's called a rape stick."

"It's probably pretty effective," I said, "but is it legal?"

"Look," said Protectstik seller, "today's Saturday. I made a special trip down here for you. It's a hundred bucks. It's my last one. Do you want it or not?"

I paid him the hundred and went home and checked my copy of the Criminal Code. If the umbrella qualified as either a concealed weapon under section 85, or a prohibited weapon under section 89, I was risking five years in the big house. Now what! On one side was the law. On the other, visions of those wild, primitive Peruvians and Brazilians I'd seen in old *National Geographic* magazines leapt into view. Bugger it, I thought, and the innocent looking black umbrella disappeared behind the false camper wall. At the last minute, I tossed in a hand line and hooks for fishing, and after a round of goodbyes to both our families, we boarded the ferry for Port Angeles in the State of Washington.

. . . .

Diary

July 24th: At long last, south of Victoria. Today, Martin turned one and twenty days ago, the old U.S. of A. hit 200. It was 1976, the big Bicentennial. Red, white, and blue colours were everywhere. Even lampposts and fire hydrants were painted red, white, and blue, for Christ's sake. The Stars and Stripes flew from the porches of the little wooden white houses in the little towns of Middle America. Love these names down here in northern Washington: Sequim, Dosewallips, Skokomish, and Squaxin.

July 26th: Reached Oregon. Signs along the highway now sounded more rugged and western, more what I'd expected from Oregon Trail country, names like Jumpoff Joe Creek and the Valley of the Rogue and my two personal favourites to date, Hooker Creek and Balls Ferry.

July 31st: Reached California. Thought my new favourite name for a town was Weed, until saw Los Baños, or the bathrooms in English. Think about it. Who would name their town 'the bathrooms.' Then saw a sign. "TO LODI - 9 MILES." We kept on I-5. I mean, like the C.C.R. song, who wants to get stuck in Lodi.

August 2nd: Reached Los Angeles, took a wrong turn looking for a motel, ended up near the University of Southern California. Now mid-afternoon and motel lobby door locked. Strange! Place run by a black family, all four standing in the lobby. Owner opened door. I asked why door was locked in middle of the afternoon. He said it was to keep out the undesirables. Guess I looked puzzled, because I certainly was puzzled. Then he said:

"Mexicans, a lot of Mexicans live around this area."

Very sad. Guess everybody has to look down on somebody.

Left L.A. & headed down I-5, turned off on the El Toro exit near Mission Viejo, drove past Leisure World, climbed a long hill, and finally pulled up to a ranch style home, and where standing at the open front door, and almost as if he knew we were coming, was Charles Callaghan.

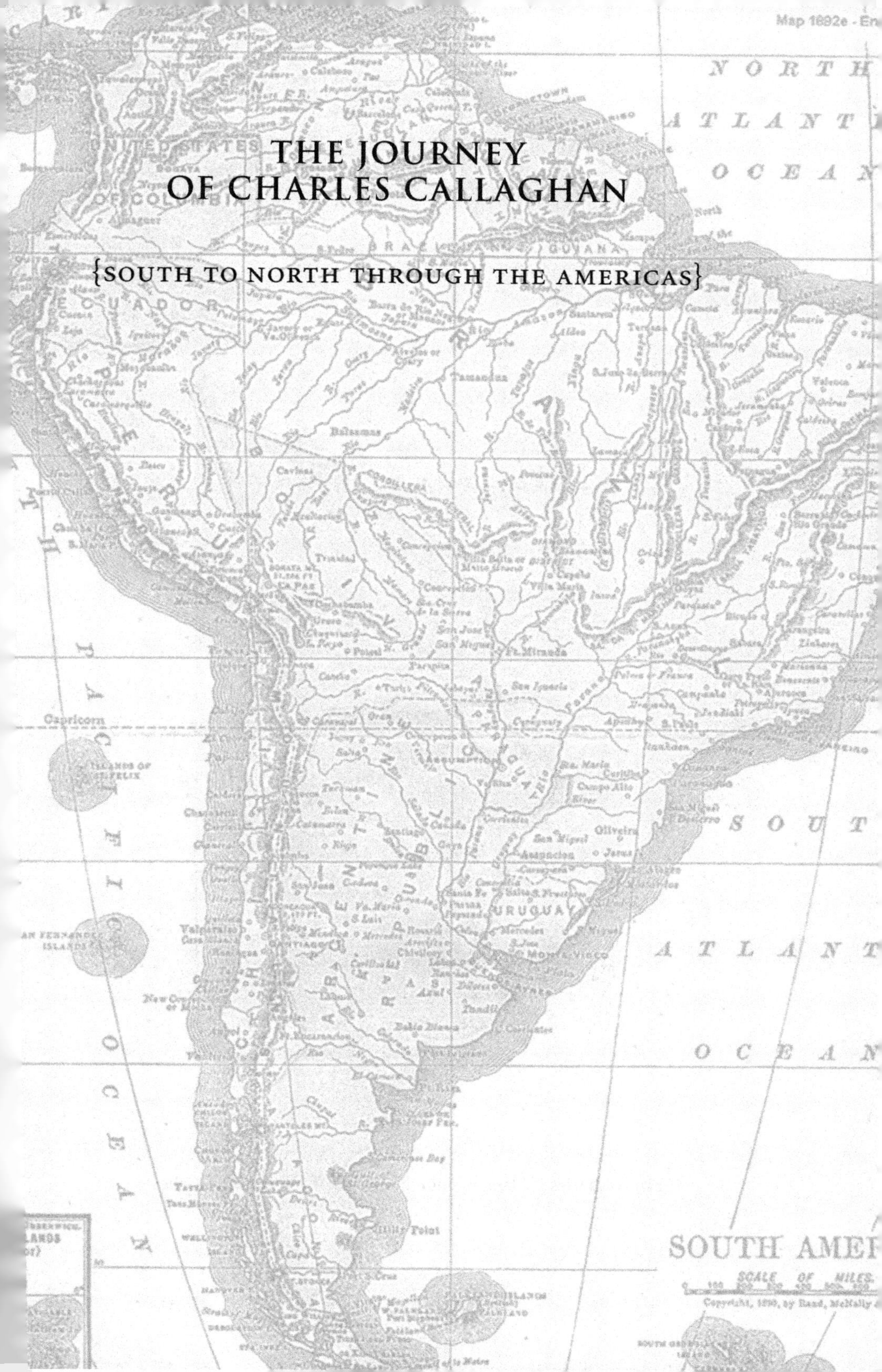

THE JOURNEY OF CHARLES CALLAGHAN

{SOUTH TO NORTH THROUGH THE AMERICAS}

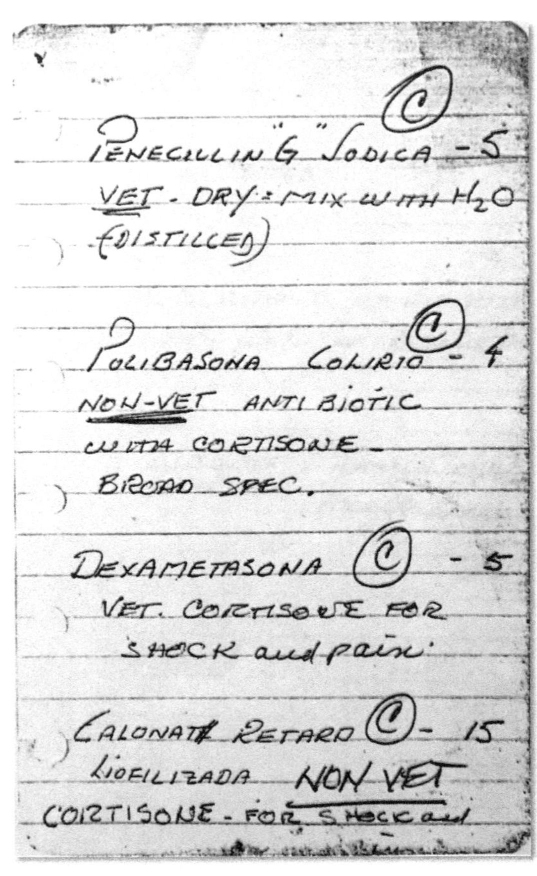

Ⓒ
PENECILLIN "G" SODICA - 5
VET - DRY: MIX WITH H_2O
(DISTILLED)

Ⓒ
POLIBASONA COLIRIO - 4
NON-VET ANTI BIOTIC
WITH CORTISONE -
BROAD SPEC.

DEXAMETASONA Ⓒ - 5
VET. CORTISONE FOR
SHOCK and pain.

CALONATH RETARD Ⓒ - 15
LIOFILIZADA NON VET
CORTISONE - FOR SHOCK and

From Charles Callaghan's notebook: list of veterinary supplies

9

THE RUBBER SADDLE MAN

The best laid schemes o' mice an' men
Gang aft a-gley,
An' lea'e us nought but grief an' pain
For promised joy.
—Robbie Burns, "To a Mouse"

On March 20, 1920, schoolteachers James and Helena Callaghan left a hospital in Brooklyn, New York. They arrived home with baby Charles, the fifth of what were to be ten children. Little, inquisitive Charlie grew up in this big family, in this big city, and with a big sack full of dreams.

By October, 1941, World War II, minus the United States, was in full swing. The Germans had advanced within two hundred kilometres of Moscow, and if Moscow fell, then Britain would be standing alone. Meanwhile, in the borough of Brooklyn, there was another battle taking place, and a battle far more important to Charlie and his neighbours on Avenue L in Flatbush. The first World Series had been held in 1903. By 1941, the Dodgers were 0 for 38. Now, for the first time since 1920, Brooklyn's beloved Dodgers had the National League pennant flying over Ebbets Field. All that remained between Reese and Reiser, and Brooklyn's first Series victory, were the Bronx Bombers of Rizzuto and the graceful DiMaggio, fresh off his fifty-six-game hitting streak.

In game four, and down two games to one, Charlie and his home team Dodgers were clinging to a 4–3 lead entering the ninth. Two groundouts and two strikes on the Yankees' Tommy Henrich later found the Dodgers on the verge of tying the Series. Casey's next pitch, an overhand curve, broke in and down to left-hitting Heinrich. Henrich missed it by a foot. In that brief instant, the Series was tied. Surely now, Charlie and his boys from Flatbush would triumph. The Bums would be Bums no more. Charlie would go on to complete his degree at Villanova and then, well who knows what would follow. All really was right with the world, or at least in the world of Charlie.

And then catcher Mickey Owens dropped the ball. Owens dropped the ball and it rolled near the Dodger dugout, and Henrich streaked safely to first. All hell then broke loose. The Yankees scored four and won the game. And that was it, really. On October 6th, the Yankees claimed the Series and darkness descended over Ebbets Field for fourteen long years until Podres and Robinson and Campy and the Duke of Flatbush gave Brooklyn its finest hour.

The heartbreak was too much for a twenty-one-year-old. Interest in Villanova vanished, and the streets of Brooklyn offered Charlie nothing. From across the Atlantic, a world of adventure called out to Charlie and his friends in Flatbush. Young Charlie dreamed of flying above the clouds and shooting down the Nazi enemy and capturing the hearts of pretty French girls. Two days later he was gone.

Charlie enlisted in the Canadian Air Force. Then, just two months after that Yankees Series victory, Pearl Harbor was attacked by the Japanese. The U.S. entered the war, Charlie jumped over to the American Air Force, and by the war's end finished up flying B-17s over North Africa. NYU came next for Charlie, and B-26s in the Korean War followed NYU.

Nine years of desk duty later, he was Colonel Charles Callaghan, husband to Shirley and father to four boys. Charles was stationed in Washington, D.C., as speech writer and Special Assistant to General Curtis LeMay, Chief of Staff of the United States

Air Force. Charlie's first twenty-one years in Brooklyn had been idyllic, his next twenty meteoric. By 1961, he had finished his climb. Charlie was atop his mountain.

His first year under LeMay proved to be difficult. In Algeria, the War of Independence had reached its seventh year. In Asia, Laos was under guerrilla attack, and the Communist North Vietnamese government of Ho Chi Minh was threatening U.S.-backed South Vietnam. Closer to home, the invasion of Cuba on the Bay of Pigs by the U.S. left twelve hundred POWs in Castro's hands as a bargaining chip. In Washington, Kennedy was slowly escalating U.S. involvement in Vietnam, and slowly edging closer to a war no high-ranking officer in the Air Force felt could be won.

By 1962, and surrounded by a deteriorating world, Charles sought refuge in his job, but it offered little. Charlie was left to produce hackneyed party line speeches that were all censored by McNamara's staff. Working secretly behind the scene, he had attempted, successfully, to persuade Senators Boggs and Goldwater to introduce a bill coordinating Armed Forces plans for Vietnam, but the bill had been shuffled off to a committee and had died in a back room.

In September of 1962, U-2 reconnaissance planes discovered Soviet missile sites in Cuba. On October 1st, Kennedy called in the National Guard to quell race riots and allow James Meredith to become the first black to enrol at the University of Mississippi. Then on October 15th, Kennedy and Khrushchev brought the world to the brink of nuclear war.

Charlie's world was falling apart. The clincher came on November 1st. On returning to his office that evening, he found two men in his office searching, they said, for bugs. Searching my ass, thought Charlie. They're planting the damn things. Charlie had climbed his mountain, and the view scared him. In December 1962, and at age 42, he retired to California.

By 1970, he was doing contract work for the military to supplement his pension, Vietnam was raging, and America's youth protesting. Charlie was restless and bored and disturbed by the racism and the drugs and the struggle of it all. To Charlie, and too many others, his country had become a nightmare. Then shortly after his fiftieth birthday, Charlie dreamed his grandest dream of all.

He would take his four boys and fly to Argentina. Then they would buy horses and ride the length of South America and right up into California. And if they got that far, why, maybe they'd just keep right on going. The idea seemed absurd to his friends, yet somehow workable, and quite exciting to Charlie, who tackled his new dream with military-like precision.

By fall, all was ready. On November 2, 1970, Greg, aged nineteen, Brian, aged seventeen, Dwayne, aged fourteen, and Charles, aged nine, or Carlitos, as they called him, crossed the tarmac at Ezeiza Airport, just outside of Buenos Aires, Argentina. They crossed with father Charlie and straight into the waiting arms of Argentina's bureaucracy.

They arrived with a .22 rifle, a shotgun, a Winchester .243, and a .357 Colt Python pistol. "Weapons of War" said the aduana official of the Winchester and pistol. "Hunting equipment" insisted Charlie, and the battle was joined. The *Buenos Aires Herald*, the local English newspaper, published an interview with Charlie, and word quickly spread in both the Anglo-Argentine and military communities of the great adventure. In due course, Charlie's military connections produced some unexpected dividends. Arriving unannounced one morning at their hotel were two coffin-sized boxes full of veterinary supplies, delivered gratis by the military. Cortizone, Novocain, penicillin, tranquillizers, syringes, vials, suture needles, and everything else possibly required for horses soon covered the hotel room floor, and from which Charlie then made a manageable selection.

Finally, and over two and a half months of expensive hotel living later, they got their guns back. Now, however, two-and-a-half good travelling summer months had been lost. Though disheartened, Charlie and his boys nevertheless boarded ship for the port town of Rio Gallegos, two thousand seven hundred kilometres south, and shortly after arrival pitched camp at the nearby Estancia [ranch] Los Pozos. Here was where, his Argentine military contacts had advised him, would be horses for sale. The plan was to purchase ten horses: five to ride, and five for pack animals. From there, they would ride 250 kilometres south to the Chilean town of Punta Arenas, located at South America's mainland tip. Then in early December, and therefore at the beginning of summer, they would start north on their unforgettable journey.

A week went by. Finally, ten horses were produced for inspection. They were tired and old and certainly not the desired Criollo horses of Charlie's dream.[2] Worse, the price was six hundred a head. The majordomo [ranch manager] had seen them coming, and no amount of haggling would reduce the price.

Now, it wasn't Charlie's stubbornness about those guns that was proving the obstacle. It was the lack of money. Six thousand dollars simply wasn't available for ten horses, let alone these pathetic rejects, and there weren't any other horse sellers in the area. And worse, it was now the end of January, and summer here nearly over. The fall and winter of the harsh windswept Patagonia was just around the corner. Their window of opportunity had been the three summer months, and they were gone.

Crushed by this setback, Charlie and his four sons bussed sixteen hundred kilometres north to the town of San Carlos de Bariloche where Charlie had some contacts. Here the five stayed through the fall and winter of '71. In October, so now in mid-

2 Criollo horses were the wild horses of the Pampas, and descendants of the horses brought to Argentina over four hundred years ago by the Spaniards. They were known as perhaps the world's best long-distance horses, with both hardiness and stamina.

spring, wife Shirley arrived from the States with some much-needed cash stuffed in her bra, and Charlie started planning another attempt.

After Shirley returned to the U.S., Charlie and the boys bussed four hours south to the small town of Esquel where he was able to purchase ten horses at a more reasonable two hundred a head. Finally, in November of 1971, so now a full year after they had arrived in Argentina, their journey began. Off they rode from Esquel and towards their starting point of Punta Arenas, Chile, now a full 1,870 kilometres to the south. They were led by ten-year-old Carlitos, proudly riding his brown mare, and with his own pack horse trailing behind and roped to his saddle.

On their third day out of Esquel, they reached a valley running north to south, and tucked into the foothills of the snow-capped Andes. Purple thistle had sprung up alongside the gravel road and mosqueta [wild rose] bushes bunched against the roadside fence, the bloom now gone and rose hips awaiting a jam maker. Ponderosa pine and poplars dotted the hills.

It had been here in the Cholila Valley, and in the Province of Chubut, that three Americans travelling under the assumed names of James Ryan and Mr. and Mrs. Harry A. Place had arrived in 1901 to homestead 3,087 hectares [7,628 acres]. Harry's 'wife' Etta at some point allegedly returned to the United States. James and Harry, whose real names were Robert Leroy Parker (aka Butch Cassidy), and Harry Longabaugh (aka The Sundance Kid), then had left their three-log-cabin setup on horseback in 1905, travelled across the Andes to Chile, and then gone north to a cluster of shacks in Bolivia named San Vicente. Here, at least if you believe that movie, they had allegedly robbed a mining company, been tracked down, and died in a hail of bullets.[3]

By now, it was clear that gravel road travel wasn't working. The

3 1969 movie, *Butch Cassidy and the Sundance Kid*, starring Paul Newman, Robert Redford, and Katherine Ross.

roads were hard on the horses, and a two-year drought had left little roadside grass for horses to eat, and certainly not the ten to thirteen kilos per day, per animal, Charlie had calculated necessary. The horses, however, had to be fed. One day, Charlie saw a six-wire-strand fence a metre high, and all that was separating their horses from a field of healthy grass. Charlie cut the fence. He had now started what became a daily routine of fence cutting, horses eating, and fence repair work.

On the fourth morning out of Esquel, they awoke to find their horses gone. A frantic search ensued, and a full two hours passed before they were located and successfully returned to camp. In the days that followed, the horses were hobbled, yet still somehow managed to hop away during the evening, making a frustrating start to every morning.

Slowly they journeyed south, passing through the Welsh settlement of Trevelin, and then the Valley of Corcovado that reminded Charlie of the Vale of Kashmir. By Lago [lake] Vintter, food and morale were low. Early one morning, Charlie sent Greg off hunting with the .22 rifle, and soon he returned with a ranch owner's lamb slung over his shoulders. Later that day, while Greg and Brian tackled the gutting and skinning, little Carlitos got the evening's fire going using Charlie's ingenious idea for a fire starter: a box of elastic bands. When lit, each elastic band burned for up to five minutes and provided a simple fire starter solution to each day's frustrating problem.

Once there was a nice pile of coals, the lamb was spread-eagled on the metal cross they were packing and the cross was then jammed into the ground at a slight tilt over the fire. It was their first and was to be their only asado [Argentine BBQ].

Two hundred kilometres south of the Cholila Valley, they reached the small settlement of Rio Pico. It was here that Americans Bob Evans and William Wilson had lived back in 1909, and here where they had kidnapped a wealthy businessman from Buenos

Aires. Depending on which historical anecdote you care to believe, Evans and Wilson were either low-life American scum, members of the Wild Bunch, or Butch Cassidy and the Sundance Kid. What is certain, however, is that in 1911, Evans and Wilson were tracked down and killed for their deeds, their journey through life ending in unmarked graves just outside of Rio Pico.

It was here also that Charlie's dream came to an inglorious end. The boys were sick and filthy and hungry. The horses were malnourished. Dwayne's packhorse had a badly infected left forelock. And attempting to hold this ragtag bunch of four kids and ten horses together was a very weary and extremely frustrated fifty-one-year-old Charles Callaghan.

It was over. The journey with his four boys that was to take them two and half years, and that would emulate the legendary ride of A. F. Tschiffely back in 1925, had lasted less than two weeks. It had ended 1,625 kilometres shy of Punta Arenas, their planned starting point. It had ended before it had even begun.

. . . .

We arrived unannounced at the home of Charles and Shirley Callaghan, old friends of Margaret's family from their stay in Margaret's hometown of Bariloche, and where Charles and the boys had wintered before attempting their journey by horseback.

"Well, David," said Charles, sipping the last of his tea, "the overall experience was quite rewarding. The boys learned leather-braiding and butchering and caring for animals, and so forth. A lot of it wouldn't help them much later on in life, but you know it's all part of life's experience. And we talked of everything, the great artists and writers, history, marijuana, Vietnam, women, anything you could imagine. Really, it was wonderful to be with my four sons for such a long time. The trip itself, the actual attempt to ride all that way, was of course a disaster, a huge personal failure.

"A while ago, you asked me why it hadn't worked out. I guess it comes down to poor planning and money. We should have just left the guns in Buenos Aires instead of wasting those two and a half months. And with more money, we could have bought those ten six-hundred-dollar horses in Rio Gallegos. Even better, maybe we could have bought a wagon to carry hay for the horses. Anyway, it's all in the past. I've come to terms with it now. Let's go down to the basement. I've got something to show you."

Downstairs, and after swearing me to secrecy, he removed a white bed sheet, and there, resting proudly on a sawhorse, was a reddish-brown saddle.

"It's a rubber saddle," announced Charles. "Indestructible and inexpensive. It's of course only a prototype, but I really think it could come to something."

A rubber saddle, I mused. A rubber saddle. Charlie's grand dream had died years ago in the Patagonia. But the dreamer? Well, the dreamer most definitely lived on.

PART III

VICTORIA, B.C. TO PANAMA

Circle City
Fairbanks
Dawson City
Whitehorse
Haines
Dawson Creek
Prince Rupert
Victoria
CANADA
San Francisco
USA
San Diego
Tucson
San Carlos
Mazatlan
Mexico City
MEXICO
PANAMA
San Salvador
EL SALVADOR
Colón
Panama City
Buenaventura
Bogota
COLOMBIA
Cali
ECUADOR
Quito
Tumbes
PERU
Cuzco
Lima
La Paz
Nazca
Arequipa
Tacna
BOLIVIA
Santiago
ARGENTINA
CHILE
Orsorno
Bariloche
Perito Moreno
El Calafate
Punta Delgada
Ushuaia

10

QUASI KEROUAC AND THE MAN FROM SWAT

Remember that new replacement water tank put in by builder Verne on our way back through Victoria, the one he said would last the entire journey? Well, it lasted to Grants Pass, Oregon. From there, it was a continuous cycle of tank leak, camper flooding, and tank repair. In San Diego, we tracked down an RV repair shop south of town and purchased six tubes of waterproof sealant. We also had installed a new water tank and a water pump. Verne's water pump had also stopped working, somewhere south of San Francisco and north of L.A. in San or Santa something. There are thirteen places in that stretch beginning San or Santa, so it's an easy place to forget.

Once the tank and pump were replaced, it was after six. Patient little Lisa had run out of patience, and in the adjoining car seat was a howling Martin. A place to sleep was needed, and needed fast. Now up north, finding a spot for the evening had been easy. A lakeside campsite near Haines, a field in Atlin, a distant cousin in Dawson Creek, an old friend in Osoyoos, there always seemed an easy answer. By Washington State, however, more imagination had been required. Gas stations had proved useful when attendants co-operated. Parking on streets in the nicer areas of towns had worked. All-night parking lots had also worked, the best being in San Francisco, near the waterfront, and three blocks from Fisherman's Wharf.

Now, on the outskirts of San Diego, those options weren't available, and there was no motel in sight. Then, looming up ahead, and alongside an artificial lake, was one of those large, super-organized, and very jammed, RV parks, the kind I had studiously avoided so far and swore I'd never enter. Reluctantly, we turned in. Slowly, we worked our way through the RVs' permanent resident section with their smoking briquette barbecues and their artificial lawns and the extra-large size brassieres and pink underwear and what-have-you's fluttering in the summer evening breeze. From wire fences dangled little unlit lanterns, all installed by each resident and to clearly define their own little permanent piece of motor home heaven.

The husbands were slouched silently in their aluminum recliners, some clutching a beer, some perhaps contemplating days gone by and what might have been, others perhaps coveting their neighbour's far slimmer and more attractive wife, and the rest probably just contemplating when it was time to pound another beer.

The wives were standing in small groups, the chattier ones undoubtedly discussing the week's little triumphs and failures, and the contemplative ones off by themselves, perhaps contemplating the high-school studs they'd married, and the duds they were now stuck with. Maybe, I thought, I was overthinking things. Maybe they were just thinking of their next round of cocktails.

God, I couldn't believe I was really here. I mean, would that old beat Jack Kerouac have pulled in here? "Say Neal, I'm exhausted. Let's pull into that nice RV park over on your right, yeh, that one, the one on the fake lake."

Now, no one had ever confused me, or accused me, of being anything remotely like Jack Kerouac.[4] On the other hand, I wasn't anything like Willie Loman from *Death of a Salesman*. Perhaps, I guess, somewhere in the middle of a Kerouac and a Loman. Perhaps a quasi-Kerouac. Quasi-Kerouac in a camper.

---

4 Before the tune in, turn on, tune out counterculture generation of the sixties, there were the writers and poets of the fifties. This was the Beat Generation (the beatniks) led by author Jack Kerouac, the author of the classic, *On the Road*.

At the far end of the park were a row of camp tables for the day visitors and the overnighters. It was here where we pulled in, and here where I met Jake. I never really got his name. Italian, and he was a Rocco, older and fatter, and he was a Ralph. But he wasn't Italian, and he wasn't old and fat, and he looked like a Jake, so that's what I'll call him. He sat at the next table, poured into tight jeans and a tight tee-shirt, and topped off with a baseball cap advertising some moving company. He was tanned, fit, maybe thirty, and most definitely drunk. Jake was on a two-week vacation from whatever he did for a living, and had with him his wife and his six packs of beer. By ten o'clock, we were surrounded by beer cans, many Jake's, and more than a few mine. There hadn't been much to say. I found out he was a recent ex-member of Special Weapons and Tactics. (SWAT). He learned I was Canadian. That's about it. Finally, when our mindless conversation petered out to total silence, Jake stood up and gestured with his right arm. He wanted to arm-wrestle. Don't know why I followed him to a nearby table, but I did. It certainly wasn't because I sensed victory.

"So Jake," said Quasi, "on our trip to South America, any ideas for protection?"

"Eighteen inches of lead pipe," offered the former Man from SWAT.

Thump, Quasi lost.

"So, uh Jake," said Quasi, "was SWAT like it's on TV or what?"

"Christ no," said X-SWAT, "I was in the drug busting squad in L.A. I love bashing those fag heads."

"Bashing heads of dealers with lead pipes," said Quasi. "Is that really necessary? I mean it's illegal, I know, but surely you don't bash their heads."

"Look, Canadian," growled X-SWAT, "those dealers are lazy fags. I hate them. They're filth."

Thump, Quasi lost round two.

"Jesus Christ," said X-SWAT, "that's all you got? This is bullshit. This ain't worth my time. And I'm part-Indian, and never went to any Junior College, so don't start running down Indians. What a bloody joke." (Say what? Now there's a man with some issues!)

X-SWAT 2. Quasi 0.

"Jake," said Quasi, "let's go left-handed. My right's kind of sore."

Then one of life's little miracles happened. Was it those thousands of golf balls I'd hit? Did the man upstairs, and on special occasions, temporarily paralyze a member of the clan of morons? Anyway, Quasi won. And then he won again, and then again. Score now: X-SWAT 2, Quasi 3.

"OK, OK," said X-SWAT. "You're all right. That's enough. Left arms don't count anyway. (Explain that to me, please.) And, uh, Canadian, don't tell my wife, OK?" (Wow! More issues than I thought!)

Quasi got up, left Mr. X-SWAT stewing in his string of humiliating lefty losses, and headed off to bed. By now, all the little lanterns were turned on, shining red and white and blue, and giving a combo Christmas-Bicentennial glow to the summer evening.

At eight the next morning, Mr. X-SWAT was still asleep. As for Quasi and family, they were doing the 'Kerouac,' on the road, heading due east, and going full tilt boogie for Tucson.

11

CHE AND EH

'EH' ON 'CHE':

What is a 'Che'? First, let me tell you what it isn't. It isn't Ernesto Guevara's middle name. In fact, it's not a name at all. And it isn't a descriptive nickname, like Red or Rookie or Swish or Slick. Che is just an expression, exclusively used by Argentines, and for so long, nobody can recall its origin. It's informal, and available for friends and strangers alike, as in:

"Hey Che, let's go to the game," or "Che, do you have the time?"

Freely translated it's "Hey you," or "Hey buddy."

So there you have it. Che is no one and everyone. All Argentines are Che.

And in a way, Che was the perfect nickname for Ernesto. It's affectionate, of the people, exclusively Argentine, so perfect for a budding revolutionary. It was certainly a definite improvement over his previous nickname, Chancho, which is pig in English. (Now seriously, would you follow someone over a ridge, and to your probable death, a person who everyone called 'pig' to his face?) 'Che' was a lucky nickname choice for Guevara. It was also lucky for him that Cuban photographer Alberto Korda snapped that famous photo, for without that nickname, and without that photo, who really would remember today the name Ernesto Guevara de la Serna.

So Che Margarita, how to describe you to the reader. I would describe you as high energy, low maintenance, easy to get along with, or 'muy simpatico,' as the Argentines say, and stunningly attractive. You can fix our lawnmower in the morning, ride a horse bareback in the afternoon, and then dance all night at the most formal of balls. You bring to the table patience, the Spanish language, and a good sense of direction. You're a person that's happy here, and if you're over there, why you're just as happy there. The thing is you never dream of over there. I guess that's where I come in.

. . . .

'Che' on 'Eh':

David may be painting the picture, but it's also my journey. So here's an insider's view of the man holding the paintbrush. Patience? It's now twenty-four-hour days with the kids. He's hanging in there at the moment, but I'm waiting to see him in action at those Latin border crossings. And handy? He's a city guy. If something breaks at home, he doesn't grab a tool, he grabs a phone. How's that going to work four kilometres high up in the Andes, and hundreds of kilometres from anywhere?

And mechanical? He always tells this story, and like he's almost proud of it, of driving through the Deas Island Tunnel just outside of Vancouver when his car starts steaming. He makes it to a gas station in Ladner, turns the car off, takes the keys out, and goes inside to ask for help. The owner looks out the window. The car is violently shaking, and in its final death throes. Then it stops shaking, and goes completely silent. The owner says to David that it's the first time he's actually seen a car seize up. When David asks him what to do, the man said he'll help push it to the junkyard that's just across the road.

And then he says two years later, he's driving through that same Deas Island Tunnel when again, his car starts steaming. He gets through the tunnel and pulls over, and figuring the problem's no water in the radiator, dumps in some beer. That doesn't work. Then he realizes the problem was just like before. It's not the radiator at all. And here, and I kid you not, he says he immediately drives to

Ladner, skips that same gas station, and goes straight to the same junkyard. Last time it was free. This time the junkyard owner charges him five bucks.

"It's called oil, David. Oil!"

Oh, and he says that long ago he once changed a tire. I believe him. And absolutely no sense of direction whatsoever. And a little compulsive. His current thing is locking the camper door, then violently twisting and pulling the knob, and to make sure it's actually locked. The knob's already come loose. One day it's going to come right off in his hand. Then he'll probably say to me, "Well dear, sure lucky I checked."

On the upside, he's determined and he's organized, a list of his lists kind of guy. A Capricorn all the way. He talks about Lindbergh flying solo across the Atlantic and cutting extra paper off his lists and maps to save space and weight. You know, writing this, I actually think they may be distantly related. Let me put it this way. I doubt we'll run out of dental floss.

Asked three months ago to describe my husband, I'd have said he's a dreamer, an armchair cowboy. Big hat, no cattle. But now? Well, now I'm not so sure. I am, however, sure of one thing. Without him, maybe I'd be at home searching for that can of Drano, but without me, he'd still be in L.A. looking for the on ramp.

12

HARRY IN MAZATLAN

It's a 671-kilometre run from San Diego to Tucson, running right through the Mojave Desert. At Gila Bend it hit 42 Celsius (109 Fahrenheit). We covered it in a day. Once again, the cab-over was bouncing on the roof, and in fact had been doing so since Sacramento. In San Diego, I had jammed in a thicker foam rubber pad but, just like up north, only had succeeded in dulling the noise, not solving the problem. Stiffer shocks than what had been installed in Victoria were clearly necessary, so stiffer ones were installed in Tucson in a final effort to prevent the cab-over's collapse once bad roads were encountered.

Repairs completed, we drove the seventy kilometres to the border town of Nogales. Here we purchased a month's vehicle insurance for Mexico and a year's policy for Central and South America at the Border Insurance Agency on Grand Avenue. Then we proceeded into Mexico to tackle the aduana and inmigración.

The engine was no sooner turned off when two large men in cartoon-sized sombreros wandered over and parked their fat butts on the newest seat in town, our hood. This, I thought, isn't a good start. By now it was noon. It was hot, dusty, and extremely quiet for a border town. I grabbed our documents and entered the nearby one-storey wooden building. Inside, a man sat engrossed in his newspaper. I moved to a nearby long counter and waited. Three minutes passed. Finally, when he felt he had proven his point, he folded his newspaper, pushed himself up, and wandered over.

"Señor?" he said.

"Si, por favor, aduana, inmigración, pasaportes, quatro personas,

I mumbled, immediately exhausting 20 per cent of my Spanish. I then proceeded to stack everything he could possibly need on his counter: passports, medical records, vehicle ownership, truck registration, Mexican insurance papers, the expensive carnet, and finally my British Columbia and my international driver's licence. He shuffled the stack, handed back the carnet, medical records, and two driver's licences, then slowly walked back to the comforts of his desk. An hour passed. Finally, his office wanderings, his paper shuffling, his mini staff meetings, his coffee cup filling, and what I assumed was the usual border rubber-stamping reached its painful end and we were free to proceed. We strapped in the kids and headed down Highway 15, having absolutely no idea what had transpired other than an exercise of 'who's the boss here' was over. We left Nogales [Walnuts] for Guaymas and leaving Señor Bureaucrat to his newspaper and the two fat-butted sombreros to their next visitor.

At seven o'clock, and still ten miles shy of Guaymas, we noticed a sign on our left. Way up on the mountainside, boulders had been painted white, and arranged to read "SAN CARLOS–8KM." An arrow pointed west. No place named San Carlos was mentioned in, and what was to be our first of many uses of, *The South American Handbook*, but whatever was there was closer than Guaymas. We left Highway 15 and fifteen minutes later reached the entrance to the Casa Moviles de San Carlos Trailer Park, locally known as Shangri-La. Here was trailer park number two of our journey, but this one was in Mexico, which somehow legitimized everything. Kerouac would have approved, I thought, so in we went.

It was huge, terraced right down to the water's edge on a lovely bay, and with space for maybe two hundred campers. Only five spots were occupied, and all five were on the upper terrace near the entrance, so far, far away from the beach. I guessed it was a new facility, and both its newness and the intense summer heat, which averaged about 32 degrees Celsius, were combining to keep people away. We drove down the slope to the terrace nearest the ocean and set up camp a nice twenty metres from the Sea of Cortez. Pelicans were dive-bombing for fish to our right, and on our left a small sailboat lay deserted on the sandy beach. That's it. Not a soul was around.

On our fifth day in heaven, I remembered seeing a small restaurant-bar at the entrance as we had driven in, so we walked up the slope and treated ourselves to a dinner of huge Guaymas shrimp sautéed in butter and garlic. Their shelled length equalled the length of a ballpoint pen.

At bedtime, Lisa realized her book she had taken to the restaurant was missing, so back I hiked up the hill to the restaurant. It was now pitch black, and a slight rain was falling. A short conversation with a German tourist led to one cerveza. That was one cerveza too many. In seconds, wind was howling and was closely followed by thunder and lightning. Rain then started pounding on the restaurant's roof. Assured by the bartender it would all stop within minutes, I stayed. Forty minutes and two more beer later, it was over. Clutching Lisa's book, I slowly worked my way through the darkness back down the hill to our camper and which now stood in a foot of water. On opening the door, I found Margaret huddled with the kids on the floor.

"Why didn't you come back?" she screamed. "The camper almost turned over!"

"What are you talking about?" I said. "It was just wind and rain. It just lasted longer than I expected. I didn't see any point in getting wet."

. . . .

CHE:

I've read David's letter to his parents from Mexico City. Here's a quote: "Luckily I was in a bar when the storm broke getting fortified."

Well, while he was safe and dry and chatting up the locals, here's what he missed. Now, there was a good reason why the trailer park was vacant. It was hurricane season. I knew it, though doubt he did, as this had been our first night in Mexico. Who would have thought? The wind had come in a flash. I heard the next day that it had reached 112 kilometres an hour. And the famous cab-over he had designed that makes the whole thing so top-heavy? The wind was getting under it, and lifting it up, and the shocks were groaning away. Honestly, I felt like we would either be pushed sideways or flipped over backwards. I was petrified. And then the rains came. I've seen rainstorms in Argentina and Canada, but this was ridiculous. It was hitting the camper so hard the windows were actually leaking.

Once the wind died down, I went outside to check if we could make it to the restaurant. I couldn't see anything, couldn't find our flashlight, and the water I was standing in reached my knees. Every inch of water that had hit the trailer park had run like the flash flood it was, straight downhill to the bottom area of the campsite, and right where we, and only we, had brilliantly camped. I think David got the picture the next morning. The entire lovely sandy beach was gone, the sand sucked back out to sea. Only boulders and gravel remained. As for that little sailboat, it had been flipped over and then been stabbed through its hull by its mast—sort of a sailboat suicide. And the wind and rain? The worst locals had seen in years. And our protector? The man of the house? B.S.'ing with the locals over a beer. Yes, I was mad, and I remained mad a lot longer than he knew. In fact, as I'm writing these thoughts down all these years later, I'm getting upset all over again.

. . . .

With our lovely beach now wiped out, we packed up and looked elsewhere. About seven kilometres south of San Carlos, we approached a mountain named Tetas de Cabra [Goats Tits]. (God, I love these Spanish names.) We turned right off the highway and began our search for a new campsite. Off the highway about a kilometre, and in the middle of nowhere, we stumbled upon an old asphalt airstrip. Margaret wondered whether it might have been a landing strip formerly used by drug smugglers. A few buildings were scattered about, their walls collapsing and their roofs a skeleton of timbers. Only one building remained intact, and on its roof was her answer. Painted in white were the letters "CATCH-22". We had inadvertently stumbled onto the 1970 movie set used by Mike Nichols in capturing Joseph Heller's novel *Catch-22* on film.[5] Nothing else was here. No parts of the B-25 bomber used in the fiery crash scene were lying around. The tree where Yossarian once sat naked had vanished.

We drove the one-and-a-half kilometre asphalt runway built for the movie until it ended at a long white sandy beach. Waves were pounding the shore, but it looked safe enough, so in we went, and me holding Martin. A big mistake! Within minutes, a huge wave smashed into us, hurtling Lisa tumbling to shore and safety, and sending me ass over tea kettle. (Now surely that's one of the most incomprehensible yet descriptive phrases in the English language.) Little Martin was torn from my grasp, rolled to shore, and was now being rapidly sucked back out to sea with next stop being Acapulco. All that grounder practice with my father then paid off and I caught him between the pipes. Meanwhile, Margaret surfaced, her bikini top around her neck and its bottom at her knees. And surfacing seconds later from nowhere, and a lucky for them ten metres away, were two black wetsuits. I could clearly see their bulging male eyeballs through their face masks. Baby grounder drills and a nude woman. What a day for scuba diving!

5 It starred Alan Arkin, Martin Sheen, Art Garfunkel, Bob Newhart, Orson Welles and Jon Voight. Today, Voight is better known as the father of Angelina Jolie. The shooting of the movie took longer than expected. With no Artie, Paul Simon was left alone to produce the bulk of the album *Bridge Over Troubled Water.* Simon wasn't happy about this turn of events. One of the songs in the album, *The Only Living Boy in New York*, references Artie's absence. "Tom, get your plane right on time, I know your part'll go fine, Fly down to Mexico." Simon and Garfunkel were originally called Tom and Jerry. Garfunkel was Tom.

Mazatlán

There were few black men in Victoria, B.C. when I grew up. The only one I ever met stood behind the plate in Victoria's first-ever Little League All Star game on upper Cook Street. I had come up with the bags loaded. It was a brief conversation:

Umpire: "Strike three, you're out."

I turned to see who'd called me out on a pitch I felt was clearly high out of my mini strike zone. The ump straightened up, looked down at me, removed his mask, and smiled. His face was black. His name was Doug Hudlin.[6]

I have never mentioned this to anyone, but I admit right here that I visited that plate three more times that game, and each time with the bags loaded. And each time it was the exact same conversation, and the exact same high fastball out of my strike zone (well, in my twelve-year-old opinion anyway), and the exact same result. Out on a called third strike.

Five years later, and playing in a men's soccer league, I collided with a player who sent me flying. I looked up. It was Doug Hudlin. After the game, I went up to him, and said he probably wouldn't remember me, but he'd umped Victoria's very first All-Star game in Victoria, and I was in it.

"Oh, yes," he had said. "I remember that game well. There was a big crowd. The *Colonist* sent a reporter, and even a photographer. It was quite exciting for everybody. And sure I remember you. You're that little slick second baseman who struck out with your bat on your shoulder four straight times with the bags loaded. I mean, it was Victoria's first All-Star game. Who could forget that?"

Eight years passed. I was working for the summer as a porter on the CPR line between Vancouver and Winnipeg. My conversation with the adjoining car's porter had gone as follows.

Black porter: "I want your room tonight to 'entertain' the

6 Doug Hudlin: Inducted into the B.C. and Canadian Baseball Hall of Fame.

conductor's wife. I'll give you ten bucks." (Well, 'entertain' wasn't the word he'd used, but we must keep things clean now, mustn't we.)

Me: "Fifteen is good."

Doug Hudlin, my very own cross-Canada brothel, and that motel owner back in L.A. By age thirty-four, that was the sum total of my black experience coming from WASP-like Victoria.

Then I met Harry. We had arrived late to Mazatlán from San Carlos. With a temperature of 36 Celsius keeping tourists away, the campground north of town was virtually empty. (This was to be our last campsite until Chile.) The next morning, the beach was ours except for a woman with two small children. Margaret agreed to watch the kids, so first swim was mine, and out I went. The waters were choppy and a strong morning wind had just started blowing off shore. I was just heading back when I heard him.

"Dolly, I can't make it honey. That's it baby. I can't do it no more."

I glanced back, and there, maybe fifty metres farther out, and belly up on an inner tube, was a very large black man.

"Hey man," he yelled, "can you help me out?"

Margaret was screaming something about undertows and currents while the woman on the beach was just plain screaming. Out I went. He looked about forty, weighing in at a good 230 pounds, and was floating on a well-patched inner tube clearly out of its weight class. His next words weren't encouraging.

"Hey man," he said, "I can't swim. And my tube's losing air."

"Don't grab me," I ordered, as I grasped the inner tube behind his head. I then started a slow tow against the wind to shore, hoping to cover the hundred or so metres before his tube totally collapsed and I sank to the bottom with 230 pounds of Americana around my neck. None too soon my feet touched bottom, and my catch of the day was immediately smothered by the woman on the beach.

Now Harry had his day's second problem. Granted, it hadn't

been the most heroic looking of rescues, but the fact remained, I had saved his life. We were bonded together for the day whether he liked it or not, and judging by his mannerisms, he didn't like it at all. Harry stared down at the sand, poking away with his right foot and rapidly jumping from one topic to another. He made no attempt at eye contact. The morning passed with the white lawyer from Canada and the black bus driver from L.A. searching for some common ground. We spent the afternoon surf casting, Harry with his brand-new rod and reel and me with my hand line. I had watched the locals in San Carlos fish off the cliffs and they'd made hand line fishing look easy. First, they secured shrimp to a triple hook attached about three feet up the line. Then a weight was tied at the line's bottom. A few twirls around the head and away the weight and baited hook went, the weight landing on the bottom, and the bait now floating temptingly above. It wasn't as easy as it looked. Unless you count two five-inchers, I caught nothing. Harry, however, proved the afternoon's hero, landing two nice sierra for dinner.

Wife Dolly then did the honours, frying them in butter, garlic, some blend or another of spices, and loads of pepper. After dinner, and now nine o'clock, Margaret left to put the kids to sleep and leaving the three of us to finish our discussion of America's great performers. I mentioned Dinah Washington for her voice, and Tina Turner for, how can I say it, being Tina Turner. It turned out that Dolly was a friend of Tina's (miracle número dos, the first being my take-down of the man from SWAT), and the introduction was mine to have if we ever visited L.A.

Before we left, we exchanged addresses as people often do, though knowing they'll probably never meet again. I have kept that address, and still have it today. I always told Margaret that maybe someday we would visit Harry and Dolly and get that fish recipe. I've never told her about Tina.

Mazatlán to Guatemala

From Mazatlán, we headed south to Tepic, eastward through the Sierra Madre Occidental mountain range to Tequila, and reached Mexico's second largest city, Guadalajara, at 1,560 metres. We had long ago settled into our driving routine, me starting the day driving, and navigation and children left to Margaret, and then two or so hours later, exchanging jobs. This routine would continue the rest of our journey. From Guadalajara, we climbed another six hundred metres, and in a day had reached Mexico City. The next morning the peso collapsed. It was its first devaluation, they said, in twenty-two years, and it went from twelve and a half pesos to the American dollar to twenty. With the Canadian dollar by some miracle (that's the third miracle of our trip so far!) at par with the American, we abandoned our cramped home for a few days of comfort in a motel.

Leaving Mexico City, we now travelled east to the Gulf of Mexico and the city of Vera Cruz, famous in Hollywood as a Burt Lancaster movie but, more importantly, as the place where Hernán Cortés landed in 1519.

Cortés was leading an expedition of ten ships at the behest of the recent conqueror and newly appointed Governor of Cuba, one Diego Velázquez. His orders were to explore the coastline and barter with the natives. Instead, Cortés sent one ship back with gold and silver to appease Velázquez, scuttled the other nine to prevent his men from retreating home, then took his little army of four hundred, fifteen or sixteen horses, and ten to fourteen cannons (totals vary according to which of writers Bernal Diaz, W.H. Prescott, or Velázquez you choose to believe), and started a march westward.

Leaving the tropical coast, Cortés and his small army struggled 450 kilometres up and over 3,600-metre-high snowy passes in the Sierra Madre Oriental, dispatched an army of forty thousand Aztec warriors, and finally reached the island city and Aztec centre of Tenochtitlan, today almost totally buried under modern day Mexico City. The Aztecs' leader, Montezuma the Second, then meekly succumbed to Cortés and Christianity. For that, his countrymen stoned poor Montezuma to death. (Montezuma's revenge, of course, came later to some tourists who dared enter Mexico.) It had taken Cortés eighty-three torturous days to cover that Vera Cruz-Tenochtitlan stretch. We covered it in reverse, and in a pleasant and air-conditioned day and a half.

In Vera Cruz, we now fully realized the enormity of the task that lay ahead. As the seasons are, of course, reversed down south, we had settled on an outside arrival date in Ushuaia of February 28th to avoid the snow-storms of fall and winter. A late arrival would mean complete failure. Side trips had therefore to be carefully chosen, and so it was that plans for a visit to the Yucatan were scrapped. Reluctantly, the beaches of Vera Cruz were abandoned, and off we pushed towards Mexico's most southwestern corner and our next border crossing challenge.

In Tapachula, Mexico, and just before reaching the Guatemalan border, we got the necessary visas for Guatemala from the local Consulado General de Guatemala, but only after some difficulty. Now remember that Nogales border crossing into Mexico, and those two men in cartoon-sized sombreros, and that border official who kept me waiting for an hour? Well, the Guatemalan official here in Tapachula pointed out that absolutely nothing had been stamped in our passports when we'd entered Mexico, no entrada stamp, no visa stamp, nada. It therefore appeared to him we had entered Mexico illegally. Fortunately, Margaret straightened out that rather serious matter with her Spanish and her smile, and then off we went to get our visas from the Consulado de El Salvador and the Consulado de Nicaragua.

A short thirty-minute drive later, we saw two white-washed

stone walls lining both sides of a bridge, and in bold black painted letters on the far wall, was the word 'Guatemala.' We lumbered over the bridge across no man's land and pulled up in front of the most official-looking building. I proceeded to gather an armload of border documents and, after insisting to Margaret that border crossings were a man's job, headed inside.

A series of four-by-ten-foot tables laid end to end ran from the entrance to the far wall, hung a left, and then continued another ten or so metres north. Behind this long line of tables sat the finest of Guatemala's border bureaucracy.

"Pasaporte," the second man at the first table muttered.

Then it all began again. Nogales revisited, only far, far worse. Review of the four passports. A request for money. Check the visas we had just obtained in Tapachula. Another request for money. Feigned interest in our carnet, which I knew was unnecessary for Central America because they built no vehicles. Pay the man. Down the line I went. Our two driver's licences and four vaccination certificates were reviewed and were followed by endless forms, rubber stamps, and police checks. Everyone had some little task, and everyone wanted a couple of quetzals. Finally, at the lines end, came the middle-aged scrutinizer of car registration papers, a thin hollow-cheeked and worry-lined man with smoke pouring out of his nose, and with a face that would surely register about ninety on an age meter. He stared at the car's registration with a glazed-over look for about two minutes, pushed them across to me, and then ceremoniously flipped over his right hand.

"Five quetzals por favor," he announced.

More dough! Well, that was it for me. Reaching into my wallet, I extracted a scrap of paper on which I had written the four words I had intended to use when we'd entered Mexico, but had never done so, words that had perhaps never before been uttered in this Guatemalan building.

"Yo quiero un recibo," I said.

"Yo quiero un recibo?" said the thin man, the words tumbling out of his mouth amidst a cloud of smoke.

"Si," I said.

He then lowered his head and very slowly and carefully scrawled the words "five quetzals" on a piece of paper torn from a magazine. "Recibo," he said, handing it over with a look more mystified than mocking. No Guatemalan letterhead, no Guatemalan stamp, no carbon copy for his records, no signature. Zip, bugger all, nada. Just a scrap of paper as my receipt.

Back to the camper I went with my useless receipt and now accompanied by two customs officers.

"You asked for a receipt?" said Margaret, clearly more mocking than mystified. The process had taken an hour and half, and I had been clearly defeated. Then in a flurry of "holas" and whatever else she said in Spanish, Margaret charmed the inquisitive duo who proceeded to enter our camper to check things out. I 'forgot' to show them our secret compartment and the fake wall. In minutes, it was all over. The last border crossing I would ever attempt on our journey had finally ended. And there's a simple lesson there folks, and one that should be remembered by you in all of life's little situations. A man has to know his limitations. Remember that please.

I slipped into the cassette player Dylan's song 'Isis,' and off we headed, due south and straight into the heartland of the Kingdom of Guatemala.

13

THE KINGDOM OF GUATEMALA

In 1523, thirty-four-year-old Captain Pedro de Alvarado left Cortés to his conquest of Mexico, gathered an army of his own of 420 Spaniards, then set off south from Vera Cruz to further Spain's control and influence in the area. Following him were various religious orders: the Franciscans, the Dominicans, the Mercedarians and, most prominently, the Jesuits. A few years later, the Kingdom of Guatemala young Pedro had created was complete and stretched from Mexico to Panama. It was ruled in the name of the king of Spain, and comprised the six ill-defined 'provinces' of Chiapas, today part of southern Mexico, Guatemala, San Salvador, Nicaragua, Honduras, and Costa Rica. Wheat and sugar cane and cattle and sheep were introduced. A mining industry thrived. For three hundred years, the Kingdom of Guatemala flourished. The various orders were granted huge tracts of land by Spain and, coupled with unlimited indigenous slave labour and Spain's tax exemptions, grew wealthy and powerful. As for Spain, it received untold riches because all trade was decreed to be with Spain, and with Spain alone.

All this economic success in the Kingdom, however, was being achieved amidst a geographical and political minefield. A hundred volcanoes were belching away, and earthquake followed earthquake. And if the land was hostile, the population was explosive. High Spanish taxes were upsetting the mestizos [Spanish and indigenous] and the mulattoes [Spanish and African] and the zambos [indigenous and African]. As for the criolles, those born locally of pure Spanish blood, they were infuriated by Spain only granting position and power to those actually born in Spain. Everybody was fed up being beholden to, and dominated by, Napoleon Bonaparte's older brother Joe, currently sitting on the Spanish throne. And topping that all off, the six 'provinces' were now fighting amongst themselves.

Then, following the lead of the American Revolution in the north, and the independence movements in the south led by Bolívar and San Martin, the Kingdom of Guatemala completely fell apart. In 1821, Guatemala declared its independence from Spain, and Chiapas seceded to Mexico. The remaining four 'provinces' bonded together as the Federal Provinces of Central America. In less than twenty years, that federation collapsed, and off spun the four little republics of today.

By 1976, little had changed. There were still the same hundred odd volcanoes, thirty-three in Guatemala alone, and some still belching away, and still the same devastating earthquakes. In the United States, the 'love affair,' if it can be called that, is between tornados and trailer parks. In Central America, it's between earthquakes and capital cities: San Salvador, El Salvador, in 1854; Managua, Nicaragua, in 1931 and 1972; Guatemala City, Guatemala, in 1541 and 1773, and then a final one in Guatemala City in 1976, and just four months before our journey began. That one killed twenty-three thousand people.

And politically, it was the still the same old B.S. Still the military dictatorships and the political assassinations and the civil wars. The last war was in 1969 between Honduras and El Salvador over a soccer game. A total of three thousand soldiers and civilians were killed in the four-day skirmish. Now those are some serious fans!

Our first day in Guatemala was spent meandering through the lush mountain countryside. By six, a light drizzle which had lasted the entire day, had turned to heavy rain. By seven, it was torrential. Slowly the truck's over-matched 460 cu. in. engine pulled us higher and higher into the heart of the old Mayan empire. Banged-up trucks and overloaded buses, many with just one headlight, pulled up alongside for a look, before dangerously passing. The hills got steeper, the rain got worse, and the darkness darker. And then the driver's side wiper stopped moving. Now with zero visibility, I pulled over and stopped, then flicked on the right-hand turn signal to show I had matters well under control. Lisa was impressed. Now what?

I had salted away in our tool box an eclectic assortment of truck and camper parts, some of which I actually recognized, and virtually all of which I couldn't possibly install. (After all, isn't that why gas station mechanics exist?) Everything, that is, except spare wiper parts and extra blades. After two minutes' silence for the dead wiper, I announced my two decisions. First, we would remain right here to sit out the storm on the edge of this cliff. And second, the tunes needed changing. Something more appropriate, something more tropical. Something like Bob Marley.

Margaret wasn't impressed. Out she stepped onto the one metre of shoulder that separated us from a thirty-metre drop to oblivion, and then carefully inched her way back to the camper door. She forgot to take the camper door key, but that was okay, because the camper door had popped open. That wasn't okay, but certainly explained the mysterious banging we'd heard for the past hour. Soon she was back, and proudly holding up her solution to our predicament: my Swiss Army knife and two potatoes.

"Seriously?" I said. "Here we're hanging on the edge of a bloody cliff waiting for some idiot to push us off, and you want me to do what? Cut up some fries?"

"No look," she said, "you just slice them up and then rub the windshield. I saw dad do it once back home on his Jeep and it worked fine. Not as good as a wiper, of course, but it works. Dad told me he'd heard that German pilots did this during the war."

Yeh, I thought, I can definitely see that happening. "Herr Hitler, my Fokker is ready to bomb England. The bombs are loaded, and

I have all the necessary petrol, but I still need my ration of Idaho potatoes."

"See that truck," she continued. "It's got no driver's side wiper but the man's still driving."

Oh, *that* truck, I thought, that huge one barrelling down the hill towards us in this blinding storm, in the dark, and with no lights.

"Well that's because he's a complete idiot," I said.

"No, dear," Margaret replied, "he probably rubbed something on his windshield. I don't know how it works, maybe like when you spit on your swim goggles. Look, give it a try."

Chef David then commenced slicing and dicing and rubbing. Within half an hour, the rain was back to a drizzle, and miracle of miracles, the spud massage actually worked. We started out again, by eight our climb was over, and a short downhill run later we had safely reached the outskirts of a little village hugging the shores of volcano-ringed Lake Atitlan. Our headlights picked out a red-apple-coloured Chevy truck and a little thatched roofed lean-to, and having found nowhere else to pull off the road, we stopped and parked between them for the night. The next morning, Margaret read the weathered sign dangling by one wire over the lean-to. "Cuerpo de bomberos," it read. We had spent the night at the town's fire hall.

Our journey continued south through extremely steep countrysides and all cultivated with bananas, coffee, and cornfields. How steep? A gas station attendant told Margaret an old man had been killed yesterday. Apparently, he'd fallen out of his cornfield.

We passed through the town of Chichicastenango, the epicentre of that recent earthquake that killed those twenty-three thousand, and on our second day out of Mexico, reached the outskirts of Guatemala City. We entered, as we now entered all large cities, with me driving and Margaret pacifying the kids, scouring for and translating road signs, and handling the maps. Her typical conversation to me as we entered towns and cities went something like this:

"Lisa, pick up Martin's bottle. Okay dear, take an easy left. Right there, just in front of that old man carrying the fridge on his back. Lisa, please pick up the bottle. Okay now, David, watch out for that blue pickup full of pigs. Now there, there, take a hard right, at that broken street-light."

After another big city white-knuckle driving job, we reached a little hotel for the night, then set out on foot to the consulates of Honduras, Costa Rica, and Panama to obtain the necessary visas. Later that day after successfully obtaining our visas, one of those usually useless phone calls to a friend of a friend of a friend resulted in a nice dinner with the Argentine ambassador and the Canadian consul to Guatemala. The Argentine was really quite amusing. The Canadian consul couldn't quite get past his self-importance.

El Salvador

El Salvador is small. Not nearly as small as Liechtenstein, but definitely small. Maybe a four-hour drive end to end. Margaret handled the border crossing like she would the rest of our journey, navigating through the polícia, aduana, and inmigración, and at El Salvador's border dealing with a fellow in a gas mask who insisted he had to fumigate our wheels using a five-foot-long spraying gadget. Back she came quite steamed.

"They all thought I couldn't speak Spanish, so kept on asking me for money," she said. "What cheek!"

"Yes," I agreed with the relaxed smile of someone who had spent the past hour half asleep, and who knew he would never again experience border stress, "what cheek!"

From the border to the capital city of San Salvador was about a hundred kilometres, and within minutes of arrival we had located the local Ford agency. By early afternoon, the driver's side wiper was fixed. Now with still part of the day remaining, we headed east out of town and towards the Mayan ruins of Copan in neighbouring northern Honduras. It was a bit of a detour, but would surely be worthwhile. Darkness was closing in as we reached the El Salvadorian side of the border. Rain started pounding down, and amazingly, the wiper again was a problem. Thanks to a lousy repair job, it worked only on its slow setting. For some strange reason, no El Salvadorian guards were in sight. Margaret got out, swung open the metal border gate, and off I drove across no man's land towards the Honduran crossing point.

Two well-armed Honduran guards instantly popped out of their shelter and one holding up his Alto [stop] sign. Margaret, originally interpreter and mother, but now also navigator and border-crossing expert, jumped out and ran over in the driving rain for a chat with the two guards. Then she almost too quickly returned.

We can't cross," she announced. "The border's closed. Apparently they're at war with El Salvador."

"What do you mean at war," I said.

"Well," she replied, "the older guard said it's to do with that same war over that soccer game seven years ago. Apparently this border's been closed ever since."[7]

Back we reluctantly headed to San Salvador and to one of its nicer residential neighbourhoods. Armed guards inside and outside of banks and supermarkets and movie theatres gave the city centre the appearance of being under siege. It was in the nicer residential areas, however, that this siege mentality was most noticeable. All homes were surrounded by high brick walls topped with barbed wire or broken glass, or both. And if a thief successfully managed to negotiate a home's walls without losing part of his parts, he would be greeted by a ferocious Doberman that the

7 The Hundred Hours' War, or the Football War, had erupted in 1969 when a World Cup qualifier was taking place. After three thousand were killed, the four-day war 'ended.' The border remained in dispute for twenty-three years until resolved in 1992.

homeowner let loose every night after dark. And on the street corners were little kiosks with armed guards peering out, San Salvador's local version of Neighbourhood Watch. Every square block of homes seemed to have the same invisible sign hovering above it: "I've got it, you haven't, and you're never going to get it."

Dobermans and armed guards, surely a perfect safe solution for big city camping. Wait until darkness and then settle in for the evening among a city's elite. That became our specialty for the remainder of our journey.

Today, when I think of El Salvador, I think of that 1969 soccer game and the resulting long-festering border dispute. That, of course, and the perfect dump and run. You see, once you leave the U. S. of A., there aren't any more handy dandy dump stations for campers. And for a very good reason. There aren't any more campsites.

Now taking your camper out for a week, you can just pack the products of your few visits to the john back home. What, however, if you've been travelling for weeks on end, and your holding tank's backing up and leaking on the camper's floor, and no dump stations are available? Well then, there's no choice, really. You are forced to execute a camper's version of baseball's hit-and-run, the little dump and run. Ours was perfectly executed. On our only night in San Salvador, we parked in a nice high-end area, and with the camper's rear end alongside a storm grate.

Then early the next morning about six, Margaret strapped in the kids, filled a thermos with coffee, and warmed the engine. Señor mechanic dipped the sticks, checked the fluid levels, and completed the usual morning start check-list.

Next, I cased the area for early morning paperboys, milkmen, garbage men, joggers (not bloody likely), and left-wing guerillas (far more likely than joggers). The coast clear, I then leaned in and removed the holding tank cap. Out shot a blue torrent of days gone by and just missing a crouched-down me. (Well just missing, unless you count the fine spray of blue matter that hit my right pant leg.) The one-metre blue arc hit the storm grate dead centre. It was over in seconds, a well-completed dump and run to make any manager proud. A short drive later, El Salvador was left behind. It was the 2nd of October. Four months had now passed to the day since we'd pulled out of our driveway with our two very young children. That, sports fans, is 2,952 consecutive hours of spouses going one-on one. Give that a try all you happily married couples and see who makes that first call to a marriage counsellor.

Honduras

Has anyone in history ever said, "Dear, let's go for a holiday to Honduras?"

Nicaragua

Crocodiles in rivers, 3.5-metre sharks in Lake Nicaragua (yes, in fresh water), twenty-three volcanoes and nineteen of them active. That 1972 earthquake I mentioned in Managua killed thousands, injured twenty thousand, and left three hundred thousand homeless. Some say the best thing to ever come out of Nicaragua is Mick Jagger's ex-wife Bianca. I just drove through. I believe it.

Costa Rica

It seemed like a pleasant place.

. . . .

Three rainstorms, one dump and run, and one earthquake-crushed capital and our run through the banana republics of Honduras, Nicaragua, and Costa Rica was in the bag. And by the way, for you very young readers, they aren't called banana republics because they each have those clothing stores. And for the rest of you, it's not because they're an impoverished group of little rather forgettable countries situated between here and there, historically riddled with coups, dictatorships, assassinations, volcanic eruptions, and violent earthquakes. Well, all of that's of course true, but the real reason is all those banana plantations. The American-owned United Fruit Company planted a hell of a lot of palm trees in the first half of the twentieth century.

Finally, on October 10th, we crossed into Panama. Finally we were able to buy some reading material in English. The world's struggles were still continuing. Down south, the left-wing youth of Argentina were clashing with the military. Cuban Airlines Flight 455 had crashed into the Atlantic after two bombs placed by terrorists, and with alleged ties to the CIA, had exploded. All seventy-three on board were killed. Up north, it was Carter versus Ford for the presidency. Cincinnati, with Rose and Bench and Morgan, had made the World Series. The Yankees were a game away from the American League pennant. And here in Panama, I was roaming the streets in a small town aptly named David, and with a seemingly unanswerable question. Here we were in Panama, so why wasn't anybody selling Panama hats?

14

THE TRIBE OF ZONIANS

Picture yourself, if you will, leaving Mexico, and on a long journey south. To be sure, the cities wouldn't surprise: noisy, congested, dirty, and downtrodden, alongside affluent, exhilarating, and fascinating, so perhaps just about the sort of mix you'd expect from Latin American cities. It's in the countryside where you would find the unexpected. An old woman struggling home, bent double by a load of firewood. Rusted-out abandoned trucks in nearby fields. Women doing their day's washing in rivers, and downstream, their husbands washing their battered old trucks. A cow, a horse, a dog, lots of dogs, all dead and rotting in the day's sun, and undoubtedly in tomorrow's. A few still standing city buildings, cracked by earthquakes and now abandoned to the homeless. And then you'd see the houses. Earth-floor little huts with walls of stones or adobe bricks and topped with a roof of corrugated sheets of tin or matted grass or cardboard held down by rocks.

Then, after three thousand or so kilometres, and in a blink of an eye, all that would vanish. You would now have entered a strange land, eighty kilometres long and sixteen wide, and sliced in half by a canal. Here again you would see the tidy little white picket fenced-in bungalows of America. And street signs in English, and a McDonald's and a Dairy Queen. Leaving the Atlantic, you would travel east to reach the Pacific, and in the morning and outside your window, there would be the sun, strangely rising over the Pacific instead of the Atlantic. You would have entered a world seemingly turned upside down. You would have entered Central America's twilight zone.

A canal linking the Atlantic and Pacific had been a dream of dreamers since the 1500s. In 1878, a Frenchman named Wyse got a concession from Colombia that granted him exclusive rights to construct a canal crossing Panama. (Panama was at that time a province of Colombia.) The Suez Canal builder Ferdinand de Lesseps came aboard. The French poured millions of dollars into the canal project, hospitals were constructed, and two thousand buildings erected. Construction of a canal started in January of 1888. Even Eiffel, the builder of the tower recently constructed for the following year's World's Fair in Paris, rendered his opinions and assistance. It was all for naught. Mud slides, malaria, yellow fever, and a small earthquake proved too much. In 1889, de Lesseps abandoned his dream and leaving behind a partially dug trench, thousands of workers dead from malaria, and tens of thousands of French investors in financial ruin.

Next to attempt connecting the oceans were the Americans. The option for a canal location had been whittled down to two locations, either Panama or Nicaragua. In 1902, the choice was put to a vote in the U.S. House of Representatives. Nicaragua was a clean, stable, and fertile country, relatively free of disease, and unlike Panama, free of political unrest. It had eighty kilometres of lakes, and as much again of navigable river, so was clearly the best choice from an engineering standpoint. More importantly, a canal in Nicaragua would be hundreds of kilometres closer to America's southern ports. On the flip side, a Nicaraguan canal would be longer than one constructed in Panama, and Nicaragua certainly did have those volcanoes and earthquakes, The vote in the House of Representatives? Nicaragua 308, Panama 2.

President Roosevelt didn't agree. With Panama having no volcanoes, and with its last major earthquake in the 1600s, and with a railway already across the isthmus, and right next to where a canal would run, and with the remnants of the French effort and a partially dug canal already in place for possible purchase, Panama looked to Roosevelt the far better bet. With all that in mind, Roosevelt offered to Colombia the sum of ten million dollars for control of a sixteen-kilometre strip across its province of Panama. Colombian bureaucrats were insulted and negotiations ground to a standstill.

Now at this very time, the province of Panama was seeking to gain its independence from Colombia. If Panama could somehow get the canal instead of Nicaragua, Panamanians sensed instant prosperity. Panama wanted that canal and their solution was pure Latin American. Make a little revolution against Colombia, but in this particular case an American-supported revolution.

Immediately, and so quickly it was crystal clear that the U.S. had been behind the revolution from the very beginning, the States sent its navy south to blockade Panama's ports of Panama City and Colón from Colombian entry. That took care of Colombia's navy. That left the Colombian government with just one remaining option to defend its claim to its province of Panama, and that was to attack by land through the Darién Gap. So off into the Darién, that inhospitable stretch of jungle and swamp between Colombia and Panama, went a Colombian army of around two thousand. The army was unprepared for its Darién opponent, soon admitted defeat, and sadly for Colombia, was forced to return home. Panama, and its strategic position between the two continents, was lost to Colombia forever. The resulting provisional government of Panama was, to no one's amazement, immediately recognized by the United States. So humiliated were the people of Colombia at the loss of its province of Panama that they refused to recognize the Republic of Panama for twenty years.

There were two winners. Panama now had its canal investor, it had U.S. military protection, and it received that ten million dollars originally offered to Colombia as a new government start-up fund. The Republic of Panama had now obtained its long-desired independence from Colombia, and in 1903, the Republic of Panama came into being. The other winner was the United States. It received the rights to construct and operate a canal until December 31, 1999, which would slice the Isthmus of Panama permanently in half. (The U.S., of course, also received the never-ending hatred of Latin Americans for its gun-boat diplomacy.)

There were two losers. Colombia was diddled out of the canal, the ten million, and their province of Panama. The other loser was Nicaragua, left just as it was before, and as it remains today, still impoverished, and still with its volcanoes and its earthquakes.

Leaving the Canal Zone and Panama City, the solid black line on our South American map denoting the Pan-American Highway continued for five centimetres, then ended abruptly at some place named Chepo. From Chepo, the line became a series of dashes that ran to the Colombian border. The line of dashes was the long dreamed of link between the Americas that neither Panama nor Colombia could ever afford. It was also the link that the U.S. would never support, as any road link would increase the threat of hoof and mouth disease which hadn't been seen in the U.S. since 1954. It would also increase the flow of illegal aliens and make its recent struggle against drug smuggling even more difficult. The line of dashes represented the 160-or-so-kilometre wide strip of swamp and jungle linking North and South America known as the Darién Gap.

In 1959, the first crossing of the Darién by vehicle was made by thirty-year-old British-born Richard Bevir and a twenty-seven-year-old Aussie in Bevir's Land Rover. Days before they were to leave Panama City, something called the Pan-American Highway Congress decided to send a jeep to join them. With the jeep came a cartographer, an anthropologist, a historian, a jungle expert from the Congress's Darién Subcommittee, a member of the National Geographic Society, and nine Panamanian woodsmen. It took this little band a total of 136 days to cover the 160-kilometre Darién. They averaged 201 metres an hour and forded 26 rivers and 180 creeks. It's recorded in the March 1961 edition of *National Geographic* magazine.

Two years later came a second attempt, this time by three Corvairs sponsored by Chicago car dealer Dick Doane and backed up by a couple of Chev four-wheel-drive trucks and a substantial team. Two Corvairs apparently got across, with the third abandoned in the jungle. It took 109 days. That's the same car that outspoken political activist Ralph Nader claimed in his 1965 book was the most dangerous vehicle on the road in the sixties. Don't know if Dick's promotional attempt sold any extra Corvairs, but do know that in 1969, Corvair production was discontinued.

Then in 1972 the British Trans-Americas Expedition and partly to promote the recently released Range Rover, came, saw, pushed, pulled, winched, and carried a pair of Range Rovers through the Darién in ninety-nine days.

And finally we arrive at the amazing exploits of American Loren Upton, surely one of history's most persistent human beings. In 1975, this ex-Marine tackled the Darién in his Ford F-250 pickup. A member of his group was shot and killed. Attempt abandoned. Round one to the Darién. Undeterred, Upton tried again in 1977 in a jeep. He made it through the Darién in forty-nine days, but for twenty of the 160 kilometres, his jeep had been lashed to two dugout canoes. That wasn't legit enough for Loren Upton. He wanted to do it right. Round two to the Darién by disqualification.

Round three was in 1979, and again by jeep. This time, he encountered what he thought were corrupt Colombian officials who wouldn't let him into Colombia without the proper papers for his jeep. (Too bad Loren didn't give me a call. He was undoubtedly missing that Carnet de Passages en Douane.) Discouraged, and to everybody but himself seemingly defeated, he headed back home. He abandoned his jeep in the jungle. Round three to the Darién.

Still determined to cross unaided, and amazingly (to me anyway) by now not permanently confined to a mental institution, he got up off the canvas in 1984 for round four, and again in a jeep. Although trapped this time by the rainy season, Upton persevered and this time pulled it off. It took him 741 days, so over two years, to cover 160 kilometres. By my math, I make that about two lengths of a soccer pitch per day, or about nine metres an hour. There certainly must have been a lot of winching and whingeing. Now that, sports fans, is what I call persistence!

Other than a couple of motor-bike crossings, that's about it for vehicles and the Darién. If you're interested in trying on the Darién, and you've got a couple of years to spare, maybe you'd like to give it a go. The Kuna and Choco Indians live here, scratching out their meagre existence, as do descendants of African slaves, small pockets of farmers, a few Colombian guerrillas, and, of course, those cocaine smugglers. It's also home to jaguars, pumas, deadly coral and bushmaster snakes, rabid vampire bats, ticks, lice, monster ants, and swarms of mosquitoes. And if you're lucky enough to survive all of that, why all you would have left to deal with would be the mud, the swamps, about fifteen dozen rivers and streams, the thick jungle, and the rain that pounds down nine months of the year. And we can't, of course, forget the threat of malaria and dysentery, and those inevitable vehicle breakdowns in a place inaccessible to your favourite automobile club.

Who knows, if you go, and if you luck out, maybe you'll find traces left by Sebastian Snow and Wade Davis as they walked through the Darién back in 1973. Maybe that car dealer's Corvair. Maybe Upton's jeep. Snow is gone now, but Wade Davis is still alive and well. Give me a call. Perhaps I can direct you to him.

The Darién Gap is a forbidding land and was totally impenetrable by camper. As suspected from the very beginning, it would have to be shipped to Colombia.

After a failed search to buy that Panama hat that I insisted would be needed nearer the Equator, we set out to find a shipping agency. All shipping agencies were apparently on the Atlantic side of the isthmus, so on the morning of October 17th we left Panama City for an hour and a half's drive to check out Panama's Atlantic city of Colón [in English, Columbus]. That's pronounced 'coal on,' by the way, not 'colon' as in your anatomy class. Mispronouncing could have serious consequences.

Our first visit to a shipping office was brief, the agent quickly glancing at our camper, then rendering his decision.

"Problema. No compania en Panama puede transportar este vehiculo por embalaje. Dos embalajes, dos precios," he uttered.

"What'd he say?" I asked Margaret.

"He basically said no company in Panama had a container large enough to take our camper. It could go in two containers, but at double the price."

That would be doable, I thought, if we could be guaranteed they could get the camper off the truck and both into separate containers in Colón, and then back out and put together in Colombia, and both happening damage-free. I didn't figure that guarantee was possible.

At agencia numero dos, a prematurely balding employee announced it could be shipped intact in its freighter's hold. There was, however, otro problema. There always seemed to be another problem in Latin America.

"Señora," he said in English, and just before turning to his next customer, "you must have more than passports, and that little piece of paper in your hand that shows you own the camper. You need a special document to satisfy the authorities of Colombia. Unfortunately, you Norte Americanos never are able to produce it."

"Señora," said his young assistant, "siento mucho. Su viaje termina aqui."

"What's that mean?" I asked my translator.

"Please," said Margaret, "it's difficult enough dealing with these people without having to translate every last little thing. Anyway, he said he's sorry, but our journey ends here."

Then, after pausing just long enough to remind me who controlled these situations (that was hardly necessary, I'd known since the Guatemalan border), Margaret reached into our pile of papers on the counter and extracted the Carnet, that bond-supported document that had been obtained in Victoria, and ignored, rightly or wrongly, by every border official from Alaska to Panama.

"Ah, muy bien," declared the young assistant.

"Su marido es muy afortunado de tener una esposa que es muy organizada."

"Well?" I asked.

"Dear," replied Margaret, clearly pushed to her limit, "he said you were most fortunate to have a wife so intelligent and good-looking, and so organized. In fact, he said he wanted to meet me tonight after work for a drink if I could dump you."

Well, at least that's what she said he said, but, come on, who would believe that B.S. I mean, my Margaret, muy organizada?

The aduana was our next stop and where everything but our foreheads was rubber stamped "Salida" [leaving] on the 17th. Then off we hurried back to that shipping office to make final shipping arrangements.

Otro problema. That freighter to the port of Barranquilla in northern Colombia wasn't going to leave today, the 17th, after all. Or even tomorrow. Ship repairs were needed, so perhaps, we were told, it would leave in fourteen days. Then after a series of complicated conversations between bald man and Margaret, it surfaced that a freighter was leaving on the 20th for the west coast Colombian port of Buenaventura, so in three days. We immediately put down the required 50 per cent deposit and returned to Panama City to arrange flight tickets to Colombia's city of Cali on the 20th. From there, it would be a short bus ride to the port of Buenaventura to pick up our camper on the 21st.

The next morning we did a little final stock-taking. Again, the water pump had broken, and again it was a burned-out switch. Then there was that camper doorknob. Since the door-opening incident in Guatemala, I had regularly, perhaps compulsively, checked it. No amount of violent twisting or tugging could ever pop that lock. This time, however, and to my utter amazement, but not Margaret's, the knob came right off in my hand.

"See dear," I announced, "lucky I checked."

With supplies low and purchasing opportunities soon to be limited, we located the U.S. commissary in Panama City, picked up some canned meat and powdered milk, and then grabbed the last twelve boxes of disposable diapers on the shelf. At twelve to a box and five per day, I calculated we'd be well into the Peruvian Andes before some poor soul would have to start washing cloth diapers in nearby rivers. I also found a hardware store and bought a chain and padlock to hold the broken camper door shut. I never found a switch for our water tank, so it appeared we would have to make do with our five-gallon plastic water containers for the rest of the journey. Also, I still couldn't find that bloody Panama hat.

Finally, on the morning of October 20th, we drove back from Panama City to our shipping agent in Colón to deal with all final arrangements for shipping that day. Here the truck and camper were attacked by two of bald man's assistants wielding their tape measures. Again and again, they measured and re-measured, compared results, then measured again. Quite clearly, every single cubic centimetre they could squeeze out was increasing our shipping costs. By the conclusion of the tape-measure marathon, it was one thirty in the afternoon.

Otro problema. We had no Colombian visas and its embassy closed at two. Over we roared by taxi, grabbed those visas, then back we went to the port to pay bald man the measured shipping costs.

All that remained was a short taxi ride to the aduana we had visited back on the 17th and just to make absolutely sure that shipping the camper now on the 20th instead of the 17th was no problem.

Otro problema. All our documents for shipping the camper had already been date-stamped the October 17th by the aduana. So how, demanded our man from the aduana, could everything be stamped stating the camper had left on the 17th, when here it was the 20th, and the camper was still with the shipping agent? We must understand, he said solemnly, he couldn't stamp our documents saying the camper had left on the 20th, when according to his official record, it had left three days ago. (Now here was a Catch-22 even Joseph Heller's Yossarian would have really appreciated while sitting naked in his tree.) Here was Latin America at its non-functional best.

A Latin American problem, of course, and just like Panama's Latin American revolution solution to that canal, required a Latin American solution. Margaret offered up a little coima (yes, that's 'bribe' in English) to our man from the aduana. Suddenly all was in order. Our now extremely pleasant customs officer crossed out the 17th everywhere, initialled all documents with great flare, and then re-stamped everything with the 20th. Then off he roared to catch a flight to Las Vegas. Apparently, in his spare time, he was a boxing referee and was handling Roberto Duran's next bout. Duran was, of course, a Panamanian legend. Buena suerte, I thought, to his opponent.

Back we went to the port and our camper. After chaining the broken door shut from the inside by attaching it to the table post, I stripped down, sucked in my gut, squeezed through the very narrow camper window brilliantly designed by me to align precisely with the truck's window, (ah, the genius of it all), stuck a perfect hand-stand landing on the truck's rear seat, dressed, jumped out, and locked up. The Panamanian judges held up their signs. Four 8s and a 9! (Well, they would have, I'm sure, if any had been present.)

We left our little home at Pier 6 in Colón in care of the two tape-measure boys and headed west by train (well west in my mind anyway, but east in reality) back to Panama City. At nine o'clock that night we boarded our flight for Cali, Colombia. The lights of Panama City soon vanished, and two hours later we were settled into a hotel and awaiting a call the following morning to pick up our camper in Buenaventura.

Eight countries down, and six to go before Ushuaia. Oh, and those elusive Panama hats? Never in history have they been made in Panama. All Panama hats have always been made in Ecuador. Go figure.

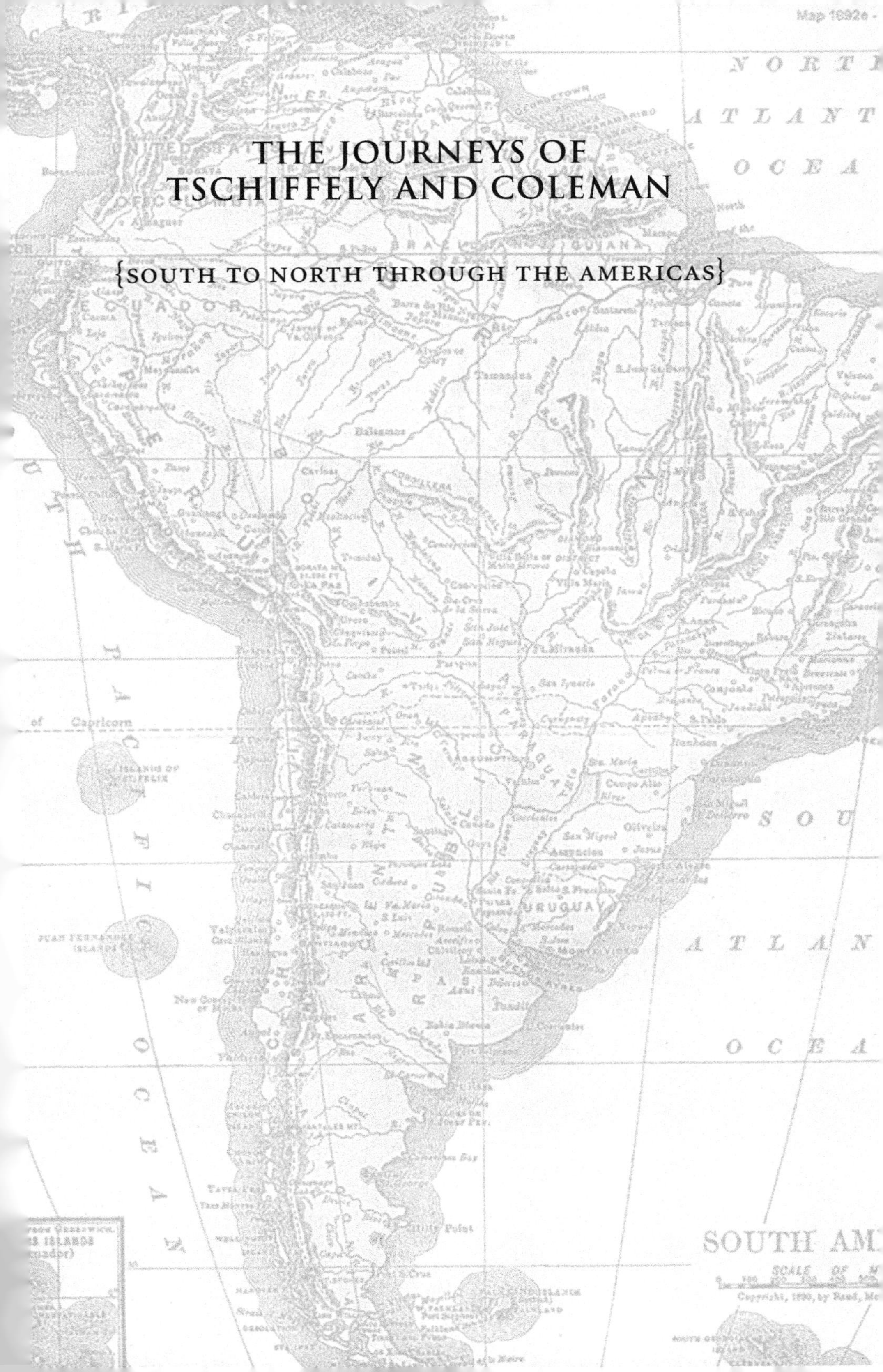

THE JOURNEYS OF TSCHIFFELY AND COLEMAN

{SOUTH TO NORTH THROUGH THE AMERICAS}

Tschiffely and Mancho

1925 Austin Seven Chummy

TWO RESTLESS TEACHERS

Part One

This is a story of a schoolteacher from England who grew tired of his job, followed a dream, and rode into history. Aimé (James) Félix Tschiffely was born in 1895 in Berne, Switzerland, and moved to England in his twenties to teach school, box, and play professional football. Then, still in his twenties, he accepted a teaching job offer at St. George's College in Buenos Aires where he spent nine years. As he was approaching the age of thirty, James felt, and I quote here from his book *Southern Cross to Pole Star: Tschiffely's Ride*, "A school master's life, pleasant though it is in many ways, does not afford much prospect and is apt to lead one into a groove. I wanted variety: I was young and fit; the idea of this journey had been in my head for years, and finally I determined to make the attempt."

What he had been dreaming of while teaching the young Anglo-Argentine boys the finer points of rugby and self-defence was riding a horse from Buenos Aires to the United States. After convincing the staff of the Buenos Aires newspaper, *La Nación*, that he wasn't after a cash sponsor but simply information, he was directed to a gentleman who was a breeder of Criollo horses. These horses were descendants of the few that had arrived from Spain with the founder of Buenos Aires in 1535, the Spaniard Don Pedro Mendoza. As the decades passed, these horses disappeared into the Patagonia of Argentina. They became feral and for generation after generation endured the harsh Patagonian winters and being hunted by the indigenous people and pumas. By the 1920s, and as life is with all species, only the strong and the resilient remained. The Criollo horse breeder agreed to supply Tschiffely with two horses, both formerly owned by a local Patagonian indigenous Tehuelche Chief. Mancha was eighteen, piebald, the spotted one, and the boss horse. Gato was sixteen and coffee-coloured. Both were extremely wild, but were soon tamed to a manageable level.

Tschiffely left Buenos Aires in 1925 to much fanfare and press coverage, some encouragement, and a great deal of ridicule, for the journey seemed to those Argentines who knew horses to be quite ridiculous and impossible. He left riding Gato, the calmer of the two, and with Mancha served initially as the pack horse. He carried a gun for food and protection, but no tent due to its weight. When sleeping outside, he would make do, as did the gauchos of the pampas, by wrapping himself in his poncho.

The horses became quite attached to Tschiffely and never needed tying up at night for fear of wandering off. The three friends travelled through mountain passes three thousand metres high, dense tropical jungles, and deserts. I do not intend to relate their journey other than stating that these three friends, all three with the toughness and intelligence and stamina one would expect, and over a span of two and a half years, travelled sixteen thousand kilometres from Buenos Aires, Argentina, to Washington, D.C. Here, Tschiffely was greeted by President Coolidge. It is considered to this day to be the most incredible journey by man and horse in recorded human history.

Mancha and Gato lived out their lives in comfort on an estancia in Argentina. Gato died at thirty-five, and Mancha at forty. Twelve years after Mancha, Tschiffely passed away in England at fifty-nine. His ashes were returned to Argentina and placed alongside his two beloved horses.

Part Two

Here now is a story about another schoolteacher, a schoolteacher who also grew tired of his job, and who also followed his dream. If you have by the slimmest of chances ever heard of A.F. Tschiffely, I can guarantee you've never heard of John Coleman. No surprise, really.

John Coleman was born in 1928 in England, and by his twenties was training to be a schoolteacher. Johnny had grown to love old cars and, in particular, the little Austin Seven that was being produced in England. All Austin Sevens followed the same basic design of the first one designed and produced in 1925 by Sir Herbert Austin, the Austin Seven Chummy. In 1951, Johnny saw a Chummy, now twenty-six years old, and being used to pull rowing boats out of the Thames at Oxford. Two years later he saw that same Chummy again. This time, however, it had been stripped of all its dignity and lay abandoned in a ditch. Its owner had apparently managed to break the crown-wheel and pinion, couldn't get parts to fix it, and had abandoned little Chummy to the elements. Johnny exchanged an old boat motor for Chummy plus boxes of car parts its owner was fruitlessly trying to flog. Over the next few years, he put the little Chummy all back together.

Then one day, he read a book published in 1933 called *Southern Cross to Pole Star: Tschiffely's Ride*. Coleman then got the seemingly ridiculous idea that he would duplicate Tschiffely's monumental ride in 1925 by horse, only he would do it in 1959, and in his 1925 Chummy. The naysayers of life warned him that the so-called Pan-American Highway was only about half completed and that some stretches had no roads at all. He was also warned, as Tschiffely had been warned, about the Atacama Desert, the driest place on Earth, and the tropical jungle areas near the Equator. It was pointed out that his now thirty-four-year-old car would lose 3 per cent horsepower for every three hundred metres of elevation, so between 30 and 40 per cent of power gone just crossing the Andes into Chile. Concerns were raised about getting spare parts when the inevitable breakdowns occurred, and about the unavailability of gas stations as he went along.

Young Coleman, however, had the enthusiasm and blind courage of a man of thirty-one. He shipped his little car to Buenos Aires, and on November 15, 1959, and led by a procession arranged by the Vintage Car Club Argentino that included Rolls-Royces, Jaguars, Alvises, and a Bugatti, left Buenos Aires from the Plaza del Congresso in B. A. for New York City.

He made it to Ecuador's port of Guayaquil and, as Tschiffely had done before him with Mancha and Gato, shipped Chummy past the Darién Gap to the Atlantic port of Colón in Panama. Coleman then crossed thirty-four rivers in Costa Rica, drove across Central America and Mexico and Texas, crossed eastward, and finally drove north to New York City.

In New York, he appeared on To Tell the Truth, the day's favourite TV show and watched by fifty or so million viewers. He appeared with two imposter Englishmen, and with a chance to win a nice cash prize. It would be his to keep if he could be so convincing that none of the show's panel guessed that it was he, and not one of the other two, who had completed this seemingly impossible journey. None of the panel guessed scruffy-bearded, skinny, and future Latin teacher John Coleman.

At the end of his book, *Coleman's Ride*, he writes that he asked the show's producer if he had done alright. The producer replied that he was terrific. "Until the bell rang," said the producer, "you looked as if you weren't capable of driving round Long Island, never mind from Buenos Aires."

John Coleman died in Litchfield, England, on January 5, 2010, when his Morris Minor skidded and he lost control. All that way in that little old car from Buenos Aires to New York and he died on a drive home.

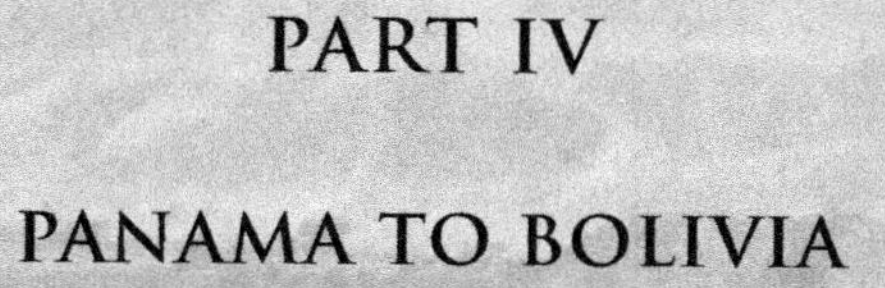

PART IV

PANAMA TO BOLIVIA

Circle City
Fairbanks
Dawson City
Whitehorse
Haines
Dawson Creek
Prince Rupert
Victoria
CANADA
San Francisco
USA
San Diego
Tucson
San Carlos
Mazatlan
Mexico City
MEXICO
San Salvador
EL SALVADOR
PANAMA
Colón
Panama City
Buenaventura
Bogota
COLOMBIA
Cali
ECUADOR
Quito
Tumbes
PERU
Lima
Cuzco
La Paz
Nazca
Arequipa
Tacna
BOLIVIA
Santiago
CHILE
ARGENTINA
Orsorno
Bariloche
Perito Moreno
El Calafate
Punta Delgada
Ushuaia

16

A COFFEE WITH YOUR COKE, SIR?

Early the following morning we headed to the local branch of the shipping company for an update on the camper. The freighter's route had been altered. Now, instead of the direct route to Buenaventura we'd been told to expect, our freighter was currently heading down the coast to the Ecuador port of Guayaquil. It would only stop in Buenaventura and drop our camper off on its return trip north. That would unfortunately be in another eight days.

That meant eight more nights in a Cali hotel and worse, eight more days for any interested crew members to strip our truck and camper. First to go, I figured, would surely be the windshield wipers. The two padlocks attaching the hood to the engine block would possibly save the engine bits and pieces, but they were small locks, and a bolt cutter could cut them with ease. The same with the small padlock on the propane tank compartment. As for the wheels, the locking lug nuts would do the job. So, as long as they couldn't get inside the camper, things would perhaps be fine.

On our ninth day of hotel living, the shipping company called and advised our camper had arrived, so off we went by bus to pick it up. The bus wound through coffee and banana plantations and tropical jungle and past houses perched on stilts to protect from tropical floods. At one moment, we passed a row of little wooden shacks hanging precariously over a fast-flowing dirty river. The portions hanging over the river were the outhouses. In three hours, we reached the Port of Buenaventura.

The freighter's hold was open to the elements and contained just one thing, our camper. Everything else had been unloaded in Guayaquil and they were deadheading back. Now we hadn't seen our truck and camper being hoisted into the ship's hold in Colón, but we sure saw it coming out. Picture an elephant in a sling. I went aboard to watch the action. Horrified, I saw they were just using two cables they had attached from stem to stern, and nothing else.

Now, before leaving Victoria, I had read about a couple who had their camper van hoisted out of a ship's hold in Buenaventura on such a sling. The camper had been dropped seven metres to the dock, bounced right off, and then had sunk fifteen metres down to the bottom of the Pacific Ocean. A diver had gone down and put a cable under it stem to stern. When hoisted up, the cables had crushed the camper van like an empty Coke can.

Up, up, and away our home went, swaying from side to side, and narrowly missing the hold's railing. The more I yelled, the more the crew laughed. Both front and back bumpers were clearly bending under the strain. Now fully suspended over the hold, it was swung out over the ocean, and then down to the wharf. Well anyway, at least down to about two metres from pay dirt. Then, and for seemingly no reason at all, the cables were released. The truck and camper landed on the wharf, bounced once into the air, and then happily came to rest in Colombia. Both bumpers were definitely now slightly bent upward, and who knew what else had been buggered up.

Steaming, I climbed into the truck's rear seat, crawled through those adjoining truck and camper windows, and then landed on the camper floor in the traditional handstand position. I glanced around. The chain and padlock used to secure the broken camper door had done its job and everything appeared in order.

Then I opened the fridge. Unfortunately, well not unfortunately, stupidly, we had left a dozen eggs in the fridge, a fridge which had now been off for nine days. Now you've probably said at least once in your life that something or other smelled like rotten eggs, but you of course have never actually smelled rotten eggs. The smell can't be described to a mixed audience. The smell, however, was the least of my concerns. Throughout the entire fridge were maggots, hundreds upon hundreds of maggots. I'd never seen a maggot. Where in hell do they come from, anyway? Had a young mister maggot been hiding out in the fridge with his girlfriend just waiting for the eggs to go off so they could feed and reproduce more little baby maggots? All I knew was that it was a disgusting mess and that someone had to clean it up and soon. I unlocked the camper door and enlisted Margaret to tackle the job.

"No, dear," said Margaret, "I have to deal with the authorities to get us out of here. I'm not cleaning up that mess. And please close the fridge before they end up all over the camper." Well, okay, I thought, I guess in the Book of Jobs (not Book of Job, Book of Jobs) for camping families, if one even existed, it probably lists 'maggots' under the heading of jobs for men. I cleaned up the stink of eggs and all those disgusting little maggots, then took the kids to find Margaret, who was undoubtedly trying her best to extricate us from the port of Buenaventura.

Ah, the Port of Buenaventura, how should I describe thee. How about humid, seamy, steamy, filthy, and diseased, the hell hole of hell holes. How about a collection of weathered, moss-covered wooden buildings, and with their remaining decades-old coating of white paint 95 per cent peeled off. The building that housed the aduana was right at the ocean's edge, and tight against the rain forest. Here was surely a place where Somerset Maugham would have been so inspired, he could have knocked off his short story "Rain" inside of a day.

I tracked down Margaret waiting in line at the aduana. First to approach us was a thin dark-skinned man in a white baseball cap who identified himself to Margaret in Spanish as a facilitator.

Apparently, the bureaucracy here was so bad that some made a living out of being a bureaucracy guide. Without him, he said, why it could take four or five days to clear customs. With him, maybe five hours. His fee was $80. I had been told at our hotel in Cali that the average daily wage in Colombia was two dollars. I told him to bugger off.

Next to approach was a missionary from the United States, and with his wife and two small children trailing behind. He, also, had been approached by the same facilitator. He, also, had refused to pay, and was tackling the job himself. Sadly, he was now into his fourth day, four days in this festering sore, this place of boils, this putrid blotch on the map, this mother of all holes. Sorry about that. Sometimes I get carried away.

Now back to the facilitator. No way, I thought, we're staying here four days. Four days here and I might be forced to kill myself. Fortunately, the facilitator didn't speak a word of English, so those words "bugger off" had never registered. Fortunately, also, he'd been totally smitten by my outstandingly good-looking wife finishing washing the inside of maggot central while in her underwear. He immediately accepted our job offer. (Well, the true part of all that is he didn't understand those words "bugger off." The part about Margaret cleaning the camper in her underwear, well, that I just made up. After all, sex sells.)

I slapped down some good old American bucks for facilitator man to do his job. By now, the day was almost gone, so he said he would finish his job the next day. We stayed the night parked in this infected scab of society, this.... Oh, sorry about that. To 'celebrate' our home's arrival, we consumed what remained in our camper: Spam, raisins, corn flakes, evaporated milk, and all washed down with a never-before-discovered combo mix of Tang and brandy. Mmm, good.

The next morning I went to our repair kit, located a couple of screws, and managed to fix the camper doorknob. By noon, all paper-work was done. The port's barrier was lifted by the military and off we went north on a side trip to Bogota and what figured to be a three-day drive. It was cloudy and gloomy and a light rain was falling. The Andean foothills were barren except for some scrub-like bushes and a few small trees along the riverside. Then, after just a thirty-minute drive, traffic started slowly piling up. We rounded a corner and stopped. Boulders were crashing down a hillside and piling up in front of the entrance to a tunnel we were just about to enter. One boulder was half the size of a Volkswagen. When the landslide finally stopped, only the upper half of the tunnel entrance was visible. Thirty minutes into Colombia and a bloody landslide! Nice start! An excavator eventually arrived, and after a five-hour delay, we were back on our way to a nearby town named Buga (pronounced the same as what I told that facilitator).

Oh yes, and the missionary? As we had driven away, I had looked back. And there he was, still looking mystified, still holding his large sheaf of papers, still with his loyal family trundling behind him, and still trusting in the Lord. And now into day five in Colombian bureaucracy land. I sometimes wonder whether he's still there and tending to his new flock. After all, they say the Lord works in mysterious ways.

We now received our first glimpse of driving in Colombia. Once the row of backed-up vehicles exited the cleared tunnel, all pent-up frustration exploded. The road consisted of very steep hills and was one lane each way. A taxi, two cars, and a small truck roared past us as we struggled up the second hill. Then, what happened next was truly extraordinary and completely ridiculous. Two buses pulled out together to pass and right behind them came three large trucks. So that's a continuous line of five large vehicles, and all passing us in one go. And on the left side of the road, and with no guardrail, was a drop-off to certain death. All that picture lacked was a sign on the left reading, "Here is your direct route to Heaven."

Poor Colombia. From the 1500s to less than two hundred years ago, it had verged on an empire. Simón Bolívar had created Gran Colombia, which for a time comprised present day Colombia, Venezuela, Ecuador, and Panama. By itself, present day Venezuela is the size of Texas. Then shortly thereafter, things fell completely apart. Venezuela and Ecuador spun off to create two separate republics. They were followed by Panama which became a republic in 1903, thanks to that United States-supported revolution with Colombia.

Yet today, what remains of Colombia is still substantial. To fill up its 1,138,910 square kilometres, you would have to toss in the states of Washington, Oregon, and California, and then touch that up with the ten states of Rhode Island, Delaware, Connecticut, New Jersey, New Hampshire, Vermont, Massachusetts, Hawaii, Maryland, and finally Indiana.

It's bisected by the Equator so its climate is dictated by altitude, not latitude. It's also somewhat schizophrenic, devoted to culture yet dominated by lawlessness, potentially wealthy yet financially unstable, legally exporting coffee yet illegally exporting marijuana and cocaine. In the seventies, hundreds of tons of marijuana and cocaine were produced annually. And virtually right next door? The United States of America, the world's largest consumer of drugs. Sadly, a match made in heaven.

On our second day out of Buenaventura, and while stopped to fill up our propane tank, a truck pulled up alongside. The driver had seen our licence plate, and asked if we would like to see their farm. Once satisfied all was legit, we followed him a few kilometres north up the highway, then turned off on a dirt road and to what turned out to be their small fish farm. They raised tropical fish to sell to pet shops. Sixteen concrete stagnant ponds were filled with fish, and, no surprise here, thousands of mosquitoes. We supplied the beer and shared their dinner, which included something we hadn't seen before, fried bananas.

Then after dinner, the four of us along with husband Jorge, his wife, their young son, and another couple with their four children, all piled into Jorge's old truck, and off we went to visit three nearby little towns. That's thirteen to save you counting. Ten of us bounced along minus seatbelts in the bed of the truck, and with us having no idea what was happening. Well, it turned out we were visiting these three little towns because it was October 31st and a big day for celebrations in Colombia, and particularly for adults. It was Halloween night and we were going trick-or-treating. I mean, who would have thought!

Our second night was spent in their living room attacked by swarms of mosquitoes and watching an old TV detective series in black and white, named *Baretta*, and starring Robert Blake. If you were born after 1960, you've never heard of it. We stayed two more days, and when leaving, Jorge's wife gave us the address of her brother Eduardo in Bogota.

Driving north and leaving behind mosquito heaven, we got our first true glimpse of rural Colombia. Homes of the poor were the size of a small living room and made completely of straw. The 'upscale' homes had walls made of adobe brick, and again with straw roofs. We saw a woman struggling towards us along the roadside and carrying a load of branches for firewood. The load must have been a metre high. Further on, we saw three younger women doing their day's washing in a river, smashing the clothes against a flat rock to get them partially dry, and then laying them out in a grassy field to finish the job. Another woman was dragging a very reluctant donkey laden with two water containers and a large canvas bag of food, up a steep dirt path to her straw house. It looked like a hard life here for women. The men, I wasn't so sure about. We left the fertile lowlands and started our final climb. By evening, our climb was over, and there below us, like millions of fire-flies in a bowl, were the lights of Bogota.

Bogota, the capital of Colombia, and the so-called Athens of

Latin America because of its devotion to culture, sits surrounded by a string of towering mountains. It's high here, at 2,639 metres, (8,660 feet sounds higher, doesn't it) the third-highest capital in the world after La Paz and Quito. It's perpetually shrouded in cloud and mist, has no seasons, and the year-round temperature is a steady fourteen degrees centigrade. It's a rather drab place and referred to as the grey city. Bring a raincoat but leave your sunglasses and sun-tan lotion at home. And as you will soon read, don't go out at night.

We tracked down brother Eduardo and stayed seven nights. Eduardo was thirty-four and married with four daughters. He ran two restaurants and a metal-working business that made chairs and bed frames and the like, and somehow was also going to law school. They ate little in the way of fruit other than fried bananas, and also few vegetables, as both are expensive here. Their children drank virtually no milk. Meals seemed to consist of meat or a stew with plenty of rice and French fries, and all washed down with enormous quantities of Coke. Colombians consume more Coke per capita than people from any other country, and apparently 40 per cent more than people in the United States. And that showed in their teeth. Every tooth of their five-year-old daughter contained either a gold filling or was black with decay. She told Margaret her teeth always hurt. So much for that Coke jingle that things go better with Coke.

Now whereas houses on the fringes of Bogota and in the rural areas were made of sticks, sheets of discarded tin, cardboard, rocks, straw, adobe bricks, and whatever else was available, and for free, their house appeared to be more typically middle class.

Here, then, is life lived by the middle class of Bogota. All windows were barred. The windows that could be opened if you so wished, were padlocked shut. The sink and bathtub had no plugs. There was hot water, but just for our first day. On day two, the hot water tank burst. And in the bathroom there was a little sign clearly for our benefit. The sign read to put all our used toilet paper into the basket next to the toilet. Now I'm sorry, and I realize that parts of the world have different customs, but that's clearly unsanitary and disgusting, let alone smelly. And at night it was cold. The house had no fireplaces and no central heating. One of the kitchen walls was strangely absent. If cold, just pile on more blankets. Sort of a little bit like the England I remember. (To prevent any reader born in England from getting his or her knickers in a knot, the comparison made was to the lack of central heating and the blankets. I have visited bathrooms in England.)

On day three, we were invited to lunch by a notary public my father had met the previous year at a notaries' convention in Costa Rica. After lunch, I noticed I'd left my watch behind in the camper so asked him the time.

"Oh, I never wear a watch when driving in the city," he said in perfect English. "Crooks go for watches and jewellery. Here you're not even safe in your car. If you're careless enough to be driving with your window open, and a crook sees you've got your left arm resting on the windowsill, he just waits for a red light. Then he pulls up alongside and cuts the leather strap of your watch. Goodbye watch. And if your watch is on your right wrist, the crook just reaches over and burns your left arm with his cigarette. Your immediate reaction is to grab your left arm with your right hand, and chau, away again goes your watch. This is a dangerous city. Be careful."

Then later that day, and while strolling across a main street, came the thing we had been warned about since leaving Canada. A robbery. Margaret was walking ahead in a crosswalk with now five-year-old Lisa, and pushing Martin in his pram. I noticed three men in their twenties heading towards me. I moved to the right to let them pass. They moved to their left. Then I moved to my left, and they then moved to their right. Then I understood. It wasn't the usual "who is going to pass on which side routine" one often encounters when crossing a street. They were heading directly for me. I had three things to protect: my wallet, my passport, and the family camera. They lunged forward and grabbed away with their six hands. It was over in an instant. Even today, I don't know how I managed it, but nothing was stolen. When we reached the other side, I turned around and starting loudly swearing at them with words I can't repeat here. The three just stood there staring at me as if they'd done nothing wrong. No fear of police, nothing.

"Cuidado," a man nearby said. "Polícia en huelga."

"What's that?" I asked Margaret.

"Be careful, the police are on strike," she said.

Be careful, the police on strike? On strike? Are you kidding me? This is one of the world's most dangerous cities, and the police are on strike?

And make no mistake, it's dangerous here. Homes are surrounded by very high walls with crushed glass cemented on top. None of this four-foot-only-high fence business found in our bylaws back home. And here in the wealthier areas, and just like we had seen in El Salvador, are serious block watches. Not the kind we have here where your neighbour's wife calls the police if a break-in's happening. Here in Bogota, people hire an armed guard who spends his nights in a phone-booth sized shelter on the street corner. No need for your neighbour's wife to pick up a phone now. She just goes outside and screams.

Then on our last night in Bogota and around two in the morning, we were awakened by a noise. I looked outside and two houses down were two men breaking into a house. An alarm went off like an air raid warning siren. The owner came running outside waving a pistol, and immediately fired five shots at the thieves, who by now were off and running into the night. After the watch story, and the broad daylight attempted robbery, and the police being on strike, and an attempted home invasion, and the bullets flying around, the penny that was apparently stuck finally dropped. The next morning, we thanked the family with the gift of a Coleman stove for their camping trips. (Maybe, I thought, it might also come in handy to heat up their guest room.) Then as we were leaving, and I was shaking hands with Eduardo, I noticed something shiny in his belt. It was a pistol. Yes sir. Definitely time to go.

We took off south back to Cali, and on what was now 550 kilometres of nice paved highway, paved alright, but barely wide enough for two trucks to pass. In places, the road was carved into cliffs sometimes one hundred metres above a riverbed. Guardrails were nonexistent. Careless driving here is not recommended. Above the highway, we could see cultivated fields of coffee bean plants on slopes a good forty-five degrees. We left the mountain area and drove through the Cauca Valley, rich with coffee, sugar cane, tobacco, rice, cotton, and cattle. Plots of land had been cleared of all rocks, which were then used to construct corrals for sheep, goats, donkeys, horses, and llamas. A few women were drying coffee beans at the roadside in large one-metre-wide flat woven cane baskets.

Then at long last, and on the outskirts of a small village, I got the answer to something I'd been wondering about for some time, something that has definitely never crossed your mind. How exactly did people make enough mud to manufacture all those adobe bricks needed to build all those houses and fences we were seeing?

. . . .

Sixteen steps to a successful career as an adobe brick maker:

1. Obtain a parcel of flat land of soil, not consisting of rocks and sand and about fifteen metres in diameter.
2. Hire two men who like going around and around in circles day after day for the rest of their working life. People perhaps like a couple of your friends.

3. Purchase two shovels, one machete, one yoke, two oxen, and three bales of straw or a pile of grass (purchase of a horse is optional).
4. Find some scrap rope about three metres long and a stick about the same length.
5. Rest while crew constructs a dozen wooden molds.
6. Keep at rest while crew prep soil by digging it up with those shovels.
7. Continue resting until rains come and soften the soil.
8. Attach yoke to oxen, then tie horse by rope to oxen to lead the parade of three.
9. Rest while watching crew whack oxen on their butts with that stick getting them going around and around in the fifteen metre prep area. Note how soil turns into a quagmire of mud worthy of your child's best mud pie.
10. Add sprinkling of straw or grass you chopped up with that machete to the mud to strengthen the mix, and to taste.
11. Shovel mud mix into those wooden molds and set aside in the sun to dry, then remove molds and set bricks on flat ground.
12. Rest while bricks dry, four to five days.
13. Stack dried adobe bricks.
14. Get crew to load countless more wheelbarrows of soil and dump them into the now empty fifteen diameter circle prep area.
15. Rest while step fourteen takes place.
16. Repeat steps seven through fifteen.

. . . .

We had watched one of the world's most boring jobs now for some time and I was filming it all on my Super 8 movie camera. The film's final scene was provided by a boy looking about ten or so. I noticed a man, probably his father, go over to him and say something. The boy then immediately turned directly at us, unzipped his fly, extracted the little fellow, and in full view, proceeded to take a pee. Lisa thought it quite funny and couldn't stop laughing. Me, I wasn't so sure. I mean, surely his dad hadn't told him to do it. Surely his dad wasn't suggesting that we piss off, was he?

Now before we leave coffee and cocaine production, let me not forget to acknowledge the most recognizable Colombian face of all time. Yes, that man from the cartel-riddled and cocaine city of Medellín, and the man who graced the television sets of the U.S. and Canada for three decades before being forcibly retired.

No, you have guessed incorrectly. It isn't drug lord and Medellín cartel leader Pablo Escobar, who at one point had fifteen planes and six helicopters and was, by some estimates, worth thirty billion dollars. The winner, and most recognized Colombian face of all time, is Medellín-born actor Carlos Sánchez, better known to you as Juan Valdez. Carlos was the man who, with his little mule Luna, promoted Colombia's coffee industry. So there you have it. The two most famous people in the entire history of Colombia are a drug lord and a shill for Colombian coffee.

Two days of hard driving from Bogota, and 550 kilometres later, we returned to Cali. It's pleasant climate-wise, but like most cities of the world, just a collection of unimaginative high-rises and plenty of concrete. Also found here were some interesting pre-Colombian antique shops, some nice restaurants, and a few colourful street vendors. Not much here for a tourist. Earlier, and while waiting for our camper to arrive, we had purchased three hand-knotted rugs from two guys for two grand with full price paid up front, and with delivery allegedly to be in eight months, and right to customs in Victoria, B.C. Now hands up if you think I was an idiot to have coughed up that kind of money to businessmen in one of the world's most corrupt countries. And now hands up again, and for your total score out of two, if you believe that these three carpets actually arrived here, and in proper condition.[8]

8 The three rugs arrived here two weeks after we returned to Victoria. I'll give you an automatic point for thinking I was an idiot.

The eldest of the sellers was a member of the high-end Club Campestre and where he had earlier taken us for a visit. Now having described, at least to some extent, how the poor and the middle class live in Colombia, it's only fair to give you a glimpse of life lived by the wealthy. This club had an 18-hole golf course second to none, twenty-eight clay tennis courts, twelve with flood lights, a polo field, an artificial lake with boats, swimming pools, a children's pool complete with a children's bar at poolside (and probably with lots of Coke on hand), two restaurants, a four-storey hotel for your out-of-town guests, a five-lane bowling alley, maids available for the kids, and, well, you get the idea. That's a far cry from those surviving on a two-dollar-a-day wage. We pulled in, and after receiving permission, parked for the evening in the clubs parking lot. It had three well-armed guards. Ah, the benefits of a low handicap. Or perhaps just a benefit of my wife's charm. Well, you decide.

The next day we ripped off a further 475 kilometres and late in the day reached the Andean border town of Ipiales. We were now four kilometres from the Ecuadorean border. It appeared a quiet town and with little to see or do, so was perfect. As had become our custom, we found a quiet street in the nicest part of town and Margaret asked and received permission from a homeowner to park in front of their house. I noticed there was an armed guard seated in a curbside cubicle so that was all the better. And that, for the rest of my life, was it for Colombia.

17

REPÚBLICA DEL ECUADOR

On November 18th, we left Ipiales, drove across the recently completed Rumichaca International Bridge over the Rio Carchi, and then entered the República del Ecuador, translating as the Republic of the Equator. Ecuador is small, about seven hundred kilometres north to south, and somewhat longer by road, so discounting any road or traffic issues, about a two days' drive. Historically, it was part of the Incan empire in the 1400s, colonized by Spain in the 1500s, and in 1832 became a sovereign state. By the 1970s, the military had taken over ruling the country. That's it for your history lesson. If you want more, please check the internet.

Since then, Ecuador has had a consistent record in both war and peace. It has managed to lose every single war and every single peace treaty negotiation with its stronger neighbours, Colombia, Peru, and Brazil. It has also managed to have never won a single Olympic medal in anything, nor a World Cup in football. It has, however, an unbeatable lead in the volcano contest with Brazil, currently pitching a 27 to 0 shutout. That's twenty-seven potentially active volcanoes for Ecuador to zero for Brazil. One always must look for the silver lining.

Now that description of little Ecuador may have seemed rather harsh, so quick now, can you name just one Ecuadorean tennis player, golfer, boxer, any athlete at all, ever? Or one famous food, one explorer, one musician, one poet, one writer, one president, one painter, one butcher, one baker, one candle-stick maker. No further questions, my Lord, your witness.

It does, however, have those Galapagos Islands, its greatest tourist attraction, and one of the world's great wonders. Unfortunately, they're 926 kilometres off the mainland, so rather hard to reach for a weekend little look-see. Of course, you can always pick up one of those misnamed Panama hats in the cities of Cuenca, Montecristi, and Jipijapa to impress your friends on the golf course. Before World War II, the Panama hat industry was a multimillion-dollar business for Ecuador, and 25 per cent of its exports. Sadly, however, styles changed after WWII, and in just twenty years, exports dropped to almost zero. They still make them, however, but now more as a novelty and tourist item. The word for winner in Spanish is ganador. You don't hear that word much here.

We travelled down the paved Pan-American for three and a half hours to the town of Otavalo, where the best market in Ecuador is held every Saturday in the Plaza de los Ponchos. Here we found a few indigenous Otavalenos selling woven sweaters and carpets, jackets, antiques, those famous Panama hats, various Andean handicrafts, and, of course what else in Plaza de los Ponchos, but ponchos. Unfortunately we arrived on a Wednesday so three days early for the big show.

Twenty-five kilometres later, we reached a six-foot-high globe of the Earth made of concrete. The globe marked the Equator and here we stopped for the rest of the day. And towering over the area, and the only point on the Equator with snow cover, was the Cayambe volcano, which last erupted less than 190 years ago. Here, I thought, would be a good place for a small hostel or a tourist bureau. Perhaps even a roadside stand flogging coffee beans or bananas, or those Panama hats. None of that was the case. Other than a dozen sheep milling around, the area was deserted. Where are those capitalists when you need them?

The next morning, we reached Ecuador's capital city of Quito of approximately six hundred and seventy thousand people. After first getting permission to park for the evening without having to check in, we pulled into the Hotel Quito parking lot. At 2,850 metres, it's the world's second-highest capital city. Being now on the Equator, we expected to find a hot tropical climate, but instead found it more like spring in England. This was due to the altitude of Quito, for it's altitude not latitude at the Equator that dictates the temperature.

Towering 3,000 metres above Quito, visible on a clear day, and fifty kilometres southeast, is the slumbering volcano of Cotopaxi at 5,897 metres [19,347 feet]. It last erupted in 1914. And even closer to Quito is the Pichincha volcano at 4,784 metres [15,696 feet]. In fact, Quito wraps itself around its eastern slopes. I somehow doubt that hotel staff was receiving danger pay. We stayed two days, explored the city, and then before being caught by any volcanic eruption, took off south in a cloud of Ecuadorean dust towards Peru.[9]

About a four-hour drive short of the Peruvian border, we were halted by a crew of construction workers. Two bulldozers were digging up a steep hill of the Pan-American and rain was pounding down hard. The traffic going north was waved ahead, and a string of vehicles then took off and led by a blue and white Ford bus with luggage piled high on top. They were descending what was now a hill of mud, so all managed with no difficulty. Then traffic heading south was waved forward to have a go at climbing this heap of slippery muck. The pickup and jeep ahead of us took a shot and managed to climb up and over. Then it was our turn. With our top-heavy camper, we were forced to proceed slowly, and couldn't get a good run at the hill. The road crew graded the road three times to help, but it was of no use. Guilt started setting in because we were now holding up progress of vehicles heading in both directions. After those three tries, I threw in the towel. Skidding over the embankment into the adjoining swamp wasn't my

9 Cotopaxi erupted in 2015. Pichincha erupted in 1999 and again in 2002.

idea of a happy ending. We were motioned to head west, and for what we gathered was a little detour. By now, it was after 4 p.m.

And that little detour? Seven hours! The road was hard to imagine. It was just a single lane of earth gouged out of the sides of huge mountains. Up and up we climbed into the Andes. Soon, the valley floor below vanished completely. We were now above the clouds. Now, Ecuador's wet season had ended in May and any vehicles on this 'road' in the wet season had left two trenches about six to twelve inches deep. Then in the drier months that followed, those mud trenches had solidified.

I tried to keep our right-side tires in the right trench. If they came out, and they often did, the camper would lean dangerously left. And if lean left turned into tip left, that would be it. On the driver's side, it was a good two hundred metres straight down to certain death. At times, we proceeded at ten kilometres an hour, unable now to turn and go back and, with no turn-out areas, unable to get off this horrible excuse for a road.

Now worse than the road, if that was possible, was what was happening to our new truck. First of all, the brake pads were shot and the braking system was overheating and rapidly failing. Next, the overload spring on the left-rear side had snapped, which left the truck and camper leaning precariously left, and towards that valley floor hidden by the clouds. And topping that all off was the power steering. It was virtually nonexistent. Forgetting to add power steering fluid wasn't the issue. I had been putting in a litre every second day for the last week. There was clearly, and even to me, a leak. Our extra supply of fluid was now reduced to one litre. Then it started raining harder. And both wiper blades were not working properly. Probably some careless gas station attendant had bent them when cleaning the windshield. (OK, more likely, yours truly.) The stress was becoming unbearable. Surely it couldn't get any worse. But it did. At the higher levels, it was getting foggy, which didn't go well with the recent arrival of darkness.

After sweating and swearing and kids crying and crawling along for hours, we finally crested the Andes and started our descent to the coastal area. Descending the Andes with failing brakes, by the way, is not something I would recommend. In that entire time struggling to not to end up dead on the valley floor, we had not met one single vehicle in either direction, which was both extremely fortunate and a good hint at the road's quality. Finally, we reached the coast by eleven p.m., and close to the little border town of Huaquillas. I pulled over to the roadside for the night. The kids and Margaret quickly vanished to bed. I stayed up another fifteen minutes. It was now November 23rd. The level in the bottle of scotch I had packed since Panama quickly dropped three inches.

A final word. To all you Ecuadoreans out there who were lucky enough to get a copy of this book in Spanish, and there probably are thousands of you, I can't in all sincerity apologize if you feel your country was disrespected by the shortness of this chapter and the shortness of our stay. But come on now, Ecuador was just one week out of our fifty-two-week journey. Do the math. The total number of words in this chapter exceeds 2 per cent of this book.

And as for the shortness of our stay? Well, let me put it this way. If you had been doing the driving, would you have hung around Quito checking out all those 'exciting' churches and wonderful museums? Or, would you have headed off to Machu Picchu, the Lost City of the Incas, and the Nazca Lines, considered by some as evidence of a visit by extraterrestrials, and Chan Chan, constructed over a thousand years ago, and considered to be the largest adobe city ever built in history. I thought so.

18

CONQUISTADORS, MUD CITY, AND THE BREAKFAST OF CHAMPIONS

We left Huaquillas early the next morning for Peru, crossed the international bridge over the dirty Zarumilla River, and proceeded to the aduana and inmigración offices, where Margaret faced the usual two-hour border hassle she always seemed to navigate with her charm and patience. We exchanged the remainder of our sucres for Peruvian soles, then entered Peru at the port town of Tumbes, where Francisco Pizarro had landed in 1531 to begin his conquest of the Incas.

Pizarro had come from Spain to the New World in 1509, and by 1523 had just been replaced as mayor of the newly founded city of Panama. Now for the previous hundred years, tales had circulated of a South American king covered in gold dust, the golden king, El Dorado. That apparently wasn't a story fantastic enough. The story of El Dorado grew and grew, and from a man to a place, a lake filled with gold and emeralds and other precious stones tossed in as part of ancient rituals. Then the story of El Dorado grew even more, and now from a place to a golden city, a city perhaps near present day Quito, or perhaps near present day Bogota, or perhaps in the very heart of Peru. This was just too much to ignore for Pizarro, who by now had reached his mid-fifties and wished to return to Spain and to live out his days in comfort. In 1531, and after two prior failed attempts, but this time with the backing of Spain, Pizarro gave it one more go to capture this land of the Inca and its apparent wealth, both for himself and for Spain.

In 1532, Pizarro learned that the Inca chieftain Atahualpa was near Peru's village of Cajamarca. Pizarro and his little army went to Cajamarca, then sent Atahualpa a message that a feast would be held the next day in his honour. Now what man can turn down a feast given in his honour. Pizarro had with him 110 foot soldiers, sixty-seven more on horseback, two small cannons, and three arquebuses, the forerunner to the musket and modern rifle. Atahualpa brought to the party an army of six thousand. It wasn't enough. Tricked by the Spaniards, he was captured, his army defeated, and he was held for ransom. Over the next nine months, the Incas proceeded to fill a five-by-seven-metre room with gold, and two other similar sized rooms with silver. Well, thank you very much indeed said the Spaniards. Atahualpa was then immediately tried and convicted on twelve bogus charges. A cord was placed around his neck, and on August 29, 1533, the Incan chieftain was strangled. Melted down, that was over six thousand kilos of gold and twelve thousand in silver. The treasure then went off to Spain to fund its religious wars. Pizarro, and his now reinforced army of five hundred, then proceeded eastward, and on November 15, 1533, captured Cuzco (or Cusco), the capital of the Inca Empire.

By that time, the Inca Empire had existed for three hundred years. It stretched along the Pacific coast from southern Colombia to south of Santiago, Chile, a stretch of over five thousand kilometres. It's a shorter walk from L.A. to New York. Eastward, the Inca Empire exerted control well into the Amazon jungles. The population it controlled was around twelve million. Its road system for commerce and for communicating with the far reaches of the empire exceeded forty thousand kilometres. Its army numbered fifty thousand. Sadly for the Incas, the death of Atahualpa and capture of Cuzco spelled the beginning of the end of their empire. In a span of a mere forty years, the Inca Empire had completely disappeared.

The first 150 or so kilometres of highway south of Tumbes

hugged the Pacific Ocean. It was hot and dead quiet. No cars, no humans, and no animals. Here began a desert we had read about that stretched from northern Peru a full 1,550 kilometres to the Peruvian border with Chile, and then continued into Chile for another eleven hundred kilometres. We were back on the Pan-American again and it was straight and flat and paved. Our camper was moving along at a nice clip and with the camper's cab-over no longer bouncing off the truck's roof. Wave after wave crashed onto kilometre after kilometre of deserted beach. In one short stretch, sand dunes had engulfed the highway, forcing us to stop and clear a path. The cold Humboldt Current from Antarctica runs past this part of the Peruvian coast bringing plankton for feeding a rich variety of fish, and fish in apparently enormous numbers. Along the shoreline, fishermen were catching their family dinner. We watched as they tied a weight to the end of their fishing lines and baited hooks about a metre up their lines. Then they whirled their lines overhead and fired them into the surf. Just like we'd seen in San Carlos.

We were finally making good progress in spite of the brake and steering issues that had started in Ecuador. The plastic switch for the water tank was toast now, and the tank itself had cracked again. I promised myself I would never again attempt to fix that bloody tank. From now on, we would just have to make do with our two five-gallon plastic water containers, plus a third we planned to pick up shortly in Lima.

By mid-afternoon on day two in Peru, we pulled into the little fishing village of Huanchaco, about twelve kilometres shy of the town of Trujillo, and after lunch we wandered down to the shore.

Leaning stern down and against two wooden support racks were five strange-shaped boats about three metres long. Each was made of four tapering bundles of what we learned were totora reeds, two large bundles for the hull, and two thinner ones on top. The four bundles were tied together to make a pointed bow which was then turned upward to assist in cutting through the surf. Each stern was open-ended, and with a portion carved out of the bundles where a person could sit or kneel. One of the fishermen told Margaret that these caballitos, or little horses in English, weigh thirty-five or so kilos and last around two months before getting waterlogged or starting to decompose. They're propelled by split-cane bamboo paddles and used to lay fishing nets and lobster pots and also for line fishing. When coming to shore, these caballitos apparently surf the waves. Locals consider this the birthplace of surfing, and not Hawaii.

These exact same style vessels have apparently been continuously used here for thousands of years, first by the Moche people, then the Chimu, then the conquerors of the Chimu, the Inca, and finally, right up to today. Alongside these caballitos was a raft also made of totora reeds. It was flat, maybe three by four metres, and with a triangular sail attached to a bamboo mast supported by guy lines.

By the time we'd arrived, the fishermen had already finished loading their nets, fishing gear, food, and water, and minutes later were off and heading many kilometres out into the Pacific. Margaret asked one of the women when they would return, and was told the following morning. She was also told they navigated by the stars, and they never used any lights, for lights apparently attracted sharks. The movie *Jaws* had come out the year before we had left, so yes, I thought, no lights was a very good idea.

These little caballitos and that reed raft reminded me of the voyage by that *Kon-Tiki*-famous Norwegian Thor Heyerdahl. Heyerdahl had noted that reed boats, and referred to in the Bible, were still being used in Sardinia, Morocco, and Corfu. He had noted that these same reed-style boats were also still in use when the Spaniards arrived in Peru in the sixteenth century, and, more amazingly, were still in use in the 1960s on Lake Titicaca, the enormous Andean lake situated half in Peru and half in Bolivia.

Heyerdahl decided to prove that man could have long, long ago populated the continent of South America by intentionally sailing across the Atlantic in reed boats rather than just being accidentally blown off course.

So in 1970, Heyerdahl had a twelve-metre-long reed boat with a cabin and a sail constructed in Morocco from reeds collected at the head of the Nile. For boat-builders, he brought over indigenous builders from Bolivia. The boat's hull consisted of two main bundles of reeds and a smaller centre one, so essentially what had been used for centuries in South America, but on a more grand scale. In what was baptized the *Ra II*, Heyerdahl and his crew of seven, and a cameraman who had once ridden a ferry, and a Moroccan businessman who had once been in a rowboat, then proceeded to sail for fifty-seven days across the Atlantic to Barbados, a total of six thousand five hundred kilometres.

Now, before getting any deeper into Peru, a one-paragraph review of the politics of Peru is necessary to give a better sense of Peru's political temperature. In 1968, so eight years prior, a coup d'état had taken place. The president had been tossed, and a military dictatorship, calling themselves the Revolutionary Government of the Armed Forces, had stepped in to run matters. Unlike other right-wing military dictatorships, however, this one initiated Soviet-Cuban communist policies. Industries were nationalized and companies expropriated. The government then began agrarian reform by dismantling the existing large hacienda landowning system in which some forty families controlled virtually all of Peru's coastline. It was replaced by cooperativas run by peasants. Simultaneously, the indigenous Andean culture was promoted, and the Quechua language of the Inca was elevated alongside Spanish as a national language. However, just like the other right-wing dictatorships found in South America, this regime didn't tolerate any dissent. Suspected political opponents were jailed, tortured, or deported, and some newspapers were expropriated. As Peruvian politics wasn't a feature item in our local newspaper or television, I can without embarrassment freely admit that we were completely oblivious as to who was in power and what was taking place.

We parked in little Huanchaco for the night and at a nice quiet spot along the shoreline. While out for a short walk before going to bed, I was stopped by a man with a concerned look on his face. In broken English, he explained that there was a curfew here at eleven o'clock, and I had better get off the street because the military would soon be out, and the curfew was strictly enforced. My watch read ten fifty-five. At that moment, I still didn't understand the political situation in Peru, but did understand the words 'curfew' and 'military' and quickly returned to the family.

The next day before breakfast we went down to the shore to see the action. The fishermen had returned an hour earlier and the townspeople were down to greet them. Some fish had already been shared among the crew and the rest were in large baskets for delivery to market. On the raft lay a shark with its head hanging over the side. I measured it at four metres. It had already been hacked up and its entrails tossed into the ocean, as had most of the fish guts. Some guts were in baskets, which we learned would be taken down the coast and dumped into the ocean to attract fish for the men fishing from shore.

After breakfast, we were on the road again, and a few kilometres short of the city of Trujillo we drove up alongside a black-and-white sign:

"INSTITUTO NACIONAL DE CULTURAL CHAN CHAN.
CIUDAD DE BARRO MAS GRANDE DEL MUNDO"

It was described in our travelling bible, *The South American Handbook*, as a large oceanside adobe city, and constructed by the Chimu people about a thousand years ago. The description didn't do it justice. There were no people around, no guards, and no ticket-takers, if guards or ticket-takers even existed. Chan Chan, considered to be the largest adobe city ever built in world history, had an estimated population in its day of between forty and sixty thousand. It was approximately eight hundred metres from the Pacific and near the mouth of the Moche River. The city covered twenty square kilometres, was constructed in stages from 850 to 1350 AD, and was surrounded by an adobe brick wall fifteen to eighteen metres high. The adobe walls of the buildings inside the complex were still relatively smooth, and we could clearly see reliefs of pelicans, fish, fishing nets, and the inhabitants themselves.

Chan Chan, the capital of the Chimu Empire, had been overrun by the Incas in the fifteenth century and abandoned shortly thereafter, and then in the sixteenth century was sacked by the Spaniards looking for gold and silver. Today, huaqueros [grave robbers] dig indiscriminately for treasure and artifacts to sell, and nearby farmers illegally plow areas of Chan Chan to grow their crops. It was now in some disrepair, as one would imagine of a structure made of mud and constructed over a thousand years ago, but was still quite extraordinary. It had lasted until now because it had been constructed in one of the world's bleakest coastal deserts. The annual average rainfall is 2.5 millimetres. Strange, I thought, that the Peruvian government hadn't kept it in better repair and brought it more to the forefront of the tourist industry alongside Machu Picchu, that famous Lost City of the Incas.

Anyway, it was not for me to worry about the preservation of Chan Chan. We had our own mini-crisis developing, and a crisis never before encountered by Canadians who'd travelled by camper from Alaska to South America with a one-year-old. (Actually, as we were undoubtedly the first Canadians to travel by camper from Alaska to South America with a one-year-old, I guess the 'never before encountered' bit is rather redundant.) And the crisis? Margaret had just determined that in exactly seven days we would be out of disposable diapers. We had seen none since Panama, so expected to see perhaps none the rest of the way. That would mean some poor unfortunate would have to wash cloth diapers for the remainder of the journey in nearby lakes and rivers. I immediately went to the camper's bible, the Book of Jobs. (That's the bible I was creating as we went along.) And there, miraculously, was the entry I was hoping to find. Under the heading, 'Mother's Jobs,' was 'cleaning of cloth diapers.' How fortunate for me!

Five kilometres later we drove through the city of Trujillo, and shortly came upon two pyramids constructed of adobe bricks, and given no mention at all in the *The South American Handbook*. They were named Huaca de la Luna [Pyramid of the Moon] and Huaca del Sol [Pyramid of the Sun]. The Moche people had inhabited this area before the Chimu and had constructed them between 100 AD and 800 AD, so they were perhaps nineteen hundred years old. The Huaca de la Luna was still intact, although pockmarked by huaqueros.

The larger of the two, the Huaca del Sol, was 350 metres long by 160 wide and 50 high and estimates are it was constructed with one hundred and thirty million bricks. Now that's a lot of mud-making! It apparently took several hundred years to construct. Sadly, however, those plundering Spaniards were at it again, this time diverting the nearby Moche River to wash away part of it hoping to expose some treasures. More damage was done to it by an earthquake in 1970. Today, only a third is still standing and also pockmarked with gaping holes made by grave robbers. Again, I noticed no evidence of preservation by the Peruvian government. Here we stayed the night.

Two days of easy driving on the paved Pan-American later, and we reached Lima. Our mission here was very simple, the truck. We located the Ford agency and took it in for brake repairs. The shoes were totalled along with God knows what, assuming, of course, that God is more of a mechanic than myself. The virtual lack of power steering and the slow destruction of the brakes hadn't been much of an issue once we had reached coastal Peru, because the highway had been paved, flat, and relatively free of traffic. That, however, would not be the case much longer. The left overload on our F-250 Ford needed repair. Two tires were shot and needed replacing. The hand brake was loose, as was the distributor cap. The air filter needed replacing. We went off to a nice hotel, the name of which I've forgotten, but which I do recall had an excellent shower, then waited out the next a couple of days for the repair work.

Now a city is not my favourite place of choice, except for a very few in the world such as London and Paris and New York, and as I was later to discover, Buenos Aires, so if you aren't too offended, I will simply move through Lima in very short order. And if you are offended well, sorry, I offer no refund. Check with your travel agent.

I would, however, like to comment on one particular meal. Now along the way, we had done our best to eat properly by eating chicken, beef, seafood, pasta, fruit, vegetables, and so forth. Before we left Lima, however, I felt we should at least try one typical Peruvian meal. So late that night, and after our sightseeing was over, we popped into what looked like an eatery for locals rather than the fancy tourist restaurants always found near large hotels.

The first items listed on the menu all involved potatoes, and probably because there are apparently two thousand eight hundred kinds of potatoes in Peru, the home of the potato. Potatoes here are used for trading for crops grown at lower altitudes, for treatment of illnesses due to containing antioxidants, for eating, and in some marriage ceremonies. And as discovered in Guatemala, they also can substitute for windshield wipers.

(Older readers will be interested to learn that a study I read somewhere in our journey reached the conclusion that glucose from eating potatoes could improve one's memory. Unfortunately, I have forgotten exactly when the study was done, and by whom, and in what country it had taken place. I plan to have an extra helping of potatoes with dinner tonight. I will leave you those missing details at the end of this chapter. If the spuds don't help, nothing will be there.)

The first menu items included the words picante, chili, aji, and peppers, all hot-sounding and, as we know, not particularly good for one's insides, let alone children's.

Aji de Gallina [creamy chicken with chili and potatoes]
Causa [potato casserole]
Ceviche [sea bass, lime juice, onion, salt, and chilis]
Papas a la Huancaina [potatoes in Spicy Cheese Sauce]
Carapulcra [pork and potato stew with peppers]
Rocato Relleno [Stuffed Spicy Peppers]
Arroz con Cebolla [rice boiled with onions and picante]

Then the menu items turned nasty:

Anticuchos de Corazon [grilled heart on skewers]
Chinchulin [grilled beef of small intestine]
Cuy [grilled guinea pig, with head, teeth, nails, and feet all intact, and served with potatoes and salad]
Cananes [The house specialty if available – small lizards caught, disemboweled, then dried in the sun, bundled into a dozen or so, cut into small pieces, boiled, and then eaten, head, feet, tail, and all, and served with vegetables]. Cananes were also served upon request as appetizers—reputed to have super aphrodisiacal powers.

At the bottom of the page was a separate item and apparently only available on occasion. The item was headed "Resaca," or hangover in Spanish. Here now is the national hangover dish in Peru, and I warn you that this is not for the squeamish.

Caldo de Cardon [A soup consisting of one bull's penis and two testicles, nicely displayed among potatoes, eggs, corn, and beef jerky. NOTE: The menu stated that the testicles could be deleted upon request as some feel they leave a bad aftertaste.]

Well, bad aftertaste was certainly my first thought!! And that's really good news for someone suffering from a hangover! He (or she) could skip those testicles without running the risk of offending the chef and, instead, just gobble up the rest of the cure. What a 'relief'!

Some Peruvians say that caldo de cardon is the true breakfast of champions. Some say that it grows hair on the chests of small children. Some say it will give you strength if you're run down or nervous. Some say it will, how can I say it, improve the late evening (just like those little lizards). Some say that a young bull's penis is best. Well, after reading this disgusting item, I say to hell with what 'some say.' What 'I say' is, just give me a drink, and right now. In fact, I ordered two of Peru's national cocktails, the Pisco Sour, both for me, and both just for starters. I asked Margaret to order me the safest thing listed, the potato casserole, and with a side of potatoes to keep my memory sharp.

After our extremely late dinner we headed directly back to the hotel to get the kids to bed. There were two other reasons to head back right away. The first was the eleven o'clock curfew. The entire city of almost four million was in total lockdown. The previous day, we had gone to the Canadian Embassy to pick up our mail. The receptionist had told us that the brother of one of their secretaries had been out in his car after curfew hour. He'd been accosted by the military and shot dead. And the other reason to get right home? I wasn't feeling, as we golfers say, up to par, having had too much Pisco. I wasn't sure if the area our hotel was in was patrolled by the military after curfew time, but did know one thing for sure. If I was hung over the next day, there would be no Peruvian hangover cure for me, with or without the deletion of those cojones [balls]. My hangover could last all week for all I cared.

After two days of hotel living, we returned to Ford. All repairs had been successfully completed except for the power steering leak. It had been fixed to a point, but I understood there still was some sort of an issue, and we should carry extra power steering fluid and get it checked again sometime soon.

As for the camper, lights had fallen off the walls, and screws had popped out, and when it rained, water was leaking in the windows. On the outside, some of the aluminum siding had come loose. I had noticed shortly after reaching Colombia that Verne the builder had used screws to attach the siding that could only be tightened with a Robertson screwdriver. That was a Canadian invention that unfortunately had not made its way this far south, and the very screwdriver I had forgotten to pack. Electrical tape had to suffice. The camper had taken such a beating that the door was now off centre and wouldn't close properly. I tossed a plastic gas can into the camper for our third water container, fixed what I could fix, and then chained the door shut from the outside. The door never shut properly ever again.

The coastal highway south of Lima snaked its way up, over, and down the dry and barren coastal mountains. Other than the paved strip of highway, here coastal Peru appeared the way I always imagined I would find the moon if I could ever catch a flight. Then, 450 kilometres south of Lima, and still on a paved coastal section of the Pan-American, we reached something I had read about in *Time* magazine six months before our journey started. What I had read was an article about a German researcher named Maria Reiche who was dedicating her life to the study of what are today called the Nazca Lines.

In 1926, a Peruvian archeologist discovered them just off the shore of the Pacific and near the town of Nazca, and they remain today one of the world's oldest mysteries. The Nazca Lines were created by just removing, and in particular patterns, the reddish-brown iron-oxide-coated pebbles covering the desert floor. In giant proportions, images of about seventy plants, birds, and animals were then produced, including a spider, hummingbird, shark, parrot, flamingo, dog, jaguar, fox, llama, lizard, pelican, condor, and monkey. The last three have each been measured at close to a hundred metres long, so about the length of a soccer field.

And also created were geometric figures: circles, triangles, and parallel lines running across the desert for some four hundred metres. The entire area covers approximately fifty square kilometres. Some of the lines can be seen from outer space. Studies have concluded they were created approximately two thousand years ago by the Nazca people and have lasted such a long time because the area has virtually no annual rainfall or wind.

The images are so enormous that they couldn't have been seen from the ground by their ancient creators. Some thought that because the Nazca people couldn't see what they were creating, perhaps they had someone up in a balloon directing the drawings. Reiche didn't buy that and concluded that the Nazca did the work themselves without balloons, and by just sketching on the ground a small image and then by using stakes, simply scaling up that smaller image.

And one other person postulated another way the Nazca Lines had been created. He was another German, Erich von Däniken. At age thirty-three and in 1970, he published a book in English, *The Chariots of the Gods*. Erich suggested that science confirmed that some of the ancient structures of the world such as Stonehenge and the Egyptian pyramids and the moai of Easter Island were produced either by extraterrestrial visitors or by ancient earthlings having been given the necessary technical knowledge by these men from outer space. Some thought Erich had an interesting theory. Some completely believed him, and some still do. Others think his theories insult the ancients. His book sold sixty-seven million copies.

Upon arrival, we turned off the Pan-American, and hoping not to disturb the desert floor, parked a few metres off the road. Like Chan Chan, there wasn't a soul around, so again we had the entire place to ourselves. After some difficulty, I climbed up to the camper's roof for a look and for some picture-taking. I panned the movie camera around and suddenly saw where we had inadvertently parked. We were parked in the belly of the lizard. The Peruvian road engineers, in their infinite wisdom, had managed to construct the Pan-American Highway so that it cut the lizard completely in half. Again, where was the Peruvian government protection of this incredible two-thousand-year-old site?[10]

Now to be fair to the government, there was a yellow four-by-eight-foot plywood sign to discourage defacing of the site.

ZONA ARQUEOLOGICA.
Los infractores seran sancionados con multa,
arresto, y decomiso del vehiculo.

Margaret translated the second line to me. It read that offenders will be fined, arrested, and the vehicle will be seized. Well, I thought, quite a severe punishment for an inadvertent poor parking job.

On the other hand, Peruvian punishments had somewhat mellowed. To discourage dissidents, the Inca had sometimes cut off people's hands. Worse, well far worse actually, was what befell a particular Spaniard who had over-taxed the local Incas. The Incas executed him by pouring molten gold down his throat. Apparently steam came out of the other end. The gold then immediately congealed. It goes without saying that the now 'wealthy' Spaniard was then sliced open and the gold recovered. 'Waste not, want not, saith the Lord,' the Jesuits had taught the Inca upon their arrival back in 1568, and the average Inca had no problems with his hearing. Fortunately for us, there weren't any army personnel stationed in the area to make an arrest and seize our camper. The camper would have made a nice addition to a general's toy collection.

Our drive south was over. It was time now to head into the Andes and the heartland of Peru, to Cuzco, the capital of the old Inca Empire, and to Machu Picchu, the legendary Lost City of the Incas.

---

10 Chan Chan was designated a World Heritage Site in 1986, as were the Nazca Lines in 1994. Two years later, Nazca, the town nearest the Nazca Lines, was completely destroyed by an earthquake.

19

THE ROADS NOT TAKEN

I checked our 'official road map for South America' obtained from the AAA in Tucson. In the 1,220-kilometre coastal stretch in Peru from Lima to the Chilean border, there were exactly three roads inland to reach Cuzco and Machu Picchu. All three showed as broken lines on our map, so all were gravel. Door number one meant backtracking from the Nazca Lines 440 kilometres north to Lima, then east into the Andes, then south to Cuzco, so a total of about 835 kilometres. Although I guessed any gravel road out of Lima would possibly be decent, backtracking seemed a waste of time, so this was discarded.

Door number three meant going south down the coast, then east into the Andes, and then north to Cuzco, so about eleven hundred kilometres. It ran through Peru's third largest city, Arequipa, so again could possibly be decent. However, this road meant even more backtracking as we were planning on using it later to return to the coast before entering Chile. Door number three was also out. I also checked out door number three in *The South American Handbook*, hereinafter described as the '*Handbook*.' Its high sierra road portions were described as "dangerous, narrow, unsurfaced, and liable to landslides: many accidents." Sounds wonderful! Can't wait!

That left door number two. The *Handbook* referred to a gravel road located just north of the town of Nazca going to Cuzco, but gave no road description other than that it was "extremely rough, but offers wild scenery," was 506 kilometres long, and would be a seventeen-hour drive over a three-day stretch. I did the math.

That averaged out to thirty kilometres an hour so gave a clear idea as to the road's quality. It didn't sound very encouraging. A few miles south of the Nazca Lines we found the turnoff from the Pan-American to door number two but only with help from a passerby. Funny, I thought, there's no roadside sign pointing to Cuzco. We hesitated for a bit, then off we slowly drove east, up a steep hill into the Andes and into the unknown.

The words 'gravel road' and 'extremely rough' were misleading. A more proper Canadian road description would have been 'a long-ago abandoned logging road.' A more proper local description would have been 'a road given a four-out-of-ten by a panel of Inca road builders five hundred years ago.' The initial stretch of road wasn't gravel. It was a bed of jagged rocks and clearly a portion of the original Inca road system constructed by road builders who had never seen a wheel. This explained that estimated thirty kilometres an hour average speed noted in the *Handbook*.

Within minutes we saw thirteen small piles of rocks on our right and with each pile supporting a little wooden cross. Next to one of the crosses was a tin can stuffed with wildflowers, an empty beer bottle, and a faded picture of the Virgin Mary. South Americans are fond of creating little shrines where their loved ones had met their maker on dangerous roadways. Here was obviously a dangerous corner but nothing compared to what we had encountered in Ecuador and, as it turned out, nothing compared to what was to come. Only one cross had a name on it, the name Victor Sola. I felt sorry for poor Victor, but more sorry for the other twelve. At least Victor's cross had his name on it.

By afternoon's end we reached a flat area, pulled off the road and stopped for the night. In eight hours' driving we had seen a total of four trucks and one bus. I glanced at the odometer. It had advanced an even hundred kilometres. That's twelve and a half kilometres an hour. I could jog that fast. (Well, of course, after a little training.)

The following morning we were off again and soon had stopped for a morning break near a little cluster of shacks. Two children approached the camper, one an expressionless and dirty-faced little girl of maybe three and holding a newborn dog. She was like a little toy. Her face was the saddest you could possibly imagine. The other was a barefoot boy. His pants had holes in both knees, were held up by a piece of rope, and there was a vertical space where there used to be a fly. His head was covered by an oversized blue toque. In his right hand, he held a red plastic bowl holding a large metal spoon. By height, he was maybe five. By his worn face, he looked maybe ten. He looked like he'd already lost the battle, the battle he was going to have for the rest of his life, and a life that had barely started. The bowl was empty. I hope Margaret gave him some food. I can't remember.

On day two into the Andes we saw one truck more than the day before, no cars, no towns, no people and, except for a solitary two-metre-high cactus, no vegetation. It made the more desolate parts of Alaska we remembered appear actually quite hospitable. A few alpacas and llamas wandered along the roadside. The road was somewhat improved, but extremely narrow. In places, a mistake on a patch of slippery gravel would result in four more of those roadside crosses. The area was a moonscape of desolate grey rolling hills, of complete and utter silence, and left me with a feeling of absolute loneliness. Sorry, that's the best I can do.

At day's end, I stopped, backed up off the road maybe three metres, and turned off the engine. Three metres were plenty, because three or twenty, it didn't really matter. There wasn't any traffic anyway. I backed in on the off chance the truck failed to start the next day. At least jumper cables could be attached if a truck ever came along.

Above the road where we'd parked we noticed a little windowless house with rock walls and a roof of matted straw. Adobe bricks required mud, and the ground here was rock hard. And brick-making required water, and water here appeared to be non-existent. Rock walls were not just the preferred choice, they were the only choice. Outside its door were two rusted oil drums that probably held the family drinking water collected from recent rains. There was a little rock corral next to the house containing three alpacas and four llamas. The wool from the llamas would provide some much-needed warmth for the cold Andean evenings. When their time came, these animals would provide food for the family and their skins some useful leather. Their dried dung was the only available fuel for a fire. The family certainly had a convenient and renewable fuel source but unfortunately the house had no chimney. I could hazard a guess what a dung fire smelled like, so hoped mum did her cooking outside.

After dinner, Margaret saw movement up above, and shortly thereafter the man of the house appeared at our door. He had on dark baggy pants that were two or three sizes too large. He was wearing a heavy-looking sweater and jacket and a poncho and on his head was a fedora, that popular hat from back in the forties. His hands were clasped in front of him and held a sling made of wool. Margaret figured he used it to fire pebbles at his alpacas and llamas to herd them into the rock corral, or shoo them out to eat the few yellow tufts of grass that were struggling to grow nearby. She tried striking up a conversation, but he spoke no Spanish, just the indigenous Andean Quechua language of the Inca Empire, and still spoken 450 years later by 25 per cent of Peruvians.

After a few minutes, he made an unmistakable gesture with his fingers near his mouth requesting some food. Now what's eaten up here are potatoes, a little meat when an animal has outlived its usefulness, and maybe a few vegetables if some decent soil can be located to grow something. For drinking in the high Andes, locals chew coca leaves and drink coca tea to enhance their physical endurance at this high altitude. I imagine they also consume it to numb themselves from their struggle. Three or four cups of coca tea would slightly register on a cocaine meter if a person ever got tested. If a tea lover, guys, best to let the wife drive.

So here was the dilemma. If their food supply was running low, where exactly would this family get food for the day? It was 150 kilometres back to the small town of Puquoi and the same ahead to Abancay, and they had no transportation. On the flip side, here we were in the middle of absolutely nowhere, driving a truck with continuous issues, having zero knowledge of engines, and with our own supply of food and drink getting dangerously low. By now, we were reduced to eating tinned meat, tinned vegetables, powdered milk, crackers, and eggs, if we could find them. If we had truck trouble, we could be stuck here for days. And by the way, just what were the odds of one of the few large trucks we were seeing daily actually going east not west, and actually stopping to help, and actually carrying a chain, and actually offering to tow us the 150 remaining kilometres to Abancay, and then to whatever Abancay offered in the way of a truck repair shop. In short, a truck breakdown here would be a nightmare beyond anything I could possibly imagine.

The first order of business was clearly to protect ourselves and our children and let Peruvians protect Peruvians. I looked around for something we could spare, and finally found something I had for some long-forgotten reason bought in Panama City. I handed him a full bottle of Martini & Rossi for their next family dinner. I hoped that sweet vermouth went well with fried alpaca.

The next morning was day three on the road to Cuzco. It carried on up and down through some rough mountainous terrain. By now, we were 2,400 metres above sea level, high up, but still far, far higher to go. Snowcapped mountains could be seen in the distance. Even with the truck heater on, it was cold driving. We saw a few alpacas in the distance and spotted dozens of pink flamingos in small areas flooded by a recent rainfall. More rock and straw-roofed and windowless houses appeared alongside rock corrals, some which were a hundred metres in diameter.

I was now starting to wonder if we were on the right road. There was a reference in the *Handbook* to exactly one turnoff going off this road and which went to the government's vicuña reserve—those rare cousins of the alpacas, llamas, and guanacos. No road signs existed offering help for direction or how far we were from anywhere or anything. Concern was mounting we had inadvertently taken that one and only turnoff and suddenly hundreds of vicuñas would appear around the next bend.

Eventually, we noticed a tidy rock and straw-covered house coming up on our right, so stopped for directions. A man was sitting outside on a chair weaving away and using a backstrap loom, with the other end tied to a post in the ground. He spoke some Spanish and confirmed to Margaret we were on the right road. I noticed he was wearing a miner's hard hat. Dangerous work, apparently, that weaving.

The day's 'excitement' was seeing a large produce truck coming up a steep hill just as we were about to descend. I pulled off to the side as best I could and stopped to let it pass. Margaret looked down. The road ahead descended into a valley far below, snaked back and forth with four hairpin turns, and then finally disappeared. It was a long, long way down. That was the only vehicle we saw in our four-hour drive to Abancay.

We passed through Abancay without stopping. The rugged mountainous wasteland was slowly replaced by green hillsides and neatly terraced fields irrigated by systems installed five hundred years ago by the Inca. Finally, and four hours out of Abancay, we reached Cuzco, the oldest continuously inhabited city in the Americas.

Now in addition to parking some nights in those high-end neighbourhoods for safety, we had also formed the habit of parking in town centres. If, based on Spain's plan of a town, a town's square or plaza would have a cathedral, perhaps also the seat of local government, and probably a place to eat. It would be a place for people to gather at night and would be safe, for who would attack us or our camper with so many people around? At least, that was the plan anyway. We headed straight for the centre, the Plaza de Armas de Cuzco, but finding it swarming with early evening's strollers and with no place available to park, checked instead into a nearby parking lot for the evening. I paid the necessary amount of soles for the night and then backed the camper tight to a concrete wall. That left the truck's two doors as the only break-in entry points to the camper. To enter, a thief would have to first access the truck and then access the camper through the two small adjoining sliding windows. All fat thieves were automatically eliminated.

The parking lot had a guard, which was encouraging, yet somehow left me with a bad feeling. This was not Lima, with its population of close to four million. I tipped him heavily. As I walked away, I turned for a last look at our home. The right side of the camper was sagging. The right overload had now snapped. We located what was apparently the best hotel in town and checked in. It unfortunately had tourist prices and second-class service, but what it did have was hot water and a shower.

Cuzco, or Cusco, as it was just recently being referred to, is a town of twenty thousand or so, and stands at 3,500 metres. It was virtually destroyed in both 1650 and 1950 by earthquakes, but rebuilt both times. The perfect Incan stonework from the fifteenth century can still be seen today and forms the foundation of many of the current adobe dwellings.

The following morning, Margaret immediately left the hotel in her urgent quest for the now much-needed disposable diapers. Finding none, she had reluctantly settled on finding cloth ones. Not finding those either, she returned in an hour with a pile of white cotton cloth and scissors.

After a look around Cuzco we took a short drive up a nearby hill on the northern outskirts of town and reached the fortress of Sacsayhuaman. Much of the stonework of this ancient site had long ago been removed and used as construction material elsewhere. Today, little remained other than three towering and parallel zigzag walls that carried on for about four hundred metres. The enormous stones of the walls were stacked two, three, and sometimes four high. The walls themselves reached a height of five metres. One estimate puts the weight of the larger stones at one hundred and ten thousand kilos! (That's 120 tons, for you older readers.) Other estimates of the larger stones range as high as two hundred and seventy-two thousand kilos, so three hundred tons. The stones are precision-cut and shaped to remain in place by their own weight without the use of mortar. The work was so precisely done that a piece of paper couldn't be slipped between them. I know, because I tried.

The first mystery surrounding Sacsayhuaman is why it even exists at all. Was it an ancient religious centre? Was it a fortress for Cuzco? And if so, why had it been built so high up and so far away and why didn't the three parallel walls fully surround Cuzco instead of just three walls to nowhere? Or was it something else entirely? As the Inca had no written language, no one really knows.

The other mystery is just how the Inca, with no use of the wheel, no draft animals other than llamas, and no nearby trees for wooden rollers, could somehow quarry these enormous stones, transport them many kilometres to this location, shape them, and then hoist them into place. That writer von Däniken, who thought extraterrestrials assisted with the construction of the Nazca Lines, also theorized they were involved with Sacsayhuaman. I read his book before we left. I have now seen Sacsayhuaman with my own eyes. It is difficult to not be a believer.

We camped here our second night in Cuzco. No tours, no tourists, no tickets, no lines, nobody. It was as if this place, which must surely rank as one of the Earth's great mysteries, wasn't even here. Our only visitors that evening were four llamas loaded with straw bundles that trotted past, closely followed by an old woman running hard to keep up. And farther back still was her husband, slowly, very slowly, walking along. Again, a woman doing all the work. What can I say.[11]

The next day, we headed for the raison d'être up here, Machu Picchu. It was constructed by the Inca five hundred years ago at 2,430 metres above sea level, and rests on a saddle between the mountains Machu Picchu and Huayna Picchu. It was therefore invisible from below to the marauding Spaniards and so never destroyed. It remained buried in the remote jungle and lost to the world until 1911, when an American explorer named Hiram Bingham made its discovery. The mystery remains today why it was built. Was it a refuge, or a summer retreat, or something else?

The little train to Machu Picchu took just over three hours and ended at a cluster of buildings called Aguas Calientes. The train ride was followed by a climb of 400 metres straight to the top in a van with six other tourists, and by a series of fourteen dangerous switchbacks. The driver drove for some inexplicable reason at a speed that was truly terrifying. There were no other tourists waiting for the trip up, so what, I thought, was the rush? He was quite an old man, so perhaps in desperate need of a pee.

At the top were another five tourists and two hundred stone-walled buildings. On the far side of the site were narrow terraced fields for agriculture. I am not exaggerating when I state that if an Inca, while collecting his corn on the cob for dinner from his private terrace, had slipped and fallen due to an excess of alcoholic chicha consumption, he would sustain more than a broken ankle.

11 Today, Sacsayhuaman receives about four thousand one hundred visitors a day. That's 4,098 more than we saw on our overnight stay. In 1983, it was declared by UNESCO, along with Cuzco, as a World Heritage Site. Today Cuzco has an international airport, so you can avoid that drive.

He—well, probably she, as the women seemed to be the workers—would fall those four hundred metres, and after a maximum of three bounces, straight into the Vilcanota River below.

Just a quick comment now on that chicha booze. This Inca beer was made by chewing kernels of corn. The spit activated the fermentation process of the carbs in corn. It wasn't a strong beer, so they had to consume up to two litres a day to get their daily buzz. This was just a regular day's consumption and at festival time, considerably more. It's apparently still made that way today. And the next day, to relieve that hangover from your neighbour's homemade spit beer, the key was apparently to have that breakfast of champions, bull penis and testicle soup. Seriously, I may never drink again.

Machu Picchu was, and remains to this day, the most amazing sight I've ever seen in my life, other than of course my wife, when I first saw her walk into the Empress Hotel in Victoria, B.C. This is not a tourist brochure, so I will leave it for you to discover Machu Picchu for yourself. I will, however, leave you with just this one thought. Machu Picchu is ranked by many as the third wonder of the world, just behind the pyramids of Giza in Egypt and the Great Wall of China. Call your favourite travel agent right away (and perhaps just skip Ecuador).

20

THE REPUBLIC OF BOLÍVAR

Please clear the exits. Next stop, Bolivia. The road reached its peak at 4,321 metres, and by day's end had descended about five hundred to the towns of Juliaca and Puno, both nestled next to the shores of Lake Titicaca. The highway, or so-called highway as pavement had vanished since the coast, carried on the entire 190-kilometre length of the lake, the largest in South America and the highest navigable lake in the world. It's here on the lake, and I literally mean on the lake, where we found the homes of the Uru.

These indigenous people live on fifty and counting floating man-made islands made of those totora reeds we had seen on the coast used for boat-building and growing here along the lake's shoreline. As their free land becomes waterlogged and liable to sink, the Uru just hack off more reeds and then pile them on top of the old ones. These little man-made islands are tied together with ropes, and usually anchored. Centuries ago, the islands were constructed by the Uru to escape enemies. Then, if in apparent danger, they just pulled anchor and moved their homes farther from shore. Today, there seemed little need to move away. Perhaps a move would be in order if a neighbour fancied your wife. Perhaps a move if your neighbour's son inherited a set of drums.

Now those totora reeds do more than supply the Uru with free land. The reeds are eaten. The reed bottoms are a source of iodine. The white part of the reeds is used to relieve hangovers. (I agree. A far better solution than that disgusting hangover remedy used on shore.) The reeds are used to construct their homes. The reeds are used to construct boats that can haul people and supplies, unlike those one-man coastal boats better suited for surfing large coastal waves. A fire extinguisher would clearly be a best-seller here for a trade if a person fancied something the Uru possessed for a souvenir. Sorry, I can't provide you with an example of anything you might wish. I do not intend to discuss the disposal of toilet waste and will leave that to your imagination.

There was nothing here in the way of vegetation, not one tree, not one cactus, and nothing that could qualify as a shrub. As we drove south along the shoreline, we spotted what could be described as three Peruvian political billboards, each about three or so metres high by five wide and made of whitewashed adobe bricks. On one was painted "Molloko, Defender a la Patria es Hacer Revolución," and alongside that message was a painted caricature of four terrifying men with guns and knives. Like Che Guevara's attempt in neighbouring Bolivia ten years earlier, Señor Molloko's Peruvian political platform was apparently to defend the country's soul by a peasant revolution. Had he never read what happened to Che?

Just before lunchtime we stopped. In front of us was a slow-moving river about three hundred metres wide. I glanced down-river and spotted the bridge. It had completely fallen apart and a crew had started repairs. It would clearly be weeks before it would be available.

Now with all supply trucks and locals having to somehow cross the river, those bridge repairmen had rigged up a makeshift and leaking 'dam' out of river rocks. Our choice was to either cross the river protected by this 'dam' with water halfway up the wheel wells or turn back. And if we turned back, that would be it for Bolivia. We sat awhile debating what to do and watched as three trucks successfully made it across. There were no government people or locals on hand for guidance. There also were no signs. Hoping no local knowledge was required to avoid getting stuck in soft spots or deep holes in the riverbed, we nervously entered the river and, after a lot of bouncing around, safely crossed to the other side.

And I mustn't forget to mention the five curious men who approached our camper when we parked shortly after crossing that river for lunch. One was carrying the most primitive of wooden plows. If Bolivians didn't have two oxen to pull their plow, and most wouldn't because of the cost, they just pulled it themselves to till their fields. These fellows were plow pullers. I hoped they hadn't noticed Margaret down at the river washing Martin's diapers. I also hoped they lived upriver.

After two hours' drive from Puno, which included that necessary amphibious river crossing and necessary river pollution, we reached the Bolivian border at the village of Desaguadero. Here we go again. We entered the Peruvian offices and got our exit stamp, proceeded to the Bolivian inmigración for our ninety-day entry stamp, and finally to the Bolivian aduana. The minutes went by, and the document studies continued, and the few bolivianos in my wallet flowed out for the usual very 'important' reasons. In the end, however, it was faster than expected and soon we reached country number twelve in our journey.

Bolivia was named after Simón José Antonio de la Santisima Trinidad Bolívar y Palacios Ponte-Andrade y Blanca, the liberator who led Venezuela, Bolivia, Colombia, Ecuador, Peru, and Panama to independence from Spain in the early 1800s, and today better known as Simón Bolívar. Some wished to use his full name to name the country. Others argued it wouldn't fit on a map, and would be impossible for little children to memorize and for old people to remember. The latter group won the day. It was originally named the Republic of Bolívar, but later was changed to Bolivia.

We were now in the third country in a row run by an oppressive military government, and now in the heart of what is described as the Altiplano. The best way to describe the Altiplano [high plateau] is to picture the Andes splitting lengthwise into two parts, the Western Cordillera separating Bolivia from Chile, and the Eastern Cordillera separating Bolivia from Brazil. In the middle lies the Altiplano, a plateau three and a half kilometres above sea level at its lowest point and stretching north to south close to a thousand kilometres. The Altiplano is, outside of Tibet, the most extensive high plateau area in the world. It was where we had found Lake Titicaca and where we would shortly find La Paz.

Now before leaving Lake Titicaca, I have to mention its amazing inhabitant and one almost impossible to believe. No, it isn't a creature found in the depths of the lake, a descendent from creatures that lived tens of millions years ago. And no, it isn't a remote colony of those extraterrestrials von Däniken had postulated visited Earth long ago and had recently returned to fix up our planet.

What you will find up here at 3,812 metres above sea level (now seriously, doesn't 2.368 miles sound higher) and four hundred kilometres from the Pacific Ocean, is the Bolivian navy. Yes, this country, which has been landlocked now for over a hundred years and ever since losing the War of the Pacific to Chile, has an actual navy. The Armada Boliviana consists of over 150 vessels and upwards of five thousand naval personnel. It allegedly exists for the purpose of preventing drug trafficking on Lake Titicaca. The real reason for its existence, of course, is landlocked Bolivia hopes to one day regain access to the Pacific. Well, I guess we all must live in hope.

We drove the length of the lake, and shortly before reaching La Paz came to the ruins of Tiahuanaco (Tiwanaku or Tiahuanacu). It was an ancient city constructed sometime between 15,000 BC and 400 AD, depending on which archaeologist is believed. No one knows when, exactly. What is known, however, is that when the Inca came upon this city in the fifteenth century and the Spaniards in the sixteenth century, this city, which once had a population estimated between ten and twenty thousand, had been completely destroyed. The stones were enormous. The 'smaller' ones of andesite, a hard volcanic stone. were quarried about ninety kilometres away and weigh around ten thousand kilos. The larger ones of sandstone were quarried ten kilometres away and weigh over one hundred thousand kilos. How the stones had been quarried and transported and precision-cut and fit together remains a mystery. Excavations had recently started, and wire fencing was evident around a couple of areas. One fenced-off area included the Gate of the Sun, an archway with mysterious inscriptions on it, three meters high by four across, and carved from a single piece of stone estimated to weigh close to nine thousand kilos.

Now remember that German writer von Däniken and those Nazca Lines and those sixty-seven million books he sold? Well Erich devoted four pages of that book to the mysteries of Tiahuanaco. Had the builders of Tiahuanaco been visited by extraterrestrials thousands of years ago who passed on the necessary knowledge to construct Tiahuanaco? Or had those extraterrestrials decided to hang around and supervise matters? These were the same two theories he raised about the construction of the Nazca Lines on the coast and Sacsayhuaman near Cuzco. Well, I leave that for you to decide.

Two hours from Tiahuanaco we crested a hill and down below in a bowl, so about 350 metres below the Altiplano, was the capital city of La Paz. It's actually co-capital with Sucre, Bolivia's capital since the 1500s, but which now shared its status as capital with La Paz, where the seat of government is located. The poor in La Paz live up on the bowl's rim and those living a better lifestyle live below in the canyon. In a nutshell, the poor have the view but the wealthy have the oxygen.

We parked in La Paz for a quick lunch and I pulled out the *Handbook*, that little book which had now become quite essential here in the Andes. I noticed comments about Bolivia paralleling descriptions of places in Alaska. Alaska had its 'world's most northerly' and its 'world's largest' attractions. Well, Bolivia had its own matching list of places destined for greatness. It had the world's highest golf course, the world's highest tennis club and, at 5,260 metres, so 60 per cent to the top of Everest, the world's highest ski resort. (Note: Skis, boots, and poles supplied, but please bring your own oxygen tank.) The book said that when visiting La Paz, a person must first get acclimatized to the thin air before any exertion. Well, I thought, a walk for people our age surely didn't count as exertion.

Our walkabout lasted three blocks. The Altiplano had finally taken its toll. Completely exhausted and unable to continue, we left. Forty minutes in La Paz and gone. The Altiplano is bleak, treeless, harsh, windswept, dusty, cold at night, freezing in winter, has lots of tin to mine, lousy for agriculture other than potatoes and quinoa, has wonderful ruins to explore, and is obviously short on oxygen. Oh, yes, Che Guevara died here and perhaps Butch Cassidy and the Sundance Kid as well. Sorry, that's about it. We're gone.

With the only direct route to Chile only passable by four-wheel-drive vehicles, we were now forced to backtrack to the town of Puno in Peru. From there, we planned to head west on what I had previously referred to as door number three, and to the city of Arequipa. From Arequipa, we would descend to the Peruvian coast and then continue south to Chile.

On December 21st, we returned to the two side-by-side tiny Bolivian and Peruvian border towns both named Desaguadero where we had entered two days earlier. We reached the main drag and headed for the aduana and inmigración offices. It was four days before Christmas and a large market was in progress. The market was right on the main road through town, the road that large trucks and buses and small cars and everything in between drove to and from Peru. And when I wrote those words 'right on' I meant exactly that. The market that was surely meant to be just on both sides of the road was now encroaching on the road itself. The vendors had spread out their blankets for Christmas shoppers and were displaying their wares: men's jockey shorts, long johns, socks, plastic kitchen utensils, pots and pans, piles of potatoes, women's underwear, knitted sweaters, more brassiere sizes than I knew existed and, as I soon found out, men's white dress shirts. I realized too late what was about to happen. Half a block later, the road was completely covered by vendors' displays and impassable. Margaret jumped out to direct matters as we now had to somehow back out. Now for the men, it was perhaps seeing all those brassieres and women's underpants. For the women, maybe the sight of those fabulous plastic kitchen utensils. Whatever the reasons, all shoppers and vendors appeared absolutely oblivious to our camper. Soon, we were totally surrounded by a horde of humanity.

Margaret stood in front of the camper giving the 'which way to turn the wheel' signal with her arm. I have to admit right here and now that when a person gives me that arm signal to back up I'm always baffled. A counterclockwise arm motion by the person signalling appears to the driver as a clockwise motion. So does the person signalling mean back up to the right or to the left? Got that? Anyway, one of us always gets it wrong, and it's probably me. I laid on the horn and started backing up, apparently in the wrong direction, but fortunately quite slowly. That was a good thing, because my side mirror immediately smashed into an old woman's head while she was busy selling her sweaters. God, I thought. I hope our side mirror isn't broken.

No, come on now, of course I didn't think that. I apologized profusely, but unfortunately in English. A young boy of around fifteen then spat on the car door, and followed that up by hurling three 'stupido gringos' at me. Things were getting heated.

I started backing up again. Suddenly, I felt something under the left rear tire. A man leapt to his feet and was screaming. My God, had I crushed his foot? Had I just squished a newborn babies head? I glanced down. Sadly, I had run right over the man's high stack of men's white dress shirts and sadder still, the top ones weren't wrapped in plastic. Now frustration and anger were replaced by a touch of fear. I backed up some more. The dirty left front wheel finished the job on those unwrapped shirts. Suddenly, and I swear, I haven't a religious bone in my body, Moses parted the flood of humanity in back and the camper had a clear path. I backed up, turned around, and shot away.

Margaret changed sweaters, put on sunglasses and a hat, and ventured back into the maze of vendors and shoppers and hoping she wouldn't be recognized as being related to those gringos. She safely made it through the throng and walked four blocks to the aduana and inmigración offices. Office staff, of course, looked for some forgotten document that hadn't been forgotten and, everything found to be in order, back she soon came. I wasn't a good mechanic (well, the word 'good' is certainly a waste of space) but I sure as hell wasn't disorganized.

And the moral of this border story? Guys, when roaring around town in your car doing that last-minute Christmas shopping for your wife's present (you know, the one she will probably return three days later), always watch out for those last-minute dazed and panicked shoppers.

Looking back, this border crossing anecdote gives the 'Ugly American' image some credence. In my defence, I'm not ugly and I'm not American and there was no market there two days earlier. And let me make my fourth and final argument in defence of the crime of cruelty to men's white shirts. This completely blocked road was, and I kid you not, a branch of the Pan-American Highway. I rest my case.

Desperate now to escape the elevation and very concerned as to its effect on the kids, we located a side street that bypassed the market and then took off on the two-hour drive back through Peru to Puno. From there we hung a left west on door number three and towards the city of Arequipa. In the rush, I hadn't noticed that before we could descend to Arequipa, we first of all had to climb even higher. The road crested at 4,572 metres. Then down we went at as good a clip as we could manage on what had been described in the *Handbook* as "dangerous, narrow, unsurfaced, and liable to landslides: many accidents."

Now it's possible you haven't noticed that nobody so far has ever gotten sick in this entire journey except, of course, for the truck. That was about to change. The instant change in elevation proved too much. First to throw up was Martin. Lisa followed close behind. Although not part of my job description, I cleaned up the whole stinking mess. Looking back, I probably cleaned it up in case a book was ever written and someone could accuse me of dodging another dirty job.

Arequipa is called the white city and it's called that because it was built with white volcanic stone. We checked into a nice hotel. (I've forgotten the name but no matter, we're planning on having those memory-assisting potatoes again for dinner.) A staff member told Margaret there were four volcanoes surrounding the city and the most prominent was El Misti. She said Misti hadn't erupted since 1471, so for 505 years. Sounded like a safe bet to me.[12] I went outside and discreetly cut a bushy branch off one of the hotel's trees. Margaret decorated it with three tree decorations she had brought plus a few paper chains and things she whipped up.

The next morning Lisa ran to the 'tree' and was surprised to see Santa had managed to track her down with a nice load of presents. Martin spent the morning trying to knock our 'tree' over.

Now it turned out that our upscale hotel came equipped with a restaurant and a bar. The restaurant provided us with a nice Christmas dinner celebration. And as for the bar, it allowed me to avoid for the rest of my life a spit-beer-chicha drinking experience. It was Christmas, 1976.

---

12 And that El Misti volcano in Arequipa that hadn't erupted for 505 years? It erupted eight years after we left town.

Managua, capital of Nicaragua: 1972 earthquake damage, 300,000 left homeless

Panama City: tide out

Guatemala: street market

Guatemala: backstrap weaving

Colombia: rough road

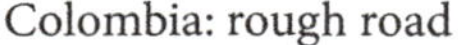

Colombia: heavy load for a woman

Colombia: river near town of Buenaventura

Ecuador: Cayambe volcano, 5,790m – only point on Equator with snow cover

Ecuador: Martin at Equator

Ecuador: at the Equator

Peru: interested children

Peru: Chan Chan – 1,000-year-old adobe wall reliefs – (l) original, (r) restored

Peru: Nazca Lines – most drawings only visible from an airplane

Peru: Nazca Lines – attempting to photograph drawings of birds and animals (some 100 meters long)

Peru: road south to Lima

Peru: road from Nazca to Cuzco; house of rocks with straw roof

Peru: camping along the road from Nazca to Cuzco

Peru: terraced fields along the road from Nazca to Cuzco

Peru: children of the Andes

Peru: remains of fortress at Sacsayhuaman (left and right)

Peru: Tambomachay; Inca baths, aqueducts, waterfalls

ru: Machu Picchu

Machu Picchu, Lost City of the Incas

Peru: Lake Titicaca; totora-reed boat

Bolivia: Tiahuanaco (monolithic statue)

Bolivia: Tiahuanaco; stairway to Temple of Kalasasaya

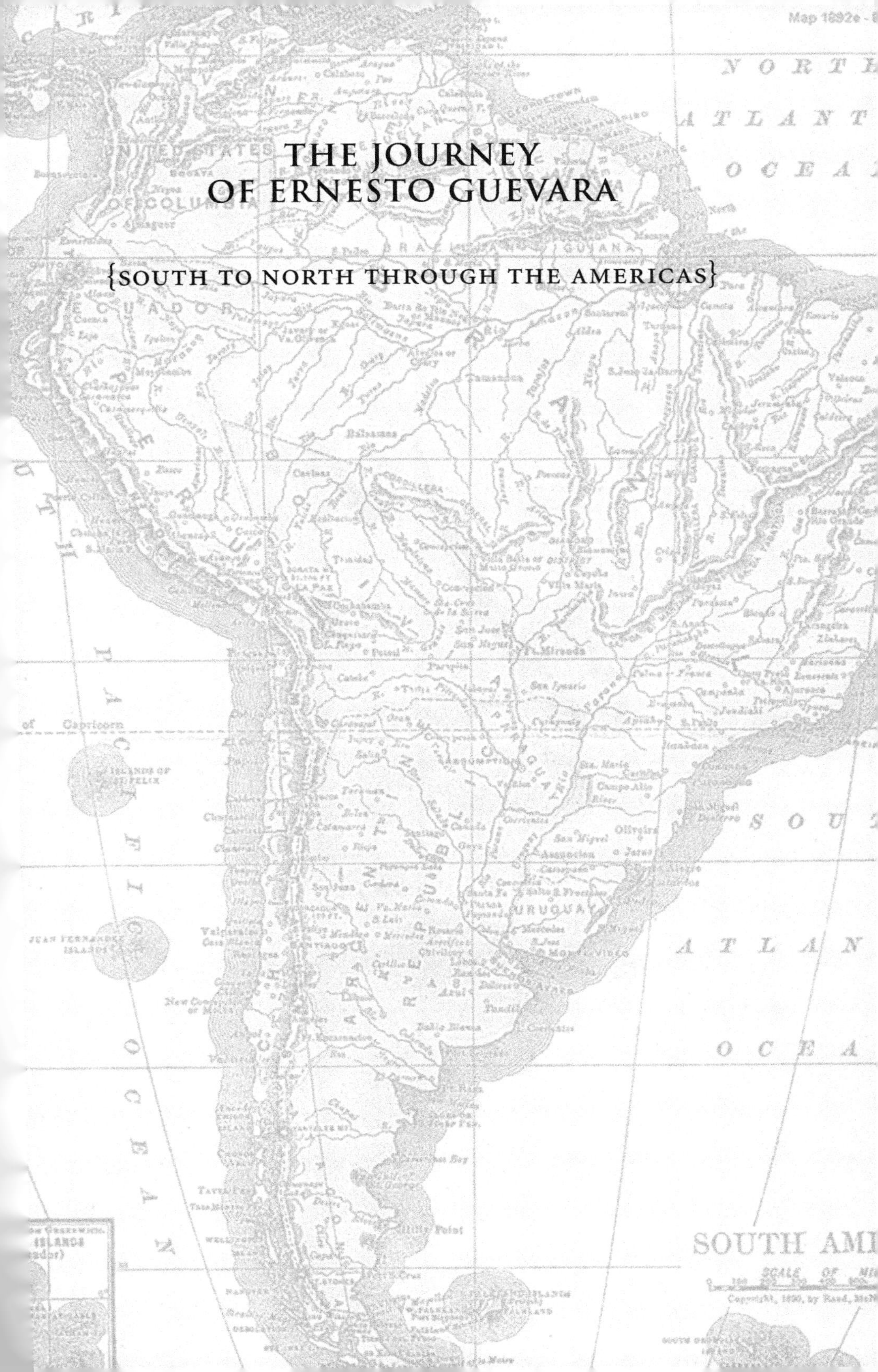

THE JOURNEY OF ERNESTO GUEVARA

{SOUTH TO NORTH THROUGH THE AMERICAS}

Ernesto (Che) Guevara signature

21

THE DOCTOR OF REVOLUTIONS

A long time ago now, an Argentine named Hansi, who was a friend of a friend of Margaret's, said to me that the life of a man was of the four seasons. By that, he meant a man's springtime was the first two decades of his life, a time carefree and simple and secure and filled with fun and laughter. A man's summer was the next two decades, full of life's little adventures and discoveries and dreams and the awakening within of who he was and what he could become. The next two decades were man's autumn. It was now the climax of his life and when he strived to fulfil those dreams and his aspirations. And his winter was man's final two decades, when he looked back at a life that had shown so much promise and the life he had lived. Hansi had turned sixty that very day and was, in his mind anyway, now in the winter of his life. He had been also incredibly drunk. I had hoped that a man's winter started much later than sixty, but I got the idea.

Ernesto's Springtime – 1928 to 1950

Little Ernesto was born in Rosario, Argentina, to Ernesto Guevara Lynch and wife Celia on June 14, 1928. He was a sickly child with chronic asthma. Who could have imagined what a life this short-for-his-age sickly boy was to lead. The family doctor advised he should live in a healthier climate, so off they went to the little spa town of Alta Gracia, outside the city of Cordoba. Here, Ernesto was home-schooled until age eight. Only then was he allowed to go to school, albeit with his asthma inhaler. After Ernesto finished his high school in Cordoba the family moved to Buenos Aires, his parents split up, and he enrolled at the Faculty of Medicine at the University of Buenos Aires. With two years remaining to get his medical degree, a now restless twenty-three-year-old Ernesto jumped on the back of friend Alberto's 500cc Norton motorcycle and off they went on an adventure.

Ernesto's Summer – 1951 to 1954

Some travellers travel away from a place and some to a place. Some travel away from themselves, and some travel to themselves. The latter was Ernesto Guevara de la Serna. The announced plan of Alberto and Ernesto was to go down the Atlantic coast of Argentina, then west across the Patagonia, and finally cross the Andes into Chile. Their secret plan was to continue north from Chile and right into North America.

The famous book, pieced together by his daughter from a detailed diary Ernesto had kept, is called *The Motorcycle Diaries*. The book's title is enticing but the reality is something else. Ernesto and Alberto first travelled east from Buenos Aires to the coastal seaside resort of Mar del Plata for a stay at Ernesto's uncle's house and then south down the Atlantic Coast. As they had planned, they traversed Patagonia to the winter resort town of Bariloche and crossed over the Andes to the Chilean town of Osorno. From there, Ernesto and Alberto rode north 250 kilometres up the Chilean coast to Temuco. That, to all intents and purposes, was it for the motorcycle they had named La Ponderosa the Second, or the 'Mighty One' in English. A few kilometres later, following a series of bike issues including a flat rear tire, a broken steering column, and a smashed gearbox, the Mighty One was finished. As the crow flies, Ernesto and Alberto were seven hundred kilometres south, not north, of where they'd started. Not much of a motorcycle ride to North America now, was it.

They ditched the bike and started hitchhiking and sleeping in hospitals and police stations. As they moved along, they were falsely billing themselves as leprosy experts. In reality, one was just a medical student and the other a biochemist. This little B.S. story of two altruistic travelling doctors got them introductions and free meals and free places to stay. However, even in spite of that cooked-up story, by the time they reached Lima, Peru, they were penniless. *The Motorcycle Diaries* recounts their stay at a hospital in Lima for lepers. These two imposters seemed to add little to the lives of the patients other than treating them as human beings. But for that minor act of humanity, they were given by the impoverished patients—and, more importantly, they accepted—one hundred soles. The *Diaries* relates how they skipped out of paying a hotel bill. It also relates how they often used what they called the 'anniversary routine.' This entailed telling people that they had been on the road for a year (lie), and wished to celebrate (true), but had no money for drinks (true), and when the unsuspecting person offered to pay for the drinks to celebrate the non-existent year's anniversary, they said that it was a custom in Argentina to eat when they drank (lie), so the snookered person also paid for their meal as well as all drinks.

In short, as they were moving north, they were conning some and taking advantage of others. They made it to Caracas, Venezuela, by thumb and bus and plane. Alberto remained there for ten years. With his uncle's connections, Ernesto flew home, free of course, to Buenos Aires. That's the end of the adventure of two guys in their twenties out to see the world. Been there, done that, except, of course, for the creative con jobs, the stiffing of poor hotel owners, and the sponging.

Returning to university, Ernesto knocked off the rest of his exams in a year and in 1953 received his degree from medical school. Then in July of that year and after hitting up every available relative for money, Ernesto left Argentina forever. He left with friend Carlos and by thumb, bus, plane, train, and ship travelled through Bolivia, Peru, Ecuador, Panama, Costa Rica, Nicaragua, Honduras,

El Salvador, and Guatemala. Ernesto reached Mexico City in 1954. By this time, he had seen the poverty of South America and the oppression of the peasants by the wealthy. By now, Ernesto Guevara was a confirmed communist.

Ernesto's Autumn – 1955 to 1965

In 1955, Fidel Castro and his brother Raúl arrived in Mexico City. They had managed to escape from Cuba before being captured by the Batista government, which was now fed up with all the threats of government agitators like the Castros. Fidel and Raúl were in Mexico and preparing for an armed revolution in Cuba. Ernesto eventually met them both and their small band of Cuban exiles. Ernesto always seemed to start every sentence with the word 'Che,' so to the Cubans he became 'Che.' Ernesto Guevara had now become Che Guevara and was to be their doctor, the doctor of revolutions.

In November 1956, a small band of Cuban guerillas, including Che Guevara, landed in Cuba to begin their planned revolution. Finally, on December 31, 1958, Batista resigned as Cuba's president and the following day he and his band of cronies were in the air flying away to the Dominican Republic. The impossible had happened. The revolutionaries had won. In short order, Guevara was appointed supreme prosecutor, commander of the La Cabaña prison, awarded citizenship, and named president of the National Bank of Cuba. He signed Cuban bank notes 'Che.'

Then in 1965, Guevara renounced his citizenship and was gone forever. He left for a visit to the Belgian Congo under the name of Ramon Benitez and to start revolution number two. Unfortunately, Che never announced to the Congo rebels that he and his mini-band of Cubans were coming, and coming to run the show and to save the revolution from itself. It was all a complete failure. His record as a guerilla was now 1 and 1, and if you consider Cuba to be Castro's win and not Che's, which would be the correct answer, then Guevara as a guerilla leader was now 0 for 2.

Ernesto in the Winter – 1966 to 1967

The winter of Che's life was not the twenty years that sixty-year-old Argentine Hansi was planning for himself. Che's 'winter' was a short eleven months. He arrived by plane on November 3, 1966, to La Paz, Bolivia, disguised as a balding, pudgy Uruguayan businessman named Aldolfo Mena Gonzáles. He had come with the intent of starting a peasant revolution in Bolivia, overthrowing the military government, and then having the conflict spread to the nearby Latin American countries, including Argentina. This, he concluded, would then draw in the United States on the one side, and on the other side, and in support of the revolutionaries, would be drawn in either Russia or China, or both. This would, in his wildest of dreams, result in the eventual conquest of communism over the imperialist United States, and in essence the creation of World War III.

By the time his hair had grown back, Che had gathered together a mini-army of twenty-four which only included nine Bolivians. Guevara was never able to attract the Bolivian Communist Party to his side for his revolution and worse, and unlike Cuba, was never able to enlist the poor peasants needed to support his little band.

In the end and high in the Andes of Bolivia, he was surrounded by the Bolivian Army. Now wounded, and with no medicine for his asthma and his rifle smashed and unworkable, he was captured. Even to the very end, Che Guevara was still keeping a diary. He was now seemingly out of touch with reality, for who would spend time each day writing a diary, while trapped in a remote part of the Andes and starving and filthy and awaiting capture and death.

October 7, 1967: Last entry in the diary of Che Guevara, and the day before his capture, a translation from Spanish:

> Eleven months since our inauguration as guerilla; the day was being spent without complications, even bucolic, until

> 12:30 when an old woman shepherding her goats came into the canyon where we had camped and it was necessary to apprehend her. The woman gave no truthful news about the soldiers, saying that she didn't know anything, as it was a long time since she had gone there. She only gave information about the roads; and according to her report, it shows that we are approximately one league from Higueras and another from Jaguey and about two from Pucara. At 17:30 Inti, Aniceto and Pablo went to the old woman's house where she has two daughters, one crippled and the other half-dwarfed. 50 pesos were given to her with the request that she not say a word, but with little hope that she would keep her promises.
>
> The 17 of us left on a waning moon, the march was very tiresome and we left many traces in the canyon where we were. There are no houses nearby, but there are some potato fields irrigated from the same creek. At 2 we stopped to rest, since it was useless to continue advancing. Chino becomes a real load when it is necessary to walk at night.
>
> The army gave strange information about the presence of 250 men in Serrano to prevent the passage of those encircled, saying that there were 37, and giving our refuge as being between the river Acero and the Aro. The news seems to be diversionary. h[hour]=2000

The day before, Guevara had heard on Chilean radio there were eighteen hundred men in the area looking for him and his now sixteen remaining followers. He was correct. The news had been diversionary. Captured October 8th, Guevara was executed by shots fired by a member of the Bolivian army the following day. Before his burial, consideration was given to decapitating him to display his head as evidence of his death. Someone suggested cutting off a finger. The compromise made was to cut off his hands, which was done. Che was then buried in an unmarked grave.

Ernesto 'Che' Guevara de la Serna, Argentine, lifelong asthma sufferer, graduate medical student, adventurer, husband, father, writer, Cuban revolutionary, high-ranking Cuban government official, and Bolivian guerilla: dead at the age of thirty-nine.

Postscript One

Thirty years later, in 1997, his body was found under a landing strip in the town of Vallegrande, Bolivia. His remains were taken to Cuba for burial in the Che Guevara Mausoleum in Santa Clara, Cuba. Santa Clara was selected in remembrance of Guevara and his troops taking the city on December 31, 1958.

Postscript Two

Years later, we returned to Buenos Aires and visited the house of a man Margaret had rowed with years before in the World Masters in the United States. A short old man was standing in the doorway grinning from ear to ear. His hair was thin, combed straight back and dyed an ugly red. His goatee was bushy and reddish brown. He was big-chested with little breasts and bow-legged. His face was free of lines, a product either of healthy living or one of Buenos Aires' many busy plastic surgeons. He had on a Masters Games tee-shirt especially for Margaret's visit. It was dirty, just like a hand-washed shirt one would expect worn by an old man living on his own.

He gave Margaret the usual one-kiss-cheek greeting, introduced himself to me as Delio Esteve, and off we went into his living room. It was 'furnished' with a rowing machine, one chair and a table. On top of the table was an old wooden radio from the thirties and a handful of rowing trophies. Half-open boxes bulging with hundreds more trophies lined the far wall. He said he had seven children with his wife, but she'd left him twelve years ago. Each had four abogados [lawyers]. He said that the abogados had cleaned him out.

His English was faulty so here's what he related in English. He had been a medical doctor and had graduated with Ernesto

Guevara in 1953. He was now seventy-seven and was five years Ernesto's senior. Ernesto was not then 'Che,' he said. Ernesto used to brag about his dirty clothes by saying things like, "It's been four months since my rugby shirt's been washed." His nickname then was 'Chancho,' or pig in Spanish. A few also called him 'El Loco,' which speaks for itself.

He related he had known the Guevara Lynch family for years and especially his eldest sister, and that the family had lived on Calle Araoz near Palermo Park in Buenos Aires, which is today the corner of Calle Arenales and Calle Uriburu. Delio said Ernesto was brilliant and charismatic and especially so with the ladies, but didn't go to dances because he couldn't dance. Delio told me that Ernesto "didn't even kill flies," and "he wasn't then a comunista."

He said Ernesto would come over to study with him and often stay the night. I asked about Ernesto's asthma attacks. Delio said Ernesto had none when staying at his place because Delio's parents fed Ernesto a lot of lettuce and tomato salads and potatoes and fruit, especially apples. Ernesto ate a lot of apples. I had no idea what food had to do with asthma attacks, if anything, but said nothing.

When we left, he gave me a book his physician-father, Juan Esteve Dulin, had written back in 1949, called *Alimentatión Racional Humana*. It was all about proper healthy eating. Delio said his family had been vegetarians for five generations. (To be a vegetarian is a difficult task in meat-eating Argentina, and to have five generations of vegetarians is mind-boggling.) It made for a lousy interview about Che Guevara, but sort of interesting if you were a rower, or a vegetarian, or always wondered if apples could cure asthma, or perhaps always wondered if Che could dance. If you're interested, and who knows, perhaps you are, go on the internet. That book by Dulin is still for sale. Sorry, my copy isn't available. I tossed it away a long time ago without reading a single page.

Ernesto Guevara at Alta Gracia, Argentina

MINISTERIO DE SALUD PUBLICA DE LA NACION
MATRICULA PROFESIONAL DE
Fecha
Apellido y Nombre
Clase 1928
M. I. Nº
Céd. I. Nº
PABLO N. C. REPETTO
FIRMA DEL INTERESADO

Ernesto Guevara's medical degree, (1953)

rnesto Guevara (middle back), Alberto Granado (front) in 1952;
otorbike christened “La Ponderosa II” – ”The Mighty One”

Che Guevara and Mao Tse-Tung in China, (1960)

Che Guevara and Fidel Castro in Cuba

Che Guevara, location unknown

Che Guevara in Cuba

Raúl Castro and Che Guevara in Cuba

Che Guevara and President Nasser of Egypt, 1959

Signature of Che Guevara on Cuban bank currency and stamps

PART V

AREQUIPA, PERU, TO PERITO MORENO, ARGENTINA

Fairbanks
Circle City
Dawson City
Whitehorse
Haines
Dawson Creek
Prince Rupert
Victoria
CANADA
San Francisco
USA
San Diego
Tucson
San Carlos
Mazatlan
MEXICO
Mexico City
San Salvador
EL SALVADOR
PANAMA
Colón
Panama City
Buenaventura
Bogota
COLOMBIA
Cali
ECUADOR
Quito
Tumbes
PERU
Lima
Nazca
Cuzco
La Paz
Arequipa
Tacna
BOLIVIA
Santiago
CHILE
ARGENTINA
Orsorno
Bariloche
Perito Moreno
El Calafate
Punta Delgada
Ushuaia

22

CHILE, BIRD SHIT, AND BOLIVIA

After Christmas, we left Arequipa and descended the final 2,380 metres to Tacna, the border town between Peru and Chile. Here we presented for inspection our yellow vaccination booklets for smallpox, our four passports, and what was now necessary for our vehicle to enter, the Carnet de Passages en Douane. And here came a new twist to crossing a border. Instead of the military completing all the entry forms, here it was to be our job, and six copies of everything were being 'requested.' Incredibly, that's the nicest word I can use, they had no carbon paper. We were told to just go across the street to the small biblioteca [library] to buy some. Now if I'd been in a bad mood, I might have asked if they were also short of pens and elastic bands and paper clips. Fortunately for me, however, my mood was good, for Chile was also under a military dictatorship. That's now four countries in a row under a military government if you're counting. Being a smartass would not have been my finest hour. One of the border guards suggested we remove our windshield wipers until we needed them in southern Chile or they'd probably be stolen. That was certainly encouraging.

Chile is a long ribbon of land and, at 4,620 kilometres, the longest north-to-south country in the world. For that matter, it's the sixth longest in the world in any direction and just short of fifth-place Brazil by ninety-five kilometres. But for the winner and undisputed champion of the world for the longest and also the narrowest country, nothing beats Chile. Its name is perhaps derived from the indigenous word 'chilli,' meaning in English 'where the land ends,' or perhaps based on the indigenous people's imitating the sound of a bird screeching out 'cheele cheele.' Whatever the derivation, in 1535 the king of Spain named it the land of Chili. Today, Chili is spelt Chile, and it's famous for, ah, just give me a minute here, for ah, wine and being a skinny country and ah....

We proceeded another twenty kilometres south through the port city of Arica and then entered the Atacama Desert. Actually, as it turned out, we were already in the Atacama, as it's technically considered to extend north of Arica, and well into coastal Peru. The Atacama is long, the Chilean portion alone is an eleven-hundred-kilometre drive from north to south, so a quarter of the country's length. And the Atacama is dry. In fact, it is the driest place on Earth. No, not the Sahara Desert, and no, not Death Valley in the U.S.A., the Atacama Desert. Some weather stations in the Atacama have never recorded rain. Contrast that with southern Chile, where rainfall averages 1,118 mm per year.

After two pleasant days of driving through the Atacama on a paved road, we came across an actual campsite, right on the shore of the Pacific, and the first campsite we had seen since Mazatlán. The campsite was completely vacant. For some reason, there was a small store to serve all the non-existent customers, and here we bought some processed meat, some wine, a six-pack of Fanta, and a few salad ingredients. Amazingly, there was a hot shower and fresh water to fill up our three water containers. The heat of the sun lifted our flagging spirits and tanned our winter bodies.

The next afternoon while wading out in the frigid Pacific, I felt little round rocks under my feet. The ocean floor was littered with dozens of clams. I immediately started scooping them up with my toes and storing them inside my bathing suit. (Try to block that out, ladies!) At dinnertime, we found enough scraps of firewood on the beach to get a little fire going and then sautéed the clams in salt, butter, lemon juice, garlic, and white wine. That was washed nicely down with a Chilean red. What a life! We stayed for five days over New Year's and my birthday.

This stretch of coastal desert was a hundred years ago part of Bolivia. It had originally been considered a completely useless area but that turned out not to be the case at all. Here there were enormous guano deposits from the anchovy-eating pelicans, something named the booby, and especially the cormorant. The cormorant, in particular, was a guano-making machine. Guano had accumulated over centuries and was in great demand worldwide as fertilizer. There were also vast sodium nitrate deposits (saltpeter), used in both fertilizers and gunpowder. Saltpeter plus charcoal plus sulfur equals a big boom.

In 1874, agreement had finally been reached between Bolivia and Chile as to their border here on the Pacific Coast and which had been in dispute for decades. The boundary settled on was that the area north of the 24th parallel (or just south of Antofagasta) would belong to Bolivia and the area south of the 24th would be Chilean. Chile agreed to this boundary with the rider that it could still mine the area north of the 24th parallel for its guano and saltpeter with an agreed upon, and set in stone, mining production tax going to Bolivia. In return, Bolivia agreed not to raise this tax for a period of twenty-five years.

Now unknown to the Chileans, Bolivia had formed a secret alliance with Peru. The new president of Bolivia then made his first mistake. Assuming he was now dealing from a position of strength with Peru in his back pocket, in 1878 he raised the tax on nitrate production by Chile north of that 24th parallel by ten cents per forty-five kilos. Why, he must have reasoned, would this matter to Chile, a mere ten cent increase in cost on forty-five kilos of sodium nitrate. And if it did matter to Chile, well Bolivia could surely count on Peru's support in any confrontation, and easily defeat their skinny little neighbour to the south. Chile offered to go to mediation on the matter but the ignorant Bolivian president refused to do so. Instead, he confiscated Chilean mining holdings in the area. That was his mistake number two.

Chile immediately invaded that area north of the 24th parallel. Bolivia then called on Peru to activate that alliance treaty and enter on its side. Now by this time, Peru had depleted its own guano reserves. Sensing a chance to replenish those reserves and perhaps to seize control of the world's best natural fertilizer, those Atacama Desert sodium nitrate deposits, Peru stepped in on the side of Bolivia. Bolivia, now emboldened, declared war against Chile. That was the Bolivian president's third mistake.

In short order, the Chilean navy wiped out Peru's navy, and its military destroyed the armies of both Bolivia and Peru. Bolivia left the war in 1880 in humiliation. Peru and Chile carried on fighting until 1883. In 1904, so twenty-four years after it ended war with Chile, Bolivia signed the Treaty of Peace and Friendship with Chile. What a classic name for a one-sided treaty.

Chile had now stretched its Pacific coast ownership 780 kilometres north of its 1884 boundary, that 24th parallel, and thereby added about 20 per cent to its total length. Chile also got those desired sodium nitrate (saltpeter) and guano deposits. Peru gained nothing but a good dose of humiliation. And Bolivia? Bolivia lost its entire coastline to Chile and those guano and sodium nitrate deposits. Bolivia, already a poor and backward country before the war, had now become the only landlocked country, other than Paraguay, in South America. The War of the Pacific, also called the Ten Cent War and the Saltpeter War, was over.[13]

13 It's hard to fathom how much bird guano would have to be dumped over centuries to be of sufficient interest to go to war over, but consider this: Calculations have shown that guano accumulates at a rate of about 1.82 metres (six feet) a century. By the nineteenth century, some Peruvian guano deposits were, in places, forty-five metres deep. Over a span of forty years, the Peruvian government alone exported an estimated eleven to twenty million tons of guano to Europe and the U.S. and for upwards of a billion dollars. With 907 kilos equal to a ton, that's 1,814,000,000 kilos. Now that really is a pile of shit! Then the guano was depleted, and by the mid-1870s, and before that stupid Ten Cent War, the Age of Guano for Peru was over.

(NOTE: For you older readers, you may recall reading that during wars of times past, some governments put saltpeter into the food of soldiers to lower their sexual urges. That's now scientifically proven to be a total pile of, well how shall I say it, guano.)

Then in 1909, German scientists discovered how to chemically produce sodium nitrate and produce it on an industrial level. Chile's nitrate mining production then started a slow decline. By 1960, the nitrate towns of the Atacama were ghost towns and all those guano deposits were long ago depleted. All that fighting and loss of life for, in the end, seemingly nothing.

It turned out, however, that Chile still got the last laugh. By the seventies, copper production from the Atacama region Chile had grabbed from Bolivia formed 70 per cent of Chile's exports, and by the 1970s, Chile was easily considered the undisputed copper heavyweight champion of the world.

And to think that if Bolivia hadn't had such a dumb president, it would still have had access to the Pacific Ocean and its guano deposits and its sodium nitrate mines and would be the world's greatest copper producer. Instead, by the mid-1970s, Bolivia ranked as one of the world's poorest countries. Some countries, like some people, always seem to just miss the boat. Well, in the case of Bolivia, it didn't just miss the boat, it missed the entire Pacific Ocean.

After our week's stay over Christmas in Arequipa and now a nice stay at the Atacama campsite over New Year's, we headed out. When we left, it was again deserted. We were anxious to move on as we had to reach Ushuaia by probably mid-February before the winter snows came to Tierra del Fuego and our journey ended short of the finish line. In our drive through the middle third of Chile, we now confronted something new, a series of military control points. As we entered and left many large and small towns, we were being forced to produce to the military our passports and car papers.

We passed through the larger centres of Antofagasta and La Serena and fertile farmlands and Chile's vineyards, and 120 kilometres short of Santiago reached the port city of Valparaiso and the nearby upscale seaside resort and beaches of Viña del Mar. I read in a brochure that the only thing cold from mid-September to mid-March here are the Pisco Sours. I also read in that same brochure that the water was warm, and so were the women. That (just the Pisco Sours and warm water, I was happily married) sounded excellent to me so we pulled over and parked for the evening at the seaside. Outside, people started milling around the back of the camper. We hadn't seen one camper so far in all of South America, so the sight of ours was clearly creating quite a stir. Our licence plates read "British Columbia," but a sticker on the back of the camper read "Circle, Alaska to Ushuaia, Argentina." This created instant confusion. "Breetisch Coalommbia, Breetisch Coalommbia," a man was uttering. He, like some others, figured we were from some special British enclave in Colombia. Another seeing the word "Alaska," figured the States. One guessed Canada. We left them guessing and went to bed.

The next morning we entered the capital city of Santiago and pulled into a parking lot. We spent the day fruitlessly checking on options to ship the camper back home and also doing the tourist thing. That evening as we were locking up for the night, an elderly lady who ran the parking lot approached our camper. She asked if we were staying the night in the camper because at 1 a.m. every morning she let loose the two vicious-looking Dobermans we'd seen tied up earlier that day. That was curfew time here in Santiago. Now if a city has a curfew, and a parking lot is guarded by Dobermans, those are pretty good indicators there were concerns about civil unrest and riots and robberies and so forth.

Before we had left Canada, we were vaguely aware of what had recently taken place in Chile. In 1970, a Marxist coalition led by Salvador Allende had assumed office. To the dismay of President

Nixon and the United States, communism was again knocking on the door of the West. Then in 1973 came a coup. A military junta headed by General Augusto Pinochet toppled the socialist Allende government and assumed power. What then followed mirrored what was currently happening in Argentina. All left-wing groups were being repressed, and communist and socialist party activity suspended. Rumours were now quietly circulating in Santiago that some of Chile's youth and intellectuals and a couple of professors and newspaper editors had vanished. We weren't crystal clear about all this but could certainly feel the tension in the air.

We left Santiago for what would surely be the safety of the countryside. The next major centre was the port city of Puerto Montt, one thousand kilometres further south. And south of Puerto Montt lay Chile's final sixteen hundred kilometres, a sparsely populated ribbon of wild forests, mountains, glaciers, fjords, islands and channels, and torrential rains, all very cold and stormy, and the exact opposite of the Atacama region up north. A hundred kilometres short of Puerto Montt was the town of Osorno, and here we hung a left and headed into the Andes.

On the other side of the Andes and in the Patagonia of Argentina, we would hopefully leave a world of robberies and military oppression and those threatening military control points far behind, and there would be the town where Margaret spent her first eighteen years, the isolated and peaceful and beautiful tourist town of San Carlos de Bariloche.

23

NAZIS IN SAN CARLOS DE BARILOCHE

Early on January 15, 1977, we headed east from Osorno into the Andes and to the Argentine-Chilean border crossing at Paso Puyehue. I shaved my scruffy beard that morning as we were now hearing more stories about the Argentine military and its dealings with anyone looking—not acting, just looking—like someone from the left. (And, of course, we all know how dangerous people are who don't shave on a daily basis!) Margaret dealt with the authorities exiting Chile and we then proceeded a few kilometres further east over the pass to the Argentine aduana and inmigración for the usual hassle. Argentina is long, just a shade shorter than a drive from L.A. to New York. It's also big, at 2,781,647 square kilometres, the world's eighth largest. We descended into Argentina through a thick forest of coihue [southern beech] and a few stands of Araucaria araucana [monkey-puzzle trees], crossed over the Rio Correntoso, and then passed through the little settlement of Villa Angostura. The gravel road continued northeast bordering 560-square-kilometre Lago Nahuel Huapi, Argentina's fourth largest lake. Rosa mosqueta [wild rose] bushes grew in clumps along the roadside. Purple lupins and white margaritas covered the nearby hills. Margaret noticed the prevailing westerly winds she remembered were picking up, and soon the lake was a sea of whitecaps. By noon, we reached the Rio Limay, Nahuel Huapi's only outlet and surging out well over the seven or so knots of the Yukon River we had seen months earlier. Just before reaching the Limay and on our right was a wooden sign hanging by two chains and fluttering back and forth in the freshening breeze and announcing the location of the El Boliche Viejo restaurant [the old general store restaurant].

Margaret said she wanted to stop here for a few minutes to see family friend Edith Jones in case we didn't come back this way, so we pulled into the parking area. The restaurant door was open and in we went. Two men were sitting at a table drinking their mate in gourds through silver bombillas [straws]. A thermos of hot water was on the table for refills.[14] No one else was around.

"Hola, que tal" [hello, how are you], said Margaret, "I'm looking for Edith Jones."

The older man replied in Spanish that Señora Jones was not there but would return later, so perhaps we could return at that time for a visit to her little house out in back. Perhaps, he continued, we might even wish to come for dinner at nine o'clock when the restaurant opened.

As we left, I noticed a few framed and faded black and white photographs on the wall of men and horses standing in front of a log cabin. I asked Margaret to ask who they were.

"Señora," the younger man answered in English, "the two on the left, they are photos of Jarred Jones, and the others, photos of the bandidos americanos who stayed here long ago. There was a movie of them, Butch something and one called Kid."

Bloody hell, I thought, Butch Cassidy and the Sundance Kid stayed here? If I remembered that movie with Newman and Redford correctly, it just placed them in the States and Bolivia and certainly not Argentina. Now we definitely had to return.

We left and headed south across the Limay towards San Carlos de Bariloche and just a twenty-minute drive from Margaret's hometown before her family came to Canada when she was eighteen. A few stands of alamos trees [poplar] hugged the shoreline of the lake, permanently leaning east due to the fierce westerlies. In the

14 Yerba, or yerba mate, is a tea made from leaves of a local holly tree placed inside a gourd and is the national drink of Argentina. Hot water and sugar are added and it's drunk through a stainless steel straw called a bombilla.

distance to the west were the Andes we'd just crossed, with snow still covering the higher peaks even now in summer.

As we approached Bariloche I saw an unfamiliar road sign, a sketch of a straight line with a dip in the middle and, underneath, the word "vado." Wonder what that's all about, I pondered, a split second before our front tires entered and exited a dip in the road, and our tailpipe smashed into the asphalt. It was Argentina's version of a speed bump, only here it was a speed dip. If you failed to slow down, chau, there went your tail pipe. Margaret spotted a YPF gas station coming up on our right and we pulled in to fill up our two seventy-five-litre gas tanks and to check the tail pipe. Miraculously, it had escaped with just a dent. For the remainder of our journey, if such a sign ever appeared, the one not driving was to yell the warning "vado."

Then on our very first day in Argentina came a military control. Even this far south there seemed no escaping South America's military. There had been a coup d'état eleven months earlier and Argentina's President Isabel Perón, Juan Perón's widow, had been given the boot. The military were on the prowl for subversives. We produced the usual papers and everything was quickly accepted, probably because Margaret was speaking Spanish with an unmistakable Argentine accent.

One thousand six hundred kilometres south of Buenos Aires, and set amid clear glacial lakes, snowcapped mountains, and lush ancient forests, lies the town of San Carlos de Bariloche. It was once said that the trick of life is not just to find paradise, it's to find paradise the way it was long, long, ago. That was San Carlos de Bariloche and the surrounding area. At the beginning of the twentieth century, Bariloche, as it's generally referred to, was just a small settlement, perhaps a hundred or so settlers in the entire surrounding area. The town had a few stores offering supplies to the pioneers in the area, a small schoolhouse, and that's about it.

As the years passed, Europeans and the English arrived and created vast sheep estancias [ranches]. The wealthy of Buenos Aires soon followed and built their summer camps to visit in the summer months of December and January and to escape the oppressive heat of Buenos Aires. (Just to be clear, that's 'camps' like the summer homes in the Hamptons of New York, not 'camps' like that summer camp your parents insisted you visit.) Former U.S. President Theodore Roosevelt came in 1913 and described it "like one of our frontier towns in the old-time west."[15] The railway arrived in 1934 and that same year the Nahuel Huapi National Park came into being. Today, at over seven thousand square kilometres, it's the largest and oldest park in the country. Ski tows on Cerro Catedral followed in 1937, and in 1939 Argentina's most celebrated hotel, the Llao Llao, was constructed. By the seventies, there was a radio station and the population had swelled to something approaching thirty thousand. It was now Argentina's destination for trout fishing, hiking, camping, and skiing. There was a golf course at the Llao Llao, and another just opening at Lago Gutiérrez. Bariloche was now the tourist centre of the Patagonia. We entered town along the costanera [waterfront] and parked for lunch.

"Leave it in neutral and the brakes off," said Margaret. "I know that sounds crazy, but when you understand how they park in Argentina it makes sense. To get in and out of parking spaces, people here use their bumpers, and just bump whatever's in front and back. I remember in Buenos Aires parking with aunt Evelina in her Mercedes. She parked at the beginning of the block. When we came back four hours later, her car was at the other end. So if you don't want the camper bashed, I think it's the best thing to do."

The town was squeezed between the lake and the Andean foothills. Alpine-style houses were constructed of wood and stone like ones I had seen years ago in Switzerland and Germany. In travel

15 Following Roosevelt's lead, Presidents Eisenhower (1960), Clinton (1997), and Obama (2016) also visited Bariloche.

books, and for good reason, Bariloche was referred to as Argentina's Lake District and also as the Switzerland of South America.

It was summer break now and students from Buenos Aires and hundreds more from Brazil were roaming the streets. We left the Centro Civico [city centre] and wandered down Calle Mitre. Stores were packed with the small items tourists could carry home such as facóns (the knife gauchos carried in a sheath tucked into a sash around their waists) and framed pictures of Eva Perón, Perón's first wife who had died twenty-five years ago. Locally made ceramics were everywhere along with brightly coloured hand-knit wool sweaters made from wool from the nearby estancias. Tea houses abounded, offering freshly made homemade scones waiting to be smothered with freshly churned butter and your choice of the locally made jams from the gooseberry, calafate, or rosa mosqueta bushes. Local crafts and beaded necklaces and candles were on display and some brought from the 'hippie' town of El Bolson, a few kilometres farther south.

And dominating the entire scene were stores selling chocolate. Aldo Fenoglio had arrived from Italy in 1947, and by the seventies, the Fenoglio family had turned Bariloche into Argentina's handmade chocolate capital. Stores sold everything imaginable: dark chocolate, milk chocolate, white chocolate, slabs of it, balls of it, sticks of it, different shapes of it, anything you could possibly imagine (well, almost anything, anyway). And Luca's little shop sold household items made from fire-blackened wood: ashtrays, butter knives, dinner plates, cutting boards, picture frames, thick-coloured pencils, serving platters, and so on.

And then there was the store selling tee-shirts. One stack of emblazoned shirts caught my attention displaying the creative 'BAR-ILO-CHE.' Then I saw a second stack of 'BARILO-CHE' shirts and then a third with 'BARI-LO-CHE,' but now 'brilliantly' stencilled vertically. Finally came stack number four emblazoned with 'BA-RI-LO-CHE.' Wow! The mind boggles at the 'creativity'!

Argentina's Che Guevara had been dead less than ten years and already had become tee-shirt fodder for budding entrepreneurs and tourists.

Inflation was rampant. It was being 'held' at just one peso a day increase. The government was hoping to 'hold' inflation to 100 per cent this year, a nightmare for sure, but not the 300 per cent experienced in each of the two previous years. When an Argentine received his or her paycheck in pesos, it was taken to a bank that very day and converted to American dolares before the next day's devaluation. After lunch, we headed west out of town and at the seventeen-kilometre mark stopped for a few nights at the large property of old family friends Teddy Wesley, wife Leo, and their four sons.

Bariloche and the lovely isolated surrounding area was a place of days gone by, and far, far away from everything. It was a perfect place for a dreamer, and perfect for a loner who never felt lonely. It was a perfect place for a man who could obtain a windmill by mail order and erect it to tap the fierce Patagonian winds and in the process of doing so avoid death or a nervous breakdown. It was a place for a fixer of anything and from anything and with just some hard work and imagination and the cojones [balls] to actually give it a go. It was also apparently a perfect place for Nazis to hide after the war.

"But of course," said Leo's son Robin, in answer to my question, "there are Nazis here for sure. I must say that just because someone here is German doesn't mean he was a member of the Nazi Party. Germans emigrated here long ago in the late 1800s to Chile and to Bariloche. Now Nazis, well I don't know for sure if Josef Mengele ever lived here, although he apparently came in the fifties and tried twice before getting his driver's licence. And Eichmann was of course captured by the Israelis in B.A. back in 1960, smuggled to Israel and tried and executed, but I've never heard good evidence he lived here, except maybe came for a visit.

And Margaret, the talk you'll hear of Hitler coming to southern Patagonia by sub, well, there have always been rumours of German subs reaching the Atlantic shore south of Viedma in 1945 and 1946, and Nazis coming with gold and hiding out here, but there's no evidence of Hitler ever coming to Bariloche. And, of course, there were those two German subs that arrived in Mar del Plata in 1945 and 'surrendered' to Perón's government, which was, of course, pro Hitler. No apparent sightings of Hitler, though. Just makes a good story, I think."[16]

"People in Argentina are writing lots of books on Nazis in Argentina. I once read there were as many as five thousand Nazis who came to Argentina after the war assisted by Perón and the Catholic Church. I personally know of two here in town right now and am certain there are many others. One actually used to be mum's accountant for her candle business. His name's Juan Maler. He's still here. Now I know for a fact that isn't his real name. It's Reinhard Kopps. He was in the SS and part of the Vatican route that helped bring Nazis here. He owned the Hotel Campana on Calle Belgrano. You know, I once went to his house on Calle Tucuman to deliver some papers for mum. It's the one with a stone wall and archway in front and hidden from the street. I noticed a sign behind a curtain in German. I wrote the first word down because I don't speak German and got it translated. The sign read 'Free Rudolf Hess.'[17]

"Today Maler's well known here as a writer and distributor of Nazi and anti-Semitic and anti-Masonic propaganda that he gets published in German over in Chile. He always talked freely of Jews and Masons and Americans and the disgusting capitalist system. He's sort of accepted here because the war was long ago, and people here weren't that affected. Anyway, once mum found out more about him, she changed accountants.

16 In December 2015, a German sub washed up on the Atlantic shore of Argentina. One wonders....

17 Deputy Führer to Hitler, Hess flew to Scotland during the war on a personal peace mission, was convicted at the Nuremburg War Crimes Trials, given a life sentence, and died as the sole remaining inmate in Spandau prison in 1983 at age ninety-three.

"Now the other Nazi's far worse. His name's Erich Priebke. He came here in the late forties and opened up a little delicatessen. He later became president of the German Argentine Cultural Association and the director of the German school, the Colegio Aleman. He's never changed his name. A book came out in the sixties about a massacre of Italians which he was involved in and which was made into a movie a couple of years ago.[18] Priebke's in the movie, well not him personally, but an actor playing him. He's quite open about it all, and just says he was under orders given by Hitler so had no choice. Don't know if that's much of an excuse, but there it is. Well, you must remember him, Margaret. You went to the German school for a few years."

"No, I don't," replied Margaret a tad defensively. "I was only there when I was in kindergarten and part of Grade 1 before we went to England for awhile. I can still count to ten in German and that's it."

The following day around lunch we drove to the local Ford agency. "Cerrado" [closed] read the sign on the door. The sign stated it was open from eight to twelve and from four to eight in the evening. It was closed like most stores from twelve to four because that was big mealtime and perhaps also little snooze time if you hadn't bothered to water down your red wine with some seltzer. We did a tour of the surrounding area and then returned at four to Ford. The oil and filter were changed, and they fixed, at least I thought they fixed, the power steering fluid leak. We had the windshield wiper blades changed and the badly frayed air conditioning belt replaced. I supplied the belt because they didn't have one in stock and at Margaret's dad's suggestion I had brought one. We drove back to the Wesleys to park for the night and the next morning, with the truck now repaired, our attention was turned to the camper.

We managed to find a switch at a ferreteria [hardware store] to deal with the water tank, which hadn't worked for thousands

18 1973 movie *Massacre in Rome*, starring Richard Burton.

of kilometres, and I somehow managed the installation. Although I had promised myself back in Lima I would never do it again, I glued the water tank seam with what was considered Argentina's super glue, Poxipol. As the cab-over still bounced on the truck's roof on bad roads, I found an even thicker sheet of stained foam rubber that was formerly someone's mattress and, after cutting it to size, jammed it between the cab-over and cab.

Now with truck and camper hopefully shipshape for the rest of the journey, we headed back for Margaret's visit with Edith Jones and for me to check up on that Butch Cassidy and Sundance Kid story. About halfway, we turned east off the main road to visit another old family friend, Eleanor Estevez, who lived on a little one hundred hectare chacra [small farm].

Three or so kilometres in, Margaret spotted the sign we were looking for, a white sign with the words "La Paloma Blanca" [The White Dove] painted in black. It was riddled with bullet holes. We crossed a guarda ganado [cattle guard], a series of wrought iron pipes spaced four or five inches apart that all chacras and estancias use to keep their cattle from wandering off, and drove in. The two-hundred-metre dirt road to the house was lined on both sides by a row of alamos plateados [silver-leafed poplar trees], which are common here and used as a windbreak against the Patagonian winds. The little chacra was overgrown in places with wild elderberry and gooseberry bushes. Adjoining the house was a water tank, gravity fed from a nearby spring.

Margaret quickly prepped me on Eleanor. Her former husband, named Boy, had been a friend of her dad's. He was a dark-skinned local of Spanish heritage, had back in the day owned the local Coca-Cola franchise, and had been very popular and outgoing, especially after a few drinks. He also liked to gamble. He had died twelve years ago with a drink in his hand and at a card table at the Rex Hotel in town. She was now married to a younger man named Ángel.

Now I should clarify something right now on the off chance that having seen the name 'Boy' and those words 'dark-skinned,' you have immediately leapt to the assumption that Argentines are racist. What they are is not politically correct, and there's a big difference. Here in Argentina, if you're chubby, your nickname could be 'El Gordo,' meaning 'the big one' or 'fatty.' If you're of Polish descent, you could be called 'El Polaco.' And if you're bald, you could be referred to as 'pelado,' or 'baldy.' I once watched two Argentine golf pros in Bariloche. One had his nickname 'negro' emblazoned on his bag and he was as white as myself. If you're dark-skinned that could be your nickname. The other pro's bag had 'Chino' on it. He wasn't Chinese. No offence is meant by these nicknames and none taken.

We entered Eleanor's kitchen through a door desperately in need of oil and sat down in the kitchen. The heating for the house, other than the fireplace in the small living room, was a wood furnace in the kitchen. The 'furnace' was completely boxed in on all sides by ceramic tiles that radiated heat into the kitchen, the adjoining eating area, and the bathroom behind. Two kerosene lamps were in the kitchen, more decorative now than functional, but quite useful if power went out. Three rifles hung on the wall from, Eleanor said, Paraguay's war with Bolivia back in the mid-1930s.

After lunch, I brought up the names Maler and Priebke.

"Well," said Eleanor, "many Nazis came here.[19] Some are here even now. I don't know any Maler but remember Priebke perfectly

19 Josef Schwammberger lived in Bariloche in the fifties—extradited to Germany, convicted on seven counts of murder and accessory to murdering five hundred Jewish prisoners, sentenced to life imprisonment, died in prison in 2004 at 92; Hans-Ulrich Rudel, ace Luftwaffe pilot, most-decorated German serviceman, and Frederich Landschner, Nazi governor of Austrian Tyrol, both members of the Club Andino hiking club in Bariloche founded by Otto Meiling, himself a former member of Hitler Youth; Walter Rauff, SS colonel instrumental in construction of mobile gas chambers responsible for killing estimated one hundred thousand—escaped, settled in Chile, and often visited friend Priebke, captured in 1962, freed by Chilean dictator Pinochet, and died in 1984.

well. Years ago, I used to push Robin's pram up Calle Quaglia and then over to Priebke's little deli on the corner of Juramento and 20 de Febrero. He sold salami, ham, cheese, cold cuts, sausages, sauerkraut, that sort of thing. The store's still there, right across from the Club Andino. I don't know if he owns it today because I now go elsewhere. Most Germans who came after the war say they came from Switzerland, but that's nonsense. He told me long ago he came from Germany. One day, I asked why he never took a holiday to Germany. He told me he'd been a Nazi officer in the SS, and if he went back he might be arrested. You know, he's lived here for almost thirty years, never having changed his name, never having said he was this or he was that. He was the director or something at the German school. Now, who will give you the real details is Odette, because she was into that, and her father was the German consul, and she is so exact. She will come in a few minutes today for tea."

"Does she speak English?" I asked.

"Claro, she speaks English, French, German, and Spanish," replied Eleanor. "No, no," she continued, "not her father, I was wrong. It was her father-in-law, Carlos Woelke. He was German consul here for years. I am not telling you she will give you classified information or anything like that, but she will give you dates, much better than I can give them, much better."

Inside of half an hour, Odette pulled up in a blue two-door Ford Falcon.

"Nice Falcon," I said. "You must have kept it in storage, because it looks in perfect condition."

"No, no," said Odette, "it's brand-new this year. I understand they don't make them anymore in the States, but Ford here in Buenos Aires, actually in La Boca, now makes them. They're very popular here and especially with the military and secret police, who toot around in those dark green ones you often see."

Knowing little about cars except how to turn them on and off, I turned the conversation to my current interest, Nazis.

"Well," Odette said, "my father-in-law, actually my step father-in-law, Carlos Woelke, was the honorary German consul here in Bariloche, so knew Priebke well. Priebke came here in 1948 or 1949. He's actually today the chairman of the board of governors of the German school. He bought a property on Calle 20th de Febrero in 1957 and built a hotel, but later changed it to a private sanatorio. That's a hospital, David. It's still there, right in front of the Plaza Belgrano. He still owns it, and lives in a house at the back."[20]

"My little Sylvana," offered Eleanor, "was born at that hospital. She's still too young to go to the German school but I was told he comes into the classroom and discusses that cave-killing business very openly."

Odette continued. "You know, a book came out about nine or ten years ago about the Ardeatine Caves massacre in 1944. The Italian resistance had killed thirty-three German soldiers, and when Hitler heard this he sent orders to the SS to execute ten Italians for every German soldier killed. They rounded up people from prison and others off the street, took them to a cave, and shot them all in the back of the head, five at a time. When almost finished, they realized they'd rounded up 335 and not the ordered 330, but shot the extra five anyway. I guess no witnesses. Priebke was captain in the Waffen-SS and right there when it all happened. Because of Vatican connections, he and wife Alicia and their two boys got out to the Argentine. Priebke excuses himself today by saying it was at a different time, wartime, and he had to follow orders."

After a late tea we headed outside.

"Eleanor," I said, "I've got a can of oil in the camper so I'll just fix your squeaking door before we leave tomorrow."

---

20 On a subsequent visit, I searched the title at the Catastro, Bariloche's Land Registry office. Maybe Priebke was getting nervous. The title showed he transferred it to his sons, Jorge and Ingo, in 1988.

"No, David," she said, "I keep it squeaky on purpose. An alarm system, like my black lab."

After a final wander around and with the children now awake from their nap, we headed back to the main road and to Edith Jones and the early twentieth century world of Jarred Jones, Butch, and Sundance.

Postscript: Nazis – Maler and Priebke

SS officer Juan Maler, aka Reinhard Kopps, aka Juan Reinhard Maler, aka Helmut Kopps, worked as assistant to Bishop Alois Hudal on one of the rat lines [Germany to Rome to Genoa to Argentina] that enabled Nazis to escape. He worked in Genoa for Father Domoter, who signed Eichmann's Red Cross passport, and in Perón's escape assistance office in Genoa. He escaped to Bariloche in 1948. He was investigated for the extermination of resistance fighters in Albania and his involvement there as an intelligence officer for Hitler.

One day in the eighties, Maler visited Victoria, B.C. Now why would a small-time accountant from a small town in the Patagonia, who spent his spare time writing anti-Semitic material and then distributing it worldwide, come all the way to little Victoria? Was it to visit my old landlord Kruger? Or was it because he had perhaps just visited his main distributor who lived in Seattle and had just popped over to Victoria as a tourist? And there was one other possible reason for his visit to Victoria. His Seattle distributor knew Canada's most notorious Holocaust denier, Ernst Zundel. And where did Zundel's trial lawyer live? Why, right here in Victoria. His name was Doug Christie.

Then in 1994 and acting on a tip, Maler was confronted in Bariloche by ABC television reporter Sam Donaldson. Kopps deflected interest to a bigger fish in town, Commander Erich Priebke, and quickly vanished to Chile until things settled down.

Sam Donaldson then cornered Priebke. Priebke's defence in

the Ardeatine cave executions, and shown on live television (and on the internet even today) was that, and I quote him exactly, "an order was an order." When that reached Italy, Italians were outraged. He was extradited to Italy for trial. The defence offered by many on trial at the Nuremberg trials that "an order was an order" hadn't been accepted there, and now wasn't accepted in Italy. And, furthermore, even if that "order was an order" defence had been accepted by the Italian court, an extra five Italians had been murdered in the Ardeatine Caves, so there went that defence. He said he'd shot no one. At trial, evidence was presented that he had shot two, so that was a lie. He said no children were shot. At trial, evidence showed three bodies were under 14, so another lie. Convicted and sentenced to life in prison, he spent his last years under house arrest at his lawyer's home in Italy and died in 2013 at age one hundred. Germany and Argentina both refused to accept his body. Italy finally buried him in a secret location. Priebke never did admit any responsibility.

JARRED, BUTCH, AND THE KID

We left Eleanor's and drove back to the main road, crossed over the Limay to El Boliche Viejo, then drove around the back and parked in front of the home of Edith Jones, widow of Andres Jones. We walked through the pantry, through the kitchen with a large woodstove, and then into the living room. Overstuffed chairs circled the large stone fireplace on the far wall. Throw rugs were scattered on the worn and tired floor. Picture frames holding black and white snapshots of days gone by covered the walls. The room appeared furnished from a warehouse owned by Ralph Lauren, only these furnishings were authentic and old, really old. The darkened walls were made of cypress from the Andean forests. Once a visitor had asked her now long ago deceased father-in-law how he'd managed to get such an unusual and quite lovely patina to the walls. Jarred Jones had allegedly answered, "Forty-five years of stove heating, a lot of coal oil lamps, and no electric light." Edith Raquel Jones was of Welsh descent, had trained as a teacher, and had married a son of Jarred Jones. Women here retained their maiden name and the husband's was tacked on at the end. Here, Margaret was Margarita Ana Moreno de Humphries. Edith was Edith Raquel Jones de Jones. After some prompting, Edith related the family story. It was related in Spanglish, a mixture of English with a few words of Spanish tossed in when an Anglo-Argentine either couldn't recall the correct word in English or just liked the Spanish word better. ("I like my bife well done," meaning, "I like my steak well done.") This is a pure English version of her story.

In 1884, a twenty-one-year-old half-Welsh, half-Cherokee, illiterate named Jarred Augustus Jones arrived by ship to Buenos Aires from Fort Worth, Texas. He arrived with his friend, John Crockett, a descendant of legendary Davy Crockett. Young John had a distant relative in Buenos Aires who had formed a partnership with local dentists Ralph and George Newbery under the name of Newbery-Crockett. They were arranging to drive cattle to Chile. Jarred Jones met John's relative and signed on for the cattle drive. Over time, his skills resulted in Newbery-Crockett hiring him to drive cattle south to the Province of Chubut and to a large six-hundred-thousand-hectare estancia formed in the nineteenth century by the British-owned Argentine Southern Land Company.

After seeing the countryside down south, Jones returned to Buenos Aires and obtained a government land grant of two thousand hectares at the mouth of the Rio Limay and just north of the small settlement of Bariloche. Then off he headed to create for himself a new life. A home and warehouse, the warehouse later converted to a boliche [dry goods store], were built and Jones raised horses, cattle, and sheep. Once a year, he would leave with his mules and horses laden with the products of a year's labour: wool, leather, feathers collected from ostriches and prized by exporters to Europe, and furs. All fruits of the country, as Edith put it. Jones travelled east to the Atlantic port of San Antonio, and then south to the new small Welsh port towns of Porto Madryn and Rawson. Finally, he headed inland to the little Welsh settlements of Gaiman and Trelew on the Chubut River. He wouldn't return to his family for months, sometimes even up to five months.

Now there had been a lot of excitement surrounding Argentina at the end of the nineteenth century. Many came to Argentina from Europe, Britain, and Scotland hoping to find for themselves a new and prosperous life. And some Americans, as Jarred Jones had done years before, were also looking to Argentina. In 1902, a twenty-two-year-old Cherokee named Will Rogers, later in life to become a vaudeville and film star, went to Argentina with a friend and with the dream of becoming ranch owners.

On February 20th of the previous year, two men and a woman boarded the British ship Herminius bound for this new land. Perhaps they'd read newspaper articles about the new Wild West, a place where they could start a new life unencumbered by their current troubles. Perhaps they'd been persuaded by stories they'd heard about American George Newbery, a land developer and dentist to Argentine President Roca, who had briefly returned to the States some years before to recruit cowboys to settle the southern reaches of Argentina. The two men were horse thieves and bank robbers. They were also train robbers and were being pursued by employees of a company specializing in capturing train robbers, the Pinkerton Detective Agency. The three that had boarded were James Ryan and Mr. and Mrs. Harry and Ethel (Etta) Place. Ryan's real name was Robert Leroy Parker, and Harry's last name was Longabaugh. They were known to United States authorities as Butch Cassidy and the Sundance Kid.

Like Jones seventeen years earlier, they also met with Dr. George Newbery, who by now was the United States vice-consul to Argentina. Although there's no record of Newbery ever venturing as far south as the Cholila Valley in Patagonia, Newbery did know a white man who had gone there, his friend Dr. Moreno. On his return to Buenos Aires, Moreno had spoken to Newbery of the fine grasslands in this sparsely populated area. With that in mind, Newbery suggested to Ryan and Place a nice parcel in the Cholila Valley on the east bank of the Blanco River, so it had a water supply. The nearest train station was over six hundred kilometres away, so extremely difficult to reach. It was located in the foothills of the Andes, so close to the Argentine-Chilean border. It sounded like an ideal place for Ryan and Place to ranch.

It also sounded like a safe place to hide and an excellent place from which to escape if local authorities, or even the Pinkertons, came calling. Ryan and Place signed all necessary homestead papers, arrived late in 1901, constructed three log cabins, and then settled in raising horses, cattle, and sheep.

On one occasion, related Edith, while driving some horses south to Cholila, Ryan and Place had been delayed by bad weather and been forced to stay a month with Jarred Jones and his family. The entries of purchases and debts at the boliche at Jones' estancia had been meticulously kept from the very beginning. Edith related that there was an entry dated either 1902 or 1903, she couldn't recall at the moment which, for a Ryan and Place. She did, however, recall the exact entry which read "one kilo yerba, one kilo sugar, two bombillas." Before leaving, they had invited Jones to visit, so the next spring, Jones and his wife and two of their children had gone south to Cholila by horse and buggy.

"David," Edith said, "those photos you saw on the wall, they were taken when my father-in-law went there. They were put up on the wall by my children over my objections and to make the restaurant more authentic for the touristas that are starting to come here after that movie. I really don't like to talk about those bandits. It makes the family look bad. You should go to Cholila on your way south, the buildings on their estancia are still standing."

We said goodbye to Edith and wandered over to El Boliche Viejo. It was now nine o'clock and had just opened. We were the only customers.

There was no menu. The restaurant served no pasta and no seafood, just meat and then more meat. Immediately after being seated, a plate of meat-filled empanadas arrived, the Argentine version of the English Cornish pasty, only far juicier, and along with a bottle of Malbec I had ordered. On the north wall was the parilla, a grill made of angle irons about three metres long by two-and-a-half deep. The parilla was tipped forward a little so much of the fat from the meat would run away from the coals, down the angle irons, into a little angle iron trench, and then over to a large empty tin can. The bed of red-hot coals under the parilla had been readied over the past two or so hours and the meat was slowly cooking for the evening's customers.

A wooden platter of meats soon arrived from which we were to select what we wished: some crispy done morcilla [blood sausage], crispy done chinchulines [cow's small intestine], kidney, sesos [sheep's brains], and liver. Apparently eating all the cow guts goes back to the days of the gauchos, who were allowed to eat as much of the cow's insides as they wanted. What we didn't wish to eat, and I certainly didn't want the intestines whether crispy or not, went back on the parilla to keep warm for others. A short while later, platter número dos arrived, this time with mollejas [veal sweetbreads from the thyroid or heart], a slice of vacio [flank steak], and a little lamb. What we didn't wish to eat again went back on the parilla. Then, after eating what we could of all that, plus a gigantic plate of papa fritas [French fries] and, as in virtually all Argentine restaurants, the only vegetable served, plus the fresh crusty bread and the wine, came platter número tres. Here was the main course: strips of tira de asado [short ribs] and two bife de chorizo [sirloin steak]. Margaret's steak was ordered and arrived cocida [well done] and mine, as requested, a punto [medium]. And if you wanted more of platters one, two, or three, you just asked. Sort of a revolving, but delivered straight to your table, meat smorgasbord.

For dessert came panqueques [crêpes] with dulce de leche [a filling made of milk, sugar, and a touch of vanilla—like melted Kraft caramels, for all you older readers.] And just to make sure we were completely happy, the waiter placed on the table a bowl full of even more dulce de leche.[21] By 10:30 p.m., the place was almost full. And still people kept arriving, and some at that late hour with small children. For us, the marathon of meat was over. Margaret,

21 Quick recipe for dulce de leche: place can of sweetened condensed milk in boiling water for three hours, open can, stir, cool in fridge to obtain correct texture & taste, serve.

who had far less wine than me, drove back to Eleanor's, where we parked for the night. She put the kids to bed, now both sound asleep, and then went to bed herself. I went inside.

Eleanor and I then proceeded to tackle the remainder of the small demijohn of red wine on the table. Her three sons with Boy had left home. She was now alone, except for three-year-old Sylvana, her daughter with Ángel, who ran a construction business. I noticed in the days we camped outside that Ángel rarely made an appearance. Eleanor and I drank some more. She was getting teary-eyed as she recounted her life's struggles. She was only forty-two but looked much older. Her long hair was prematurely grey and her body had gone soft. She appeared to be slowly losing life's struggle. Townspeople knew that much younger Ángel fancied the young beauties of Bariloche. And she knew it as well.

Eleanor was alone and lonely, and kilometres from anywhere, and anyone. She showed me her .22 pistol she always kept nearby at night. Sometimes, she said, and in those evenings when Ángel's truck was absent, she would hear the tero-tero birds nesting in the fields going crazy, which would then trigger her dog barking and a sure sign someone was nearby.[22] Occasionally, there would be an unwelcome knock at the back door. She said she just opened the kitchen window and fired a couple of shots into the night sky. That always scared off anyone with any bright ideas. By midnight, the demijohn was empty. I left Eleanor and returned to the camper. The air felt fresh and clean and the stars were brilliant, brighter down here in the non-polluted Southern Hemisphere than I had ever seen in my life. Through the kitchen window, I saw Eleanor still seated at the kitchen table, and with tears now running down her cheeks. Ángel never did come home.

---

22 The tero tero was a lapwing, specifically a plover. It nested in the fields and went crazy when humans approached, so acted like a watchdog of sorts. The noise it made sounded like how one would pronounce tero tero, so that's what they were called.

25

HIPPIEVILLE AND THE BOMB

With winter coming to Tierra del Fuego about mid-February, we had little time to waste. We left Bariloche and all remaining well-aged Nazis behind and headed south for the town of El Bolson, about 120 kilometres distant. The roadside was lined with golden Scotch broom, not native to the country, but looking quite yellow and bright and lovely in the crisp morning air and sunshine. We drove along the gravel road, throwing up a good cloud of dust, through stands of cypress and coihue [beech], past Lago Gutiérrez, where we had been swimming days earlier, and then past Lago Mascardi. There was little traffic and after two hours we reached the centre of El Bolson.

In 1949, the Soviet Union conducted its first atomic test, and in 1953 it detonated a hydrogen bomb. In the United States, the Americans were keeping pace with the Soviets at their nuclear-testing site in Nevada. Citizens in the small towns in Nevada, Utah, and Arizona, downwind from the blasts, were getting extremely concerned. Pinkish mushroom clouds filled with radiation debris were floating overhead on test days. When children played in trees and shook branches, some days radiation debris fell like snow. The Utah Cancer Registry noted that the incidence of leukemia in the late fifties in Utah was one and a half times higher than the national average.

Then in 1961, the Soviet Union detonated the largest and most powerful nuclear weapon ever detonated. Known in the Western nations as the 'Tsar Bomba,' it was the equivalent of fifty megatons (fifty million tons of TNT) and completely levelled an uninhabited village fifty-five kilometres away. By comparison, the largest nuclear blast detonated by the U.S.A. was fifteen megatons. President Kennedy announced the federal government would begin construction of fallout shelters. Tensions were escalating. The Cold War was on. Tensions ramped up further in 1962 with the Cuban Missile Crisis. And by this time, Britain, France, and China had also joined the nuclear race.

Now as the sixties moved into the seventies and Americans like Charles Callaghan sought a safer environment for their families, so also did some young Argentines. Those five noted nuclear powers all had one thing in common: they were in the Northern Hemisphere. Argentina was in the Southern Hemisphere, so in theory safer from any radiation carried by winds, yet not completely safe. And what area would be safest for Argentina's youth living in the more northerly populated centres of the country, and unburdened by family and job? The obvious answer was a little town in southern Patagonia, snuggled right next to the Andes. If radiation ever reached that far south, why, the reasoning went, the winds of the Patagonia would simply carry any such radiation up and over the high Andes, and then far, far away.

And if the threat of a nuclear war for young Argentines wasn't enough of an incentive to leave Buenos Aires and other main cities up north, they had a second and perhaps more realistic incentive. The government was facing a threat from the left, oddly enough initially triggered by one of its very own, Dr. Ernesto 'Che' Guevara. A crackdown had quietly begun. At first, there were just small irritants imposed by the current military dictator, President Ongania, such as ordering no kissing on the streets and no wearing of miniskirts and no long hair for boys. Things then got far worse. The press was censored, university professors and students were being arrested and beaten, and others were forced into exile. Some people were vanishing. This was not lost on the youth of Argentina. Something terribly wrong was going on.

So south some of Argentina's youth went to settle in the little town of El Bolson and to create what would eventually become the hippie centre of Argentina. Here in the foothills of the majestic Andes, they could squat on land for free and probably for their lifetime. Now, you may ask, how exactly could a person squat on land in such an area of pristine wilderness for his or her lifetime?

Well, here's your answer. Much of the land here had been purchased long ago by settlers who purchased and took title. Then, as the years went by, some couldn't adapt and went back to the old country, some packed up and moved elsewhere, and some simply died. Land taxes stopped being paid. Others purchasing here were members of wealthy families in Buenos Aires. They also obtained title, but soon lost interest in this remote land that they considered of little value. Again, land taxes stopped being paid. Well, you say, all that land would have long ago reverted back to the government for non-payment of land taxes. Today, that land would either be government-owned or would have been sold by government to someone else. Fortunately for those squatters, you would be incorrect.

What happens is that every few years the Argentine government has a moratorio [moratorium]. This means all outstanding land taxes that a registered owner owes, whether he's living on the land or living elsewhere or dead, are now totally forgiven. Then another few years pass by and the outstanding land tax bill of all those absentee title holders again climbs and climbs. And then, voilà, another moratorio is declared. All land taxes are again totally forgiven. This has gone on for decades.

Some squatters with cash from the bank of dad go to a notario publico, file some papers, wait a couple of years, and then pick up legal title to their chunk of heaven. The cost is the notario's account and paying some recent back taxes. And what do these new land title owners now do? Why, they don't bother to pay what is now their own tax debt, and simply wait for the next moratorio. That's how you get free land. This routine obviously leaves Argentina a little strapped for funds.

Now while on this topic of squatters and non-payment of taxes, let me describe what takes place here on an actual land sale. Let's say, for example, the sale price on the boleta [original contract of purchase and sale] is $500,000 cash. And all deals are in cash, and in good old American dollars. At closing, the executed escritura [closing] documents prepared by the notario publico for the land title office show $300,000. The boleta [original contract] that showed $500,000 is now torn up by the notario, so all that remains to be seen by the curious are those documents showing that $300,000 figure. And the result? The seller gets his $500,000 less commission, so he's a winner. The buyer pays the land transfer tax on the $300,000, not on $500,000, so he's a winner. The realtor gets his commission based on $500,000, so the realtor's a winner. And the loser? The loser is the country of Argentina, screwed again out of even more taxes. And remember that not only are the only documents in existence showing a false and far lower sale price, but the transaction was all in untraceable dollars.

And that extra $200,000 in the above example? Experienced realtors have on hand all the necessary papers for a seller to open up a bank account in the tax-free haven Cayman Islands. All a seller has to do is pack that $200,000 across the River Plate to a bank in Uruguay's capital city of Montevideo. Then off it goes to the Caymans. So buena suerte [good luck] to Argentine auditors checking for funny business on land deals or auditing realtors' commissions (see postscript).

Well, you say, all that talk of moula is sort of interesting but doesn't really affect me at all. Sorry, you are wrong again. Follow this, please. Hard-working Canadians religiously pay taxes to their government. In turn, the Canadian government funds the World

Bank and the International Monetary Fund (IMF). These two institutions grant loans to the always-short-of-cash Argentine government. The Argentine government regularly defaults on these loans because it has no money, and it has no money because Argentines aren't paying their land taxes and their full income tax debt. And Argentines aren't paying those taxes because they realize they will get little benefit back from the crooked politicians.

The end result is that Argentines now enjoy a relatively tax-free life, as do Argentine politicians who are busy ripping off the system by their own methods. Meanwhile, Joe Canuck continues year after year grinding away at his job and religiously coughing up his annual tax burden. And the beat goes on. Got that picture? Or should I repeat it?

Now Argentina's youth who came to Bolson in the late sixties and early seventies were beaten there by Willi Cordier and his flock, the Cordians. Willi, a former member of Hitler Youth and the leader of a religious Bible-reading sect expecting the doom prophesied in the Bible, had left Germany in 1948. Willi figured the group would be safe in Argentina from the 'doom' and would be welcomed with open arms by Perón and his pro-Nazi government. Unfortunately for Willi, Perón had, five months before war's end, flipped sides to the Allies. Willi and his flock of one hundred, all now personae non grata, were forced to detour and settle in the Falkland Islands. Then in the mid-sixties, so after almost twenty years in the Falklands, Willi and his gang settled in El Bolson and began squatting on the lands of those absentee landowners. Early every morning, someone would blow a German tune on a bugle to rise and shine. Defrocked priest Willi demanded that his flock live a life of self-degradation and poverty. All technology was rejected and all work was to be done by manual labour. Sure sounds like a lot of fun to me!

By the early seventies, Argentina's youth had arrived to El

Bolson. Here in Bolson was where you would find the silversmiths and rawhide rope braiders and wood turners and glass painters and bead necklace stringers and jewellery makers and dried wild flower suppliers and all those poverty-stricken Cordians. And if you wanted homemade pottery or candles or (everyone's favourite) those energizing crystals, why, they could all be found right here in the street markets of Bolson. Glass jars of jams and jellies abounded. And the Rosa mosqueta bushes grew wild, and seemingly everywhere, so provided the rosehip oil for a locally made skin cream. Shelves were loaded with jars of this skin cream, a cream which apparently solved every conceivable skin condition known to mankind, and undoubtedly all other conditions still to be discovered.

We stopped for lunch for a Fanta and a Coke and some empanadas. I had recently eaten empanadas de carne in Bariloche that had been filled with meat, raisins, onions, and egg. Here, I discovered, empanadas came with many different fillings. Sold were empanadas de pollo [chicken-filled], empanadas de jamón y queso [ham and cheese], and empanadas de humita [corn-filled]. To determine the filling you were about to bite into, you simply looked at how the pastry was folded to seal in the contents. Each empanada filling had its own distinctive pastry shape. Simple, yet ingenious. We ordered three of each filling to go, and then continued southwest to the Cholila Valley, for our rendezvous with Butch and Sundance.

Then, just at the edge of town, there it was, the little sign I had heard about: "El Bolson, a Nuclear Free Zone." Whew! It certainly was a huge personal relief to learn that all those skin-creamed-to-perfection men and women of El Bolson absolutely refuse to manufacture, or even possess, nuclear weapons. I mean, one never knows what hidden talents those marijuana-smoking jam and pottery makers actually possess, now does one?

Postscript

In 1997, the Italian clothier family, Benetton, purchased from a group of adjoining landowners a parcel of nine hundred thousand hectares (two million, two hundred thousand acres) about seventy-five kilometres south of El Bolson. The price was a purported $50,000,000. The closing of the sale was at a bank in Buenos Aires. Into the room came the Benettons and their abogados (lawyers) and their notario publicos and their accountants. Also arriving was a Dutch-born realtor from Bariloche named Federico van Ditmar.

Then in came all the sellers: old people, widows, young couples, and the corporate representatives for the large estancias. Undoubtedly also arriving were one or two of those former squatters. If they had picked up title with the help of the bank of dad they were now on the verge getting more cash out of their piece of dirt than 99 per cent of those Klondike prospectors. The sellers also arrived with their representatives, so now a room full of close to forty.

A bank draft drawn on an American bank was whipped out by the Benettons' abogado and dramatically placed on the table. Federico never disclosed the actual amount of the draft. A hush fell over the room. A bank draft was totally unacceptable. As Federico related to me in 1998:

"The Benetton representative hadn't listened closely when I said land transactions here are completed in American dollars. I meant exactly that, not a bank draft, not a certified cheque, but cash, or, as you so nicely put it, David, 'Ben Franklins.' Everyone stormed out. A week later, a plane arrived from New York with the cash and everyone who had left Buenos Aires rushed back. The pile of money on the table was half a metre high. Everyone was yelling and grabbing their share. A total disgrace."

The commission paid to realtors in Argentina on a sale was

3 per cent paid by the buyer and 3 per cent paid by the seller. On a sale of that purported $50,000,000, that's a $3,000,000 commission. Federico told me he didn't take the full 6 per cent, but said he did alright. I imagine so.

Since hearing that story from Federico, I have always wondered about two things. Was that half-metre pile of cash on the table just the purported purchase price of $50,000,000? Or were all those boletas (purchase and sale contracts) torn up at the closing by the abogados? And if torn up, then that half-metre stack of $10,000 bundles of Ben Franklins (hundred dollar bills) undoubtedly represented far more cash than $50,000,000. I have also wondered if the next day there were a few extra tickets sold for the ferry across the River Plate to Uruguay and if bank staff in the Caymans had to work late the same day. (Now don't get excited, all you Argentine and Italian readers, I'm not accusing, just wondering....)

26

BUTCH AND TRE FELIN

The drive from Bolson to the Cholila Valley was short, about seventy or so kilometres. Cholila, in the indigenous Mapuche language, means 'beautiful valley,' and it was certainly that. Someone once had written that this area was a place to dream of, and a place to dream. Perhaps that described it better. An enormous field of blue lupins greeted us as we entered the valley, which was surrounded by high Andean peaks. Purple thistle appeared here and there along the roadside, and mosqueta bushes were everywhere. Alongside the road, a carcass of a dead hare was being picked over by two hawk-look-alike chimangos. As we neared the northeastern entrance to the valley, we slowed to a crawl and started looking for something announcing Butch and the gang had once been here. After a short while, as there were no neon signs flashing "Butch and Sundance slept here," or for that matter any signs at all, we noticed a group of three deserted-looking buildings set among a clump of poplars, so wandered over for a look.

They were log cabins, constructed like those we had seen in the Yukon and Alaska, and totally unlike what existed here in the Patagonia. No one was around. On the west side of the cabins was a creek bed. It was summer now, and except for a faint trickle of water it was bone-dry. This was perhaps the Rio Blanco that Dr. Newbery had mentioned to Butch and Sundance in Buenos Aires. I looked at the photo in my hand Margaret had taken of the photo hanging on the wall at El Boliche Viejo in Bariloche. The photo showed two large framed windows to the left of a framed door, and another framed window to the door's right. I looked back at the house in front of us. Yes, this was definitely the right place.

Butch and Sundance had petitioned for a parcel of land of one square league, or about 3,087 hectares [7,628 acres], and had moved here with Etta in 1901. In a letter to a friend in Utah in 1902, Butch had written they had cattle and sheep and good horses. He had written they had a house and warehouse and stable and that the country was first-class, with mountain water and knee-high grass.

They had lived here through 1904, raising cattle, horses, and sheep. Neighbours had visited. The newly appointed governor of the Province of Chubut had visited. The Jarred Jones family from Bariloche had visited. All had been peaceful and quiet. At some point, Etta had left Cholila and probably returned to the United States.

Then in 1905, a bank robbery had occurred in the Atlantic coastal town of Rio Gallegos, about sixteen hundred kilometres south of the Cholila Valley and allegedly by two Americanos. Butch and Sundance, and known here as Ryan and Place, had been the prime suspects. Someone had blown the whistle on them. Perhaps a disgruntled neighbour, perhaps Dr. Newbery after finding out who he had dealt with, or perhaps Jarred Jones. No one knows, really. Tipped off that the local authorities were on their way by a local Welsh friend, the local police inspector named, and I am not making this up, David Humphries, they had sold off their livestock and vanished.[23] The land couldn't be sold as they had yet to obtain title. They probably had escaped by horseback to Chile through nearby Paso El León, a pass containing an ancient two-week-long cattle trail first used by Jesuit missionaries in the early eighteenth century and later used by locals to drive cattle to market in Chile.

23 Author Allan Burns, who wrote the screenplay for *Butch and Sundance, The Early Years*, refers to the police inspector as "David Humphries." I read somewhere the police inspector was named "Eduardo Humphreys." I like to think that Burns did the better research.

After crossing into Chile, did Butch and Sundance then go north by horse or train or both thirty-two hundred kilometres to the mining town of San Vicente in Bolivia and perish in a hail of bullets, as in the movie? Or did they, as some stories go, return to the United States, with Butch dying in Spokane, Washington, and Sundance in Utah? No one knows, really, and without that 1969 movie starring Paul Newman and Robert Redford, I doubt that anyone today would really care.

We entered the largest log cabin and clearly the main house. Inside was absolutely nothing, no furnishings, no floorboards, no old newspapers crammed into crannies between the logs, absolutely nothing. On the north side of the ceiling was a round hole patched over with tin. Here was where would have been their pot-bellied stove with its protruding stovepipe. Margaret took pictures outside but I wanted something more tangible for a souvenir. Perhaps a coin might have been lost in the dirt floor. Perhaps Butch had lost his pocket watch. Perhaps Etta had dropped a diamond-studded brooch given her by Sundance. Nothing! Damn it, I thought, why did I leave that metal detector behind in Victoria. The smallest of the cabins was probably the warehouse Butch had mentioned in that letter he wrote in 1902, but again, it was completely empty. We figured the third and middle-sized building we entered had been the stable. Again, nada.

And then, and just as I turned to leave, I found my souvenir. Half buried in a corner was a broken leather and iron stirrup. The leather portion was partially attached to the stirrup by two old brass-coloured coins. I could clearly see the word 'peso' on each coin.

Having now tracked down Butch and Sundance and now having my souvenir, and don't we all love souvenirs, we returned to our truck. Margaret took the wheel. I was, as my Welsh namesake, local police inspector David Humphries, would have said, excited "fel ci a dau goc," which translated from Welsh means "like a dog with two willies," or in plain English, "so excited that I don't know what to do with myself." I immediately started rubbing the tarnish off one of the coins with my sleeve to check the year. I could read the first two numbers, a one and a nine. The last two were probably 01, 02, 03, or 04, because Butch and Sundance had left in 1905. I continued cleaning until all the tarnish was gone. The last two numbers were a 7 and then a 5. The other coin was the same. Both coins were two years old! So much for souvenirs of Butch and Sundance! Margaret thought my disappointment was quite funny. Not me. My Welsh namesake would have uttered that the 'souvenir' was "dim gwerth rhech dafadz" which, translated, means that something is "not worth a sheep's fart," or in plain English, "worthless."

We left Cholila and headed southeast to the Chubut Valley and to the nearby town of Tre Felin in Welsh, Mill Town in English, and today called Trevelin. There was nothing in the *Handbook* about the area other than a small paragraph on page 93 about Welsh settlements in Argentina. According to this small-print paragraph, Welsh is still spoken in some settlements in Argentina, and even today some newspapers are published in Welsh. We pulled into town for a look-see and a bite. We had an early tea at a tearoom on Calle Perito Moreno with scones and fresh butter and home-made jams and cheese and then popped into a bookstore that seemed to sell nothing but books on the Welsh in Patagonia. I bought a small pocketbook in English and, no surprise here, on Welsh settlements in the Patagonia.

We decided to treat ourselves to a stay at a hotel that evening and have a good shower. It would also allow one of us a quiet time to give the camper a good cleanup. Margaret insisted on the cleanup job, and I got the two children. After five minutes, I understood why.

Now the hotel was quite something. In the reception area hung a picture of Jesus Christ, one of Jesus and Mary, and a small Argentine flag. The hotel clearly had quite a few rooms and with just one car parked outside, things looked promising. Only twin beds were available, said the young señorita at the reception desk, and two cots could be supplied for the kids. Well, only twin beds seemed completely ridiculous until I figured out who would actually be frequenting a hotel way down here. Most would be single men, truck drivers and travelling salesmen, and certainly not young couples doing a town with a non-existent tourist industry.

We took a room anyway out of exhaustion. The room had a little black and white TV attached high up on one wall alongside an old faded picture of Bariloche, two of the narrowest and shortest single beds ever made in the entire history of bed makers, and a small table. It had a ceiling fan about the size of an airplane propeller. Its label read The Windmaker by Martin & Martin. I pulled the cord and away it whirled at airplane lift-off speed. Then it started to wobble, and I mean really wobble. I could visualize the headline now. 'Two Canadians lose their heads in Argentina.' I pulled the cord again, and off it reluctantly went. I looked around some more. The only other thing in the entire room was a red and white plastic ashtray. Inscribed on it were the words "Cinzano" and "Raoul's Plumbing." Nice job with the advertising, Raoul.

Then I checked out the bathroom. It had a shower, and a sign on the wall read "hot water." Desperately in need of my first shower in three days, I pulled a plastic curtain in a circle around a porcelain 'tub' slightly larger than a bidet, selected which of three taps to turn, waited about three minutes for the water to get hot, then jumped inside the curtain, which was clearly four sizes too short for the job. In seconds, water covered the bathroom floor and threatened to flood the adjoining bedroom. Fortunately, the owners had planned ahead for bathroom floods and had attached to a wall a well-used squeegee. My job was to push all the floodwater down into the hole in the centre of the tile floor. What a 'shower'! You don't find these babies at home!

And the toilet was a classic. It was flushed by a button high up on the wall. When pushed, there was a roar and a terrific surge of water and in a nanosecond, anything that had accidentally fallen below—your cash, your drugs, your small child if he or she had stayed too long—vanished forever. None of that toilet water flushing counterclockwise action I had read about in the Southern Hemisphere, as opposed to up north. (You've never noticed our clockwise action?) And the toilet, of course, ran all night, so just great for sleeping. The sink was minus a plug, so matched Patagonia's par. The sign outside the hotel said it was a two star. Hard to imagine what a one star offered. Perhaps, I thought, a tent and an outhouse.

After we both had a 'fabulous shower' and the kids a nap, we headed across the road to a small restaurant for an asado [BBQ]. It was about 8:30 p.m. but the sign said "Cerrado por dia." It was strange to find a restaurant closed for the day because it was Saturday, so certainly a good day to be open for business. We were looking forward to a nice dinner of barbequed lamb, but instead settled for odds and ends from the camper. I then sat down with a bottle of Malbec and tackled my new book.

Way back in 1847, I read, a report commissioned in England had concluded that the Welsh were "ignorant, lazy, and immoral," and one of the reasons given was the continuing use of their evil language. Now before writing any further on what followed in that book, I have to comment on that "ignorant, lazy and immoral" suggestion. Having just discovering my Welsh heritage, I'm personally offended by the "ignorant and lazy and immoral" suggestion. I mean, come on now, no one's ever accused me of being lazy and immoral.

And as for the language being evil, well, that's of course

ridiculous, but for sure, it's certainly strange. As an example, what follows is not the work of a four-year-old aimlessly banging on my computer keys. It's the name of a small town in Wales.

'Llanfairpwllgwyngyllgogerychwyrndrobwllllantysiliogogogoch.'

To save you time, that's fifty-eight letters. It's usually shortened to Llanfairpwllgwyngyll. Well, that's certainly a bonus, isn't it!

Anyway, now that's out of the way, back to my reading. In 1861, and understandably tired of persecution, a group of men in north Wales discussed the possibility of founding a new Welsh colony. They wished to protect their Welsh culture and language, which they felt were threatened. They wished to create a little Wales beyond Wales where they would be free to speak their own language and practise their religion. Two options were considered, Vancouver Island in western Canada and Patagonia in southern Argentina. Patagonia won the day.

Now at this very time that the Welsh were seeking a home away from home, the Argentine government was looking for prospective settlers to populate the Patagonia to strengthen its legal claim to the area and over the competing claim of next-door Chile. Argentine authorities described to the visiting Welsh leaders that the area being offered them was like the green and fertile lowlands of Wales. The deal was clean and simple. A free 260-square-kilometre parcel of land given to the Welsh settlers in exchange for their settlement.

So on July 28, 1865, and two months after leaving Liverpool, the first of two ships reached Golfo Nuevo on the Atlantic coast of Argentina. With the arrival shortly thereafter of the second vessel, the total of Welsh immigrants reached 153. The group comprised 101 adults, including tailors, cobblers, carpenters, brick makers, and miners. Sadly, however, there were few farmers, and farmers were what would soon be needed. Then off inland went this little band of dreamers. They went on foot and with only a couple of wheelbarrows to carry their possessions. Three difficult weeks later they reached their promised land.

The parcel of land had been oversold by the Argentines. It was semi-desert, no animals for food and no trees for timber to construct homes. The friendly indigenous Teheulche tried to help them survive, but the going was difficult. Their crops were destroyed by flash floods. Supplies from the homeland had difficulty reaching their little settlement located about sixty kilometres upriver from the nearest ocean port. By 1867, they were ready to admit defeat, and many left to return home. Then, after those two years of struggle, they discovered the land could be irrigated by diverting the nearby River Camwy. Now the area, although not what had been promised, became somewhat suitable and, in 1875, they were granted title to their lands. More and more Welsh continued to come, and by 1885 the Welsh settlements of Rawson, Porto Madryn, Trelew, Dolaron, and Gaiman had been created, and received those annual visits from Butch's old friend from Bariloche, Jarred Jones.

Then in 1888, fifty of these Welsh settlers set out west towards the Andes to found a new settlement. Seventy-one days and 625 kilometres later, they stopped just short of the Cholila Valley. Currant and strawberry bushes were in bloom, forests of birch and pine and ash and cypress were available for building homes and for firewood, and the climate seemed very Mediterranean-like. The countryside had a few wild cattle, deer, nandus [relatives of the ostrich], and guanacos. This was clearly a better place to settle, and this small group immediately set about constructing their homes. The Argentine government marked out the ground for another Welsh colony here on the upper waters of the Chubut River and soon the town of Trevelin and, later, the nearby town of Esquel came into being.

Well, that's your history lesson for today, and quite interesting really if you like history and even more so if you're of Welsh descent. And let's face it, you didn't know until reading this chapter that the Welsh had settled in Argentina. And you certainly weren't aware there are towns today where you can sit with a coffee and spend the morning trying to translate your Saturday Welsh newspaper. (Perhaps the cartoon section is your better bet.)

On the other hand, if you've just read this Argentine-Welsh history and feel that you've completely wasted ten minutes of your life, well, as we Welsh say, "paid a chodi pais wedi pisio," which translates to "don't lift your petticoat after you've peed" and in plain English means "no point in crying over spilt milk."

Fort Worth, Texas (1903): (left, seated) Harry Longabaugh (Sundance Kid); (right, seated) Robert L. Parker (Butch Cassidy)

Photos on pages 246–248 courtesy of Edith Jones (except 1977 photo)

Argentina – Cholila Valley, (1903): Sundance Kid and Etta Place

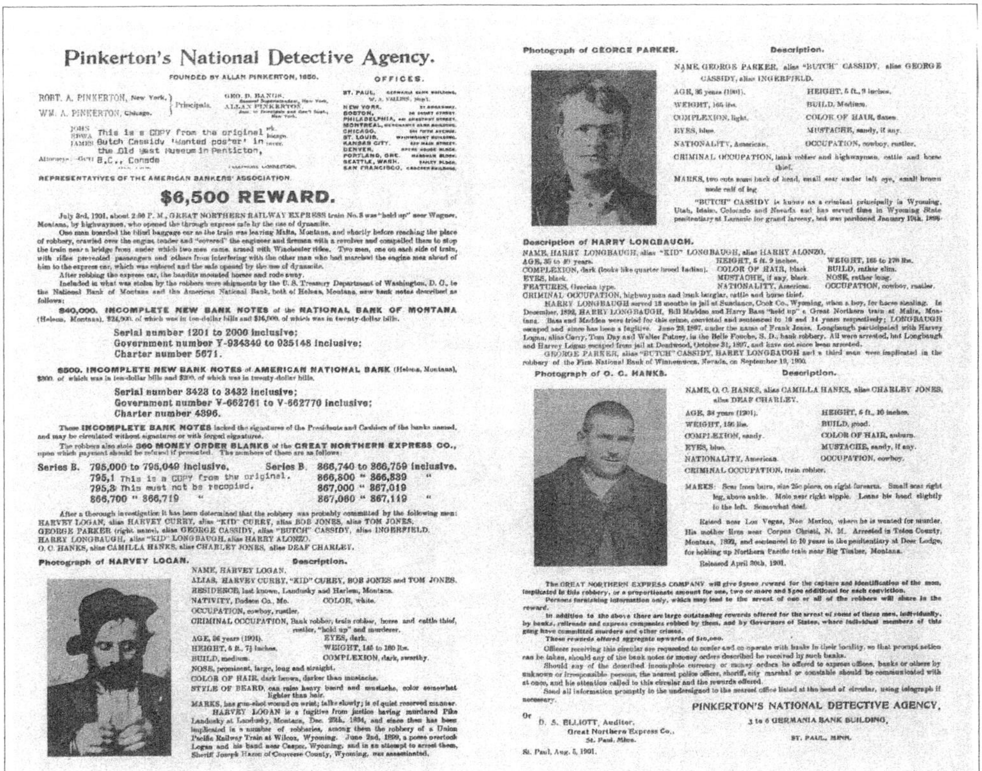

Pinkerton's National Detective Agency.

FOUNDED BY ALLAN PINKERTON, 1850.

ROBT. A. PINKERTON, New York, } Principals.
WM. A. PINKERTON, Chicago.

GEO. D. BANGS, General Superintendent, New York.
ALLAN PINKERTON, Asst. to Principals and Gen'l Supt., New York.

This is a COPY from the original Butch Cassidy 'Wanted poster' in the Old West Museum in Penticton, B.C., Canada

OFFICES.

ST. PAUL, GERMANIA BANK BUILDING. W. A. VALLINS, Supt.
NEW YORK, 57 BROADWAY.
BOSTON, 30 COURT STREET.
PHILADELPHIA, 441 CHESTNUT STREET.
MONTREAL, MERCHANTS BANK BUILDING.
CHICAGO, 201 FIFTH AVENUE.
ST. LOUIS, WAINWRIGHT BUILDING.
KANSAS CITY, 622 MAIN STREET.
DENVER, OPERA HOUSE BLOCK.
PORTLAND, ORE. MARQUAM BLOCK.
SEATTLE, WASH. BAILEY BLOCK.
SAN FRANCISCO, CROCKER BUILDING.

REPRESENTATIVES OF THE AMERICAN BANKERS' ASSOCIATION.

$6,500 REWARD.

July 3rd, 1901, about 2:30 P. M., GREAT NORTHERN RAILWAY EXPRESS train No. 3 was "held up" near Wagner, Montana, by highwaymen, who opened the through express safe by the use of dynamite.

One man boarded the blind baggage car as the train was leaving Malta, Montana, and shortly before reaching the place of robbery, crawled over the engine tender and "covered" the engineer and fireman with a revolver and compelled them to stop the train near a bridge from under which two men came, armed with Winchester rifles. Two men, one on each side of train, with rifles prevented passengers and others from interfering with the other man who had marched the engine men ahead of him to the express car, which was entered and the safe opened by the use of dynamite.

After robbing the express car, the bandits mounted horses and rode away.

Included in what was stolen by the robbers were shipments by the U. S. Treasury Department of Washington, D. C., to the National Bank of Montana and the American National Bank, both of Helena, Montana, new bank notes described as follows:

$40,000. INCOMPLETE NEW BANK NOTES of the **NATIONAL BANK OF MONTANA** (Helena, Montana), $24,000. of which was in ten-dollar bills and $16,000. of which was in twenty-dollar bills.

Serial number 1201 to 2000 inclusive;
Government number Y-934349 to 935148 inclusive;
Charter number 5671.

$500. INCOMPLETE NEW BANK NOTES of **AMERICAN NATIONAL BANK** (Helena, Montana), $300. of which was in ten-dollar bills and $200. of which was in twenty-dollar bills.

Serial number 3423 to 3432 inclusive;
Government number V-662761 to V-662770 inclusive;
Charter number 4396.

These **INCOMPLETE BANK NOTES** lacked the signatures of the Presidents and Cashiers of the banks named, and may be circulated without signatures or with forged signatures.

The robbers also stole **360 MONEY ORDER BLANKS** of the **GREAT NORTHERN EXPRESS CO.,** upon which payment should be refused if presented. The numbers of them are as follows:

Series B.	795,000 to 795,049 inclusive.	Series B.	866,740 to 866,759 inclusive.
	795,1 This is a COPY from the original.		866,800 " 866,839 "
	795,3 This must not be recopied.		867,000 " 867,019
	866,700 " 866,719 "		867,060 " 867,119 "

After a thorough investigation it has been determined that the robbery was probably committed by the following men:
HARVEY LOGAN, alias HARVEY CURRY, alias "KID" CURRY, alias BOB JONES, alias TOM JONES.
GEORGE PARKER (right name), alias GEORGE CASSIDY, alias "BUTCH" CASSIDY, alias INGERFIELD.
HARRY LONGBAUGH, alias "KID" LONGBAUGH, alias HARRY ALONZO.
O. C. HANKS, alias CAMILLA HANKS, alias CHARLEY JONES, alias DEAF CHARLEY.

Photograph of HARVEY LOGAN. **Description.**

NAME, HARVEY LOGAN.
ALIAS, HARVEY CURRY, "KID" CURRY, BOB JONES and TOM JONES.
RESIDENCE, last known, Landusky and Harlem, Montana.
NATIVITY, Dodson Co., Mo. COLOR, white.
OCCUPATION, cowboy, rustler.
CRIMINAL OCCUPATION, Bank robber, train robber, horse and cattle thief, rustler, "hold up" and murderer.
AGE, 36 years (1901). EYES, dark.
HEIGHT, 5 ft., 7½ inches. WEIGHT, 145 to 160 lbs.
BUILD, medium. COMPLEXION, dark, swarthy.
NOSE, prominent, large, long and straight.
COLOR OF HAIR, dark brown, darker than mustache.
STYLE OF BEARD, can raise heavy beard and mustache, color somewhat lighter than hair.
MARKS, has gun-shot wound on wrist; talks slowly; is of quiet reserved manner.

HARVEY LOGAN is a fugitive from justice having murdered Pike Landusky at Landusky, Montana, Dec. 27th, 1894, and since then has been implicated in a number of robberies, among them the robbery of a Union Pacific Railway Train at Wilcox, Wyoming. June 2nd, 1899, a posse overtook Logan and his band near Casper, Wyoming, and in an attempt to arrest them, Sheriff Joseph Hazen of Converse County, Wyoming, was assassinated.

Photograph of GEORGE PARKER. **Description.**

NAME, GEORGE PARKER, alias "BUTCH" CASSIDY, alias GEORGE CASSIDY, alias INGERFIELD.
AGE, 36 years (1901). HEIGHT, 5 ft., 9 inches.
WEIGHT, 165 lbs. BUILD, Medium.
COMPLEXION, light. COLOR OF HAIR, flaxen.
EYES, blue. MUSTACHE, sandy, if any.
NATIONALITY, American. OCCUPATION, cowboy, rustler.
CRIMINAL OCCUPATION, bank robber and highwayman, cattle and horse thief.
MARKS, two cuts scars back of head, small scar under left eye, small brown mole calf of leg.

"BUTCH" CASSIDY is known as a criminal principally in Wyoming, Utah, Idaho, Colorado and Nevada and has served time in Wyoming State penitentiary at Laramie for grand larceny, but was pardoned January 19th, 1896.

Description of HARRY LONGBAUGH.

NAME, HARRY LONGBAUGH, alias "KID" LONGBAUGH, alias HARRY ALONZO.
AGE, 35 to 40 years. HEIGHT, 5 ft. 9 inches. WEIGHT, 165 to 175 lbs.
COMPLEXION, dark (looks like quarter breed Indian). COLOR OF HAIR, black. BUILD, rather slim.
EYES, black. MUSTACHE, if any, black. NOSE, rather long.
FEATURES, Grecian type. NATIONALITY, American. OCCUPATION, cowboy, rustler.
CRIMINAL OCCUPATION, highwayman and bank burglar, cattle and horse thief.

HARRY LONGBAUGH served 18 months in jail at Sundance, Cook Co., Wyoming, when a boy, for horse stealing. In December, 1892, HARRY LONGBAUGH, Bill Madden and Harry Bass "held up" a Great Northern train at Malta, Montana. Bass and Madden were tried for this crime, convicted and sentenced to 10 and 14 years respectively; LONGBAUGH escaped and since has been a fugitive. June 28, 1897, under the name of Frank Jones, Longbaugh participated with Harvey Logan, alias Curry, Tom Day and Walter Putney, in the Belle Fouche, S. D., bank robbery. All were arrested, but Longbaugh and Harvey Logan escaped from jail at Deadwood, October 31, 1897, and have not since been arrested.

GEORGE PARKER, alias "BUTCH" CASSIDY, HARRY LONGBAUGH and a third man were implicated in the robbery of the First National Bank of Winnemucca, Nevada, on September 19, 1900.

Photograph of O. C. HANKS. **Description.**

NAME, O. C. HANKS, alias CAMILLA HANKS, alias CHARLEY JONES, alias DEAF CHARLEY.
AGE, 38 years (1901). HEIGHT, 5 ft., 10 inches.
WEIGHT, 156 lbs. BUILD, good.
COMPLEXION, sandy. COLOR OF HAIR, auburn.
EYES, blue. MUSTACHE, sandy, if any.
NATIONALITY, American. OCCUPATION, cowboy.
CRIMINAL OCCUPATION, train robber.
MARKS: Scar from burn, size 25c piece, on right forearm. Small scar right leg, above ankle. Mole near right nipple. Leans his head slightly to the left. Somewhat deaf.

Raised near Los Vegas, New Mexico, where he is wanted for murder. His mother lives near Corpus Christi, N. M. Arrested in Teton County, Montana, 1892, and sentenced to 10 years in the penitentiary at Deer Lodge, for holding up Northern Pacific train near Big Timber, Montana.

Released April 30th, 1901.

The GREAT NORTHERN EXPRESS COMPANY will give $5000 reward for the capture and identification of the men implicated in this robbery, or a proportionate amount for one, two or more and $500 additional for each conviction.

Persons furnishing information only, which may lead to the arrest of one or all of the robbers will share in the reward.

In addition to the above there are large outstanding rewards offered for the arrest of some of these men, individually, by banks, railroads and express companies robbed by them, and by Governors of States, where individual members of this gang have committed murders and other crimes.

These rewards offered aggregate upwards of $10,000.

Officers receiving this circular are requested to confer and co-operate with banks in their locality, so that prompt action can be taken, should any of the bank notes or money orders described be received by such banks.

Should any of the described incomplete currency or money orders be offered to express offices, banks or others by unknown or irresponsible persons, the nearest police officer, sheriff, city marshal or constable should be communicated with at once, and his attention called to this circular and the rewards offered.

Send all information promptly to the undersigned to the nearest office listed at the head of circular, using telegraph if necessary.

PINKERTON'S NATIONAL DETECTIVE AGENCY,
3 to 6 GERMANIA BANK BUILDING,
ST. PAUL, MINN.

Or
D. S. ELLIOTT, Auditor,
Great Northern Express Co.,
St. Paul, Minn.

St. Paul, Aug. 5, 1901.

Reward Poster (1901): Pinkerton's National Detective Agency, U.S.A.

Argentina – Cholila Valley, (1903): Sundance Kid, Etta, and Butch

Argentina – Cholila Valley, (1903): Bandoleros Americanos: far left, Butch Cassidy; second from right, Sundance Kid; far right, Etta Place

Argentina – Cholila Valley, (1977): Butch, Sundance, Etta – main house

THE KINGDOM OF ARAUCANIA AND PATAGONIA

Patagonia is not a country and it's not an Argentine province and it's certainly not a clothing line. It's a word that describes the southern third of Argentina bounded by the Rio Colorado in the north, about six hundred kilometres north of Bariloche, the Straits of Magellan in the south, the Atlantic Ocean in the east, and the eastern portion of the Andes in the west. Patagonia also refers to the southern part of Chile from the western half of the Andes to the Pacific Ocean, where it consists of glacial fjords and temperate rainforest. Ninety per cent of Patagonia lies in Argentina, ten in Chile.

Looking down from a plane heading south, Argentine Patagonia consists of the craggy mountain peaks of the Andes and gorges choked with glaciers. To the east of this Andean region are found deep blue and ice-cold lakes and wonderful trout-filled rivers and fertile valleys and thousands of square kilometres of deep forests. And to the east of that and comprising the majority of the Patagonia are the treeless Pampas, flat and desert-like, covered mostly with grass tussocks, in places bisected by deep gorges, and containing enormous estancias. And farthest east of all is the treeless and desolate Atlantic coast with colonies of penguins and those little Welsh towns, and little else.

All parts of the Patagonia, however, have one thing in common. Wind! Patagonia, and especially the Pampas, is windy, and I mean really windy. The biting westerlies normally blow fifteen or twenty but can sometimes reach 120 kilometres an hour. The way

I figure it, a store selling contact lenses down here would go bankrupt in about five minutes. There's no truth, however, to the saying that the winds here are sometimes so strong that small planes often fly backwards.

And Patagonia is big. It's a place where you travel with two spares, not one. Like Alaska, it's a place where a driver who sees a stranded vehicle will stop to help instead of driving past, terrified of rape or robbery. Patagonia comprises a third of the country. To fill up its 1,043,076 square kilometres, you would toss in the western states of Washington, Oregon, and California, and then touch that up with Rhode Island, Delaware, Connecticut, New Jersey, New Hampshire, Vermont, Massachusetts, Hawaii, and Maryland. It's that big.[24] In fact, Patagonia does everything big. It has big volcanoes, big lakes, big glaciers, big parks, big mountains, and big estancias. And apparently, and long ago, some big people!

When Ferdinand Magellan and his crew had circled the globe in 1520 and had amazingly arrived safely home, instead of, as most expected would happen, simply sailing off the edge of the Earth, they had sailed through a passageway between mainland South America and a large island now called Tierra del Fuego. Upon making land, they had seen huge footprints in the sand and had encountered members of the indigenous Fuegian tribes. They had been dressed only in a mantle of skins of the guanaco, that llama relative from Peru, and their feet had been covered with boots made from guanaco necks. Some men had exceeded six feet in height, so exceedingly tall to Europeans who averaged around five and a half feet.

Now there are two theories as to the derivation of the name 'Patagonia.' One theory is that those primitive skin-covered people Magellan saw eating raw meat reminded him of Patagón, the dog-headed savage creature in a 1512 Spanish romance novel written

24 Slightly larger than British Columbia's 944,735 square kilometres, if you're from Canada.

by Francisco Vázquez. A second theory is based on the enormous footprints they had seen, and logically quite enormous considering those primitive boots. Whatever the reason, Magellan had thought the land to be inhabited by giants. He had named them patagones, which in Portuguese meant big feet, hence land of the big feet, or Patagonia.

We left behind Trevelin and the Chubut Valley and my long-lost Welsh relatives early the next morning. We had gone maybe one kilometre when we were pulled over by two dark green Ford Falcons, the very ones we had been warned about in Bariloche that were driven by the military.[25] Margaret rolled down her window.

"Buenos dias," she said.

"Señora," said the driver of the first car in broken English which I will now improve, "have you seen an orange Ford Falcon with two men in it? They're accused of stealing sheep."

"No, señor, nada," Margaret replied.

So, I thought, as we drove away, that explained two things. The first was why these were the only cars to not try to pass us in about a week. And secondly, it clarified why that little restaurant in Trevelin was closed last night. Yesterday, those two rustlers were probably so busy escaping the military they hadn't dropped off the lamb they had promised the restaurant for Saturday night's asado [BBQ].

We continued through the towns of Tecka and Gobernador Costa, then a little southwest through the town of Rio Mayo and heading for the town of Perito Moreno. The drive to Perito Moreno was about 560 kilometres, not much of a drive in a car on paved roads, but quite a distance on a gravel road with the camper's cab-over back to bouncing off the truck's cab and with two children. The camper and truck had held up reasonably well since that nightmare climb in Ecuador and with the only

25 Military death squads drove green Falcons during the 1976-1983 military regime picking up people for questioning. Some of them were never seen again.

apparent damage being more loose aluminum siding, which I had again taped up.

Patagonia is definitely vast but it's also quite empty. A saying in Texas is a rancher can't see the smoke of his neighbour's chimney. In Patagonia, you can forget about that smoke analogy. Here, it could be a four days' horse ride just to pay your neighbour a visit. It's a mystery why so few people settled in this area a hundred years ago. Perhaps it was fear of the indigenous Tehuelche and the indigenous Mapuche migrating over the Andes from Chile.

Perhaps the reason even went decades further back when a young 22-year-old named Charles Darwin had stepped ashore for the shortest of visits to Patagonia, later describing it as having a dreary landscape and "the curse of sterility." Darwin had seen the filthy giants on the nearby island of Tierra del Fuego and had understood them all to be cannibals who ate their enemies and their old women. Darwin must have thought he'd seen either the missing link, or at least the closest thing to it. And seeing and hearing that, why would he then have thought that the rest of Patagonia would be any different?

And it's not just human life that's scarce here. Wildlife, other than the thousands of grazing sheep, is not exactly abundant. Once we noticed a herd of twenty to thirty guanacos grazing on a nearby hill, another time a dead armadillo on the road's edge. Lisa spotted a brown Patagonian fox sprinting alongside our camper for a short distance, momentarily trapped between our camper and the adjacent fencing. We saw two herds of nandu [ostrich relative] that, upon seeing our approaching camper, bolted off at their top speed of sixty kilometres an hour. That's about it for our 560-kilometre drive to the town of Perito Moreno. Oh, and there was that Patagonian hare that crossed the road. To Lisa's relief, we just missed it. Yup, missed it by a hair! (Sorry about that.)

Nearing dinner time, we arrived at a sign announcing the town of Perito Moreno. The sign, like that sign announcing the small chacra of Eleanor's back in Bariloche, was riddled with bullet holes. We crossed over the guarda ganado [cattle guard] in place to prevent any escaped cattle from nearby estancias from entering town and pulled up to a military control just short of town.

Now the first military control we'd seen in Argentina was that one entering Bariloche, and we had seen three more since. This one was manned by two fully armed members of the Argentine military. Margaret got out and presented our passports, which were scrutinized by the older one, who presented himself as being in full control of the situation and exactly what the doctor ordered at a military control. Margaret had handled the border crossings since Guatemala and was now also dealing with all the Argentine military controls. The reason for these controls had been made crystal clear to us in Bariloche. The military was looking for subversives or radicals or anyone who remotely looked like, not acted like, not talked like, just looked like a possible threat to the military government headed by Lieutenant General Jorge Videla and, since March of 1976, President Videla. We had so far assumed that because Argentines loved little children we didn't look particularly threatening. I was hoping that assumption remained correct.

The military control went amazingly well, but as we were pulling away, the second guard commented that the left rear tire looked low. I jumped out for a look. Flat as flat can be. Our first flat tire of the entire journey and it had occurred in the town of Perito Moreno, the town named after Margaret's father's uncle, so her grand-uncle, or great-uncle, if you prefer. I mean, what are the odds! I pulled off the road to assess the situation.

"I'm sure we can do it ourselves, dear," said Margaret. "Here in the Patagonia, you must be able to handle things yourself. You just can't call up the Automobile Club. Mum never learned to drive in Scotland so when we lived in Bariloche dad wanted someone else in the family available to drive in an emergency. Before he allowed me to drive, he made sure I could change the spark plugs, check the water and oil levels, check if the carburetor was clean, and change a tire. I was only fourteen so I'm sure we can both do it now."

Now I have to be honest here. I wasn't looking forward to attempting jacking up this giant-on-wheels of ours in front of a military audience. I also wasn't keen on risking humiliation in front of someone who I had just found out that very second was more of a car mechanic at fourteen than I probably would ever be in my lifetime.

"No, dear," I replied, hopefully convincingly, "I don't think that the jack that came with the truck can do the job." I confidentially then uttered a new word I had added to my limited Spanish vocabulary.

"Gomeria, por favor?" I enquired.

"Si, cuatro cuadras," a guard replied, and pointed where we would find the local tire repair shop four blocks down the road. Off the camper limped, trailed by two mongrels dangerously nipping at our rear wheels. I must say that whenever I see stupid dogs chasing cars, it always reminds me of that old golf saying, "What never lasts are dogs chasing cars and pros putting for pars."

By now, it was 6:30 p.m. Everything in Canada and the U.S. would be cerrado, but here, everything was open to 8:00 p.m., or even later. Brilliant! We spotted an old truck tire propped up by boulders and with the word "GOMERIA" painted on it in white, and pulled over. A handful of chickens, another two dogs, and one lonely turkey were wandering around out front. The place seemed abandoned until I spotted two men behind a garage. I walked up to the nearest one, took complete command of the situation from Margaret, and mumbled, "El precio para arreglar el neumático, por favor." (See, you just loosely translated that Spanish all by yourself.) And the price he gave me?

"Cincuenta [fifty] pesos, señor," he said. That worked out in American dolares to be the gigantic sum of thirty cents. Thirty cents! And he said to Margaret they would fix the handbrake for nada, for free! Imposible! Fantastico! Dear reader, add those three words to your growing Spanish vocabulary. Actually, the word 'vocabulary' is, in Spanish, wait for it, 'vocabulary,' so now you just added a fourth word.

We plunked Martin into his stroller and off we headed into town. The first thing we saw on the median entering town was a huge statue of Perito Moreno. This guy Moreno is everywhere, I thought—a statue here, a statue entering Bariloche, streets in every town named Moreno or Perito Moreno, the world-famous Perito Moreno glacier coming up shortly, and even a comic book I had picked up in Bariloche about his life. Margaret went up to the large statue for a photo op.

Then for some reason, a heavily armed member of the military seated nearby, and taking his fifteen-minute yerba mate break from whatever he was not doing, stood up brandishing his rifle and told her to back away from the statue. Seriously? Back away from the statue? Back away from the statue? Was the large statue an Argentine Trojan horse full of vertically challenged military personnel? Was it a nuclear weapon in disguise made by one of those El Bolson jam makers? Was he thinking Margaret might suddenly whip out a mini-can of spray paint from each side of her brassiere? I mean, what sort of IQ are we dealing with here, I pondered. Then, fortunately for me, as I was by now quite fed up with all this military business and could now have said something to perhaps qualify me for a visit to a nearby prison, Margaret spoke up. She told Mr. Military Man she'd just driven all the way from Canada and that her father was a nephew of this legendary man, Perito Moreno, and she just wanted a picture of herself with the statue to give to her father. Well, the flood of apologies that followed from this idiot became almost unbearable.

After the photo, we headed to a little nearby restaurant and had a nice dinner of gnocchis, those Italian dumplings that are extremely popular here, and an ensalada mixto of lettuce, tomato, and half rings of onions, topped with olive oil and vinegar, and finally touched up with a squeeze of lemon and pepper. After dinner and a cold cerveza, we retrieved our camper, paid the cincuenta pesos, and then parked for the evening alongside the gomeria. While Margaret struggled to put the kids to sleep, I sat outside and continued reading that book I'd picked up in Trevelin on the Patagonia.

Argentina had declared independence from Spain in 1816 and Chile the same in 1818. By the mid-nineteenth century, Chile was claiming southern Patagonia as its own on the basis that rights to the area had been granted to it by the Spanish crown. In furtherance of its claim, Chile founded the settlement of Punta Arenas on the Magellan Straits in southern Patagonia. To counter Chile and to strengthen its own claim to Patagonia, Argentina had started settling the Patagonia with those Welsh immigrant relatives of mine.

Meanwhile, the indigenous Mapuche continued migrating over the Andes from Chile, stealing the cattle of the Argentine settlers and then driving them back to Chile through mountain passes to trade for alcohol and other goods. As the years passed by, the Argentine government grew increasingly concerned about the Mapuche pouring into Patagonia and laying their own legal claim to the area.

Then in 1860, matters got even more complicated. Arriving on the scene was a thirty-five-year-old French lawyer and explorer named Orélie-Antoine de Tounens. Antoine arrived in Patagonia, lands that had not been colonized by the Spanish empire, donned a poncho and learned the Mapuche language. Antoine united the indigenous tribes by promising the support of France and the delivery of weapons to assist them in their struggle against Chile and Argentina. Undoubtedly, the Mapuche leaders thought it wise to have a white man as their front man. Then on November 17, 1860, Antoine proclaimed by a decree the founding of the Kingdom of Araucania and Patagonia, with himself as king. Coins were minted, a flag created, and an anthem for 'New France' commissioned.

The legal arguments he presented to Argentina and Chile in support of the Mapuche's legal claim were twofold. Firstly, the original Araucanians, now called the Mapuche, had signed a treaty in 1641 with Spain. Therefore, his argument went, for either Argentina or Chile to annex Patagonia as its own and from the Mapuche, now ruled by a European monarch, the self-proclaimed King Antoine, was an act in violation of international law. That was, of course, an interesting legal argument if young King Antoine was actually recognized by the world as king of something.

His second legal argument was that what Argentina and Chile had 'inherited' from Spain was never meant to include the entire Argentine area south of the Rio Colorado and all of southern Chile, so all of Patagonia comprising 1,043,076 square kilometres. Nor, for that matter, was that 'inheritance' meant to include the northern area of Chile called Araucania, a further 31,842 square kilometres, so a total area in all of 1,074,918 square kilometres. As such, and in the opinion of this young French lawyer, all Patagonia and Araucania was up for grabs, and King Antoine was grabbing it all.

Now, one has to wonder about Antoine's real motives here. Was it purely altruistic and was he just assisting the Mapuche in establishing their ancestral lands? Well, the naive, or a person on something stronger than alcohol, may believe that reason. I see it this way. The three driving forces in life are sex, power, and money. Sex here, and correct me if I'm wrong, is not applicable. Power is a possibility, certainly, but did this thirty-five-year-old man from France actually wish to spend the rest of his life living in a foreign land as ruler of the indigenous Mapuche and a people he had never heard of until recently? I doubt it. That leaves money. The countries of Argentina and Chile were already squabbling over their competing claims to Patagonia and they would, at least in his mind, have just two options to deal with him and the Mapuche. Option one was they both could acquiesce to his demands and leave him as king over what would be, outside of Brazil, the largest area in South America. That would be complete insanity.

That apparently, in the mind of Antoine, just left Argentina and Chile with option number two. The two countries could simply settle the matter like most legal matters are handled. Just pay Antoine off with perhaps legal title to say a paltry four thousand square kilometres. Remember the size of Patagonia, so that's less than one half of one per cent of the entire region. King Antoine could then negotiate a sale of his land title back to the highest bidder between Argentina and Chile. Then he could relinquish his title as king, return to France, the centre of civilization (at least in the minds of the French), and return home an exceedingly wealthy young man. Surely then the pretty jeunes filles of Paris would line up around the block to try and capture him for a husband or, better yet, if Antoine didn't wish to share his wealth, for a lover. (Sorry, guess I was wrong. Maybe sex did sneak into the picture after all.)

Sadly for that inexperienced young lawyer, there existed a third option. Antoine was captured by the Chileans, sent to trial in Santiago, declared insane by the court, and immediately sent off packing back to France. His kingdom had lasted a mere two years.[26]

That solved the King Antoine-Mapuche claim problem for Argentina, but the Mapuche were still crossing the Andes into

26 De Tounens died in 1878, no children, and no will. He did appoint a successor, who appointed another, and so on, and as king of the government-in-exile. The royal house, in exile now for over a century, is currently represented by Prince Philippe of Araucania. The kingdom has a flag, has a preserved manifesto from 1863, a museum of the kings, a royal gallery of all the monarchs of the kingdom, and even a crown for the king. Today, the Mapuche, like other indigenous groups elsewhere, are asserting their ancestral land claim rights. Perhaps young Antoine wasn't so insane after all.

Patagonia, and as they grew in strength, so did Chile's position in the Patagonia. If it came to war over title to Patagonia, and if the Mapuche sided with Chile, then Argentina would be in for a serious battle. The Patagonia could be lost to Chile forever.

The Mapuche clashes with the Argentine settlers in the south grew more and more common and culminated in 1872 when six thousand Mapuche killed hundreds of settlers and stole over two hundred thousand head of cattle. That was the final straw for the Argentine government. Its first attempt at controlling the raiding Mapuche was the construction of a trench three metres wide, two deep, and 372 kilometres long, just south of the Province of Buenos Aires. That, they reasoned, would surely stop most of these cattle drives into Chile by the Mapuche, discourage them completely, and send them off packing back to Chile. All would then be well. This solution was marginally successful, but still the Mapuche came and still the cattle disappeared into Chile.

Then came the final solution, offered by Argentina's Minister of War, General Roca. Roca decided the Mapuche had to be subdued or, more bluntly, exterminated. Thus, in 1876, the Conquest of the Desert began. Thousands of the Mapuche were killed.

By 1880, the claim of King Antoine to Patagonia was gone and the ancestral claim of the Mapuche to Patagonia seemingly finished forever. What remained, however, was Argentina's strongest adversary to its claim to Patagonia, the country next door of Chile.

Then into this long-standing clash of land claims to the Patagonia between Argentina and Chile rode a young Argentine to save the day, Francisco Pascasio Moreno.

THE MOST UNFORGETTABLE MAN I NEVER MET

Have you ever wondered why Chile's so skinny, the pencil-thin country of the world? It has an average width of only 150 kilometres, so just a rather a short drive from side to side. So why is that? Well, I'll give you your answer. In 1874, twenty-two-year-old Francisco Pascasio Moreno set off from Buenos Aires to explore and discover and survey lakes and rivers and mountains in southern Patagonia. It was an area virtually unseen by a white man and populated with the hostile indigenous tribes of Tehuelche and Mapuche. Then in 1880, he embarked south again. By this time, however, Argentina's General Roca had his war against the indigenous tribes in the south well underway, and this time young Moreno's visit wasn't as well accepted. Moreno and his little crew were captured by the Tehuelche and sentenced to death. Fourteen days later and on the very day before execution, they escaped downriver on an improvised small raft and eventually returned to civilization, although just barely alive.

By 1881, Argentina and Chile's boundary discussions had been going on for sixty years. Chile was still fighting The Ten Cent War, or The Saltpeter War, with both Peru and Bolivia and certainly didn't wish to risk another war with Argentina. Accordingly, its authorized envoy in the boundary discussions was advised not to take too strong a stance in claiming the lands in dispute. As such, in 1881, and partly based on the surveying efforts of Moreno, the boundary was defined as a line between the highest Andean peaks that was presumed to delineate the Continental Divide between watersheds draining into the Pacific Ocean (designated Chilean) and those draining into the Atlantic (designated Argentine). The treaty was signed by the presidents of both countries. It is important here to note the wording of Article One of the Treaty:

> The boundary between Chile and the Argentine Republic is from north to south, as far as the 52nd parallel of latitude, the Cordillera de los Andes. The boundary-line shall run in that extent over the highest summits of the said Cordilleras which divide the waters, and shall pass between the sources (streams) flowing down to either side.

By 1883, Chile's wars with Peru and Bolivia were over, and Chile now turned its full attention to the interpretation of Article One. The assumption on which Article One was based was that the line of the mountain peaks and the water flow direction of the rivers would always coincide. This assumption, as applied in the southern steppe region of Patagonia, was flawed.

Here in southern Patagonia, some lakes and rivers arising east of the line of the Andean mountain peaks actually flowed west to the Pacific, rather than east to the Atlantic. To accept Chile's interpretation of Article One that the watershed argument should prevail in southern Patagonia would, from Argentina's perspective, mean that Lago Buenos Aires, Argentina's largest lake, whose outflow was to the Pacific, and all the lands surrounding it, would become part of Chile. So also would all lands surrounding other lakes and rivers on Argentina's side of the Andes that flowed westward to the Pacific, including (from north to south) Lago Lacar north of Bariloche, the Rio Corcovado near Esquel, the Rio Cholila in the Cholila Valley, the Percy River near Trevelin, and the Rio Fénix near the town of Perito Moreno, to name a few. Acceptance of Chile's watershed argument here in southern Patagonia would mean that a strip of land approximately one thousand kilometres long by a width varying from twenty to fifty kilometres would be lost to Chile. Losing this huge area of fertile ground filled with lakes and rivers would be devastating. A calculation of the land loss to Argentina was approximately thirty-two thousand square kilometres.

Argentina's counterargument for location of the Argentina-Chile boundary in southern Patagonia was to simply forget this Continental Divide or watershed business and to establish the boundary using more of a straight-line approach, even if that meant cutting in half numerous rivers and lakes. The dispute over the interpretation of Article One then dragged on for a further twenty years.

Then in the late nineteenth century it all came to a head. Francisco P. Moreno was appointed lead of the Argentine Boundary Commission and to deal with the Chileans. The issue was clear. Either the Continental Divide–watershed interpretation would prevail in southern Patagonia or it would not.

Now during the course of his expeditions, Moreno had noticed numerous crevices or valleys running from the Andes eastward to the Atlantic and clearly created by long-ago-vanished rivers that had once flowed to the Atlantic. Moreno compiled evidence establishing that the easterly direction of these long-ago rivers had been blocked by the accumulation of glacial debris. In other words, events occurring over time could alter the watershed, and, that being the case, the Continental Divide–watershed stance, although appropriate up north, was simply inappropriate here in the steppe region of southern Patagonia.

Moreno then undertook a little experiment. Enlisting the help of some locals, he had a trench dug accessing the Rio Fénix, a river arising east of the Andes but actually draining west into Lago Buenos Aires, and then farther west to the Pacific Ocean. The Rio Fénix was by this temporary trench instantly diverted to the east. His point was clear. If man could divert a river's direction, then so could an earthquake or perhaps ash buildup from a volcanic eruption.

Finally, in 1902, first Argentina and then Chile submitted their cases on this boundary dispute to an arbitration tribunal set up under Britain's King Edward the Seventh. Coming out to Argentina to represent the British crown and the arbitration tribunal itself was a Colonel Sir Thomas Holdich.

The battle was joined. In one corner, representing Chile, was Señor Alejandro Bertrand, a man who had virtually nothing in the way of personal explorations under his belt nor topographical mapping of the area to produce in support of Chile's position. And in the other corner was Dr. Francisco P. Moreno, a scientist, a cultured man speaking three languages, Argentina's greatest explorer, a man awarded a doctorate from the University of Cordoba, and the founder of the La Plata Museum, South America's greatest archeological museum. Moreno knew intimately the western area of Argentina and its people and its geography. He had maps of the area—as it turned out, the only available maps—to show Holdich and to back up his position. And playing host to arbitrator Holdich? Why, none other than Dr. F.P. Moreno himself!

It wasn't a fair fight. It was like a veteran lawyer against a rookie and the veteran golfing with the judge the day before he would be rendering his judgment. On November 20, 1902, the award was made by King Edward the Seventh. The decision as to the interpretation of Article One of the 1881 Treaty was that Chile's Continental Divide–watershed argument in southern Patagonia was inapplicable. The boundary was to be selected on the basis proposed by Moreno. The winner by a knockout was Dr. Francisco Pascasio Moreno.

All the lands and rivers and lakes east of the Andes that would have gone to Chile under that Continental Divide–watershed argument now ended up in the hands of Argentina. Ownership of Lago Buenos Aires itself was split down the middle. The benefit to Argentina was calculated to be eighteen hundred leagues, or around thirty-two thousand square kilometres.

And Chile? No huge chunk of southern Patagonia. No Atlantic ports. None of those beautiful lakes and rivers and fertile areas. Chile had lost a battle that had gone on for eighty years. It would remain forever the long pencil-thin country of South America.

So there's your answer to the question why Chile's so skinny. If there never had been a Francisco Pascasio Moreno, Chile would have won its Continental Divide–watershed argument and might today be at least 25 or more per cent wider. It might even have today its long-desired Atlantic ports.

For his efforts, Moreno was awarded the title 'Perito,' meaning technical specialist or expert. The Perito Moreno glacier, Argentina's major tourist attraction, was named in his honour. In July 1903, the Argentine government presented Moreno with a gift of twenty-five square leagues [772 square kilometres] in the Andean region complete with rivers, lakes, mountains, and old-growth forests. He gifted back to Argentina three square leagues [ninety-two square kilometres], which eventually formed the core of the current eight-thousand-square-kilometre Nahuel Huapi National Park.

In 1913, Moreno escorted former U.S. President Teddy Roosevelt through parts of the Patagonia. Today, Dr. Francisco Pascasio (Perito) Moreno is undoubtedly the most revered private citizen in Argentina's history.

In a drawer found in his desk after his death in 1919 was found a note he had written:

> I am 66 years old and haven't a cent! I have given eighteen hundred leagues to my country and a National Park for the benefit of future citizens, so that they may find solace and renewed strength to serve this country. Yet, I have not so much as a square metre of land to give my children to bury my own ashes! It was I who staked the claim over eighteen hundred leagues of disputed territory for Argentina, when no one else could defend those lands and secure Argentine sovereignty

over them. Still, there is no place for my ashes, not even a 20 by 20 centimetre box.

Now that I have answered your 'skinny Chile' question, I have my own question. What exactly happened to the remaining 680 square kilometres that Moreno had been gifted? How does a brilliant man end up a tad bitter and writing a year before he died that he hasn't "a cent" and hasn't "so much as a square metre of land" to his name? Was all that land sold for a pittance? Or all gifted to friends? Or lost by negligence? Or lost by forgery? Or lost to squatters? I ask that because, again, Dr. Francisco Pascasio (Perito) Moreno was Margaret's great-uncle. Just wondering....

1912: Former U.S. President Theodore Roosevelt guided through Patagonia by Perito Moreno.

Diversion of the Rio Fénix in 1898: Experiment by Dr. Francisco Moreno (Perito Moreno) to show that the use of the Continental Divide-watershed approach in southern Patagonia to determine the boundary between Argentina and Chile was flawed.

The Author: Somewhere in Patagonia lived
a scarecrow with a nice hat

Argentina: Condor –
wingspan three metres

Argentina: Guanacos
in Patagonia

Chile: Market – Lisa, Margaret, Martin

Argentina: Gaucho and a cattle drive

Argentina: An asado for large group – lamb

Argentina: Lago Nahuel Huapi and Lago Moreno

Argentina: Rio Limay north of Bariloche

Argentine Words and Expressions [English translations are quite absurd]

"a las chapas": 'to the metals' – to drive fast

"al pedos": 'to the farts' – to drive fast

"groso": big, large – an important person or outstanding in his field: example "Mick Jagger es un groso."

"bajá un cambio": 'shift down' – calm down

"calienta la pava pero no ceba los mates": 'she heats the kettle but doesn't serve the mates' – she's a prick tease

"corchito": 'a little cork' – a short person

"echar un cloro": 'to throw a chloride' – to take a leak

"meter la mula": 'put in the mule' – trick someone, cheat

"no le llega agua al tanque": 'no water reached the tank' – he's missing something, he's not fully there

"no pesca un futbol": 'doesn't catch a football' – a person who's a bit stupid

"nunca taxi": 'was never a taxi' – a good used car

"ponerse la camiseta": 'to put on a jersey' – he's a team player

"la noche está en pañales": 'the night is in diapers' – the night is young

"tirame las agujas": 'throw me the needles' – what time is it?

"tirar la casa por la ventana": 'to throw the house out the window' – have a wild party

"tomalo con soda": 'drink it with soda' – take it easy

—adapted from Bracken, James, *Che Boludo*

Bariloche: Lago Nahuel Huapi

Ruta Cuarenta: Route 40

A book of Verses underneath the Bough,
A jug of Wine, a Loaf of Bread – and Thou
Beside me singing in the Wilderness –
Oh, Wilderness were Paradise enow!

—The Rubaiyat of Omar Khayyam

(Oh yes, and $240,000 in Ben Franklins! You didn't believe me when I wrote in chapter 25 that land sales in Argentina completed in American dollars?)

THE JOURNEY OF GEORGE MEEGAN

{SOUTH TO NORTH THROUGH THE AMERICAS}

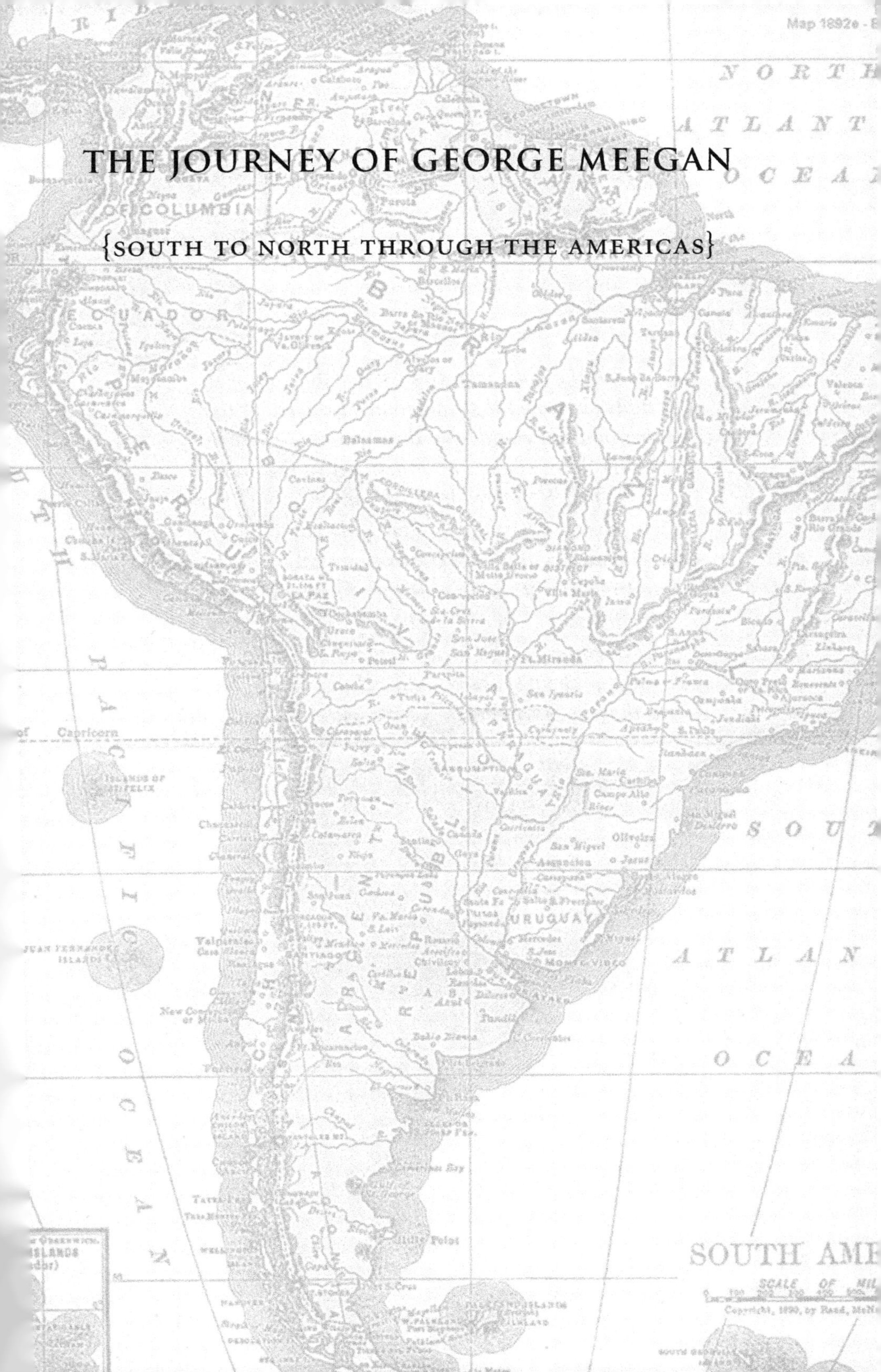

It is not the critic who counts, nor the man who points out how the strong man stumbled, or the doer of deeds could have done better. The credit belongs to the man who is actually in the arena; whose face is marred by dust and sweat and blood; who strives valiantly, who errs and comes up short again and again; who knows the great enthusiasm, the great devotions, and spends himself in a worthy cause, who, at his best, knows in the end the triumph of high achievements; and who, at his worst, if he fails, at least fails while daring greatly, so that his place shall never be with those cold and timid souls who know neither victory nor defeat.

—Theodore Roosevelt, Paris, April 23, 1910
President of the United States, 1901–1909

29

THE WALKERMAN

I wonder where I'm going tomorrow.
Over which hill will I climb and climb
Until I can see...
Until I can see the next hill.
The hills march into infinity,
Preceding the tomorrows and the
Tomorrows precede me.
I guess I'm getting ahead of myself.
—D.A.H.

George Killingbeck was born on December 2, 1952. By age three, his mother had died of cancer, his father had left him, and he'd been adopted by his mother's brother Geoffrey Meegan and wife Frieda. Young George was raised in Rainham, Kent, one and a half kilometres from where Sir Francis Drake grew up and had long ago left to circumnavigate the Earth. George left school at sixteen, like Drake found the oceans, joined the merchant navy, and finished up in 1976 as second mate in navigation. George had saved $11,500 and was now ready to tackle a dream he had harboured for many years, something that would define his entire life.

Encouraged by a meeting with fellow countryman Sebastian Snow, young George decided that he would attempt to walk the entire length of the Americas. It would be, if successful, the longest journey on foot from south to north in recorded history and thus completing what Snow had tried but failed to accomplish when his journey from Ushuaia had ended in Panama.

On January 26, 1977, almost four years to the day since Snow had left Ushuaia on his epic walk north and almost four hundred years to the day since Drake had set off to circumnavigate the globe, twenty-four-year old George Meegan walked out of Ushuaia. George left with $500 in his pocket, about $11,000 in a bank in England, and an English boot sponsor.

PART VI

PERITO MORENO TO USHUAIA TO HOME

Fairbanks
Circle City
Dawson City
Whitehorse
Haines
Dawson Creek
Prince Rupert
Victoria
CANADA
Blackpool, Quebec
New York City
San Francisco
USA
San Diego
Tucson
San Carlos
Mazatlan
MEXICO
Mexico City
San Salvador
EL SALVADOR
PANAMA
Colón
Panama City
Buenaventura
Bogota
COLOMBIA
Cali
ECUADOR
Quito
Tumbes
PERU
Lima
Nazca
Cuzco
La Paz
Arequipa
Tacna
BOLIVIA
Asunción
PARAGUAY
Iguazú Falls
Montevideo
URUGUAY
Santiago
Buenos Aires
ARGENTINA
CHILE
Orsorno
Bariloche
Perito Moreno
Comodoro Rivadavia
El Calafate
Punta Arenas
Punta Delgada
Porvenir Ferry
Ushuaia

30

FIRELAND

We could sense the end now. It was a hard day's drive of 625 kilometres to the town of El Calafate, a good drive at the best of times and made more so by the potholed gravel road. At 7 p.m. we passed through the log archway entrance to El Calafate and parked for the night completely exhausted. The next morning we drove the remaining sixty-five kilometres to the parking lot near the Perito Moreno Glacier. The gravel road was decent and lined with the calafate bushes with their little yellow flowers and dark blue edible berries that gave the town its name. The temperature was about thirteen degrees, so quite pleasant and average for February.

This is not a tourist plug, but it must be said right here and now that this glacier is simply spectacular. It's Argentina's leading tourist attraction and completely dwarfs anything else you care to name. It rises approximately eighty metres above Lago Argentino and drops under the lake another 170 metres. And it's long—thirty kilometres long. Glaciers worldwide are receding. This one recedes in winter but advances more in summer, so is one of the few advancing glaciers in the world. Then every three to five years the glacier dams up one particular arm of the lake. With water coming in and no outlet, this arm's water level rises and rises, sometimes up to thirty metres above the main lake's level. Then, at some point, the water pressure is just too much for the glacier and it collapses. A massive wall of water thunders through the rupture and the flow continues for a couple of days until the water levels of both lake portions are even. A local told us that the

Argentine military had been called in on prior occasions to dynamite the plugged area to prevent all adjacent farmland from being flooded.[27] We returned to the outskirts of Calafate for the night. A nearby sign stated we were now 863 kilometres, so perhaps three days now, from Ushuaia.

We awoke early the next morning and took off at 7 a.m. We drove for two hours before I saw another vehicle, which was coming hard from behind. The driver pulled right up to our rear bumper, just like in those movies when a man sees the bad guy pull up tight to his rear bumper and seconds before he's pushed off a cliff. This was an Argentine's 'polite' way of saying, "I'm passing, so get out of my way." I slowed. He passed. There was no cliff. By afternoon, we reached the small Chilean town of Punta Delgada and the nearby Puerto Espora ferry terminal located at the narrowest part of the Magellan Straits. We parked for the remainder of the day.

The next morning we crossed by ferry in twenty minutes to the Island of Tierra del Fuego. It's a large island, about three times the size of the Big Island of Hawaii, and the largest of the string of islands off the tip of South America. The western 60 per cent of it is Chilean, and the eastern 40 belongs to Argentina. When Ferdinand Magellan, that Portuguese sailor in service to King Carlos V of Spain, passed by in 1520 and saw the fires of the indigenous tribes, he called the island Tierra del Humos. King Carlos, however, liked the name Tierra del Fuego better. Land of Fire (Fireland) had a nicer ring to it than Land of Smoke. I agree with Carlos completely. We drove for a while and finally stopped for the evening in the natural gas production area of Chile, just shy of the border crossing at San Sabastian, and where we would cross back

27 Shortly after our visit, the glacier ruptured. As the years passed by, Argentina grasped the value of the glacier rupture as a tourist attraction. The practice of dynamiting essentially disappeared. Good news for the tourist industry. Bad news for those repeatedly flooded-out adjacent landowners.

into Argentina the next day. Summer here was over and tomorrow would be our last day south.

We arose early the next day for the home stretch. It had rained in the night and a thin layer of ice covered the pools of water that now surrounded our camper. A light snow was falling. In the distance we could see gas fires jetting out of pipes and ridding the Chilean production fields of excess gas. After we finished the last of breakfast, I bundled up and went outside with my morning coffee. Margaret let the kids outside to run around. I checked the tire pressure, checked the oil and water levels and made sure, as I always did, that all locks were in place. Then I warmed up the engine, Margaret hustled the kids into their car seats, and off we went along the gravel road to the finish line.

About five minutes later, walking towards us and bent low into a now cold and biting wind and light snowfall, were two people in dark-hooded rain gear and each pulling what looked like golf carts. I pulled to a stop, lowered my window and found myself staring into the faces of a young Englishman and a Japanese girl. He introduced himself as George Meegan and his girlfriend as Yoshiko. We explained what in about four hours' time we were about to accomplish. He congratulated us and then said they had left Ushuaia twenty-one days earlier on January 26th and were planning to walk to Alaska. Now having seen exactly four trucks and two cars pass us heading north since reaching Tierra del Fuego yesterday, what they were doing seemed completely ridiculous.

"Don't you find it difficult getting rides down here?" I asked. "I mean, with the two of you, and those golf cart things, you'll need a truck to give you rides, and we sure haven't seen many trucks."

"You don't quite understand," said George. "We're planning to walk the entire way."

Are you kidding me? Is this actually happening? Here we'd just driven, except for the Darién Gap, eight and a half straight months from Alaska and this guy is telling me they're planning to walk the same entire route. Now was that not the definition of insanity?

"But that could take years," I said.

"I figure about six," said George, "and that includes some jungle survival training in Colombia before we tackle the 160-kilometre Darién Gap which, as you must have found out, is not passable by vehicles. We should be there by sometime in 1983.

George asked for and we gave him our remaining bread and took a film of them, for some unknown reason. Then off they merrily went, each pulling a two-wheeled cart loaded with their tent, sleeping bags, clothes, food, and plastic collapsible water containers. Each cart also had strapped to it a bright yellow air mattress so they could be spotted by drivers. Well, buena suerte, I thought. Good luck, however, surely wouldn't be enough. At the rate they were going and with snow now starting to fall, they wouldn't even get off Tierra del Fuego. Their fantasy trip would probably end well short of the Straits of Magellan, in the middle of absolutely nowhere, and probably inside of a week.

We continued on to the small village of San Sebastian, where we cleared the aduana and inmigración and crossed back into Argentina. Finally, at 4 p.m. on February 15, 1977, we crested the last remaining hill. Through a mixture of rain and snow that was now pelting our windshield we could see a small town on the shores of the Beagle Channel. And there on the right side of the road was a sign we had dreamed of seeing for a long, long time. "USHUAIA."

As George and Yoshiko continued their seemingly hopeless walk to their unattainable goal, we drove into town. A brochure pegged the current population at five thousand and annual rainfall at 304 centimetres. It stated that Ushuaia had been founded in the mid 1860s by Englishmen Thomas Bridges and Reverend Waite Stirling. In 1884, an Argentine naval base had been established. In 1896, construction of a prison in Ushuaia had been proposed and twenty-three prisoners had been sent by ship from Buenos Aires to build it. It grew to house six hundred convicts until finally closing in 1947.

Today, Ushuaia is supported by its fishing industry and duty-free shops. It has a Chinese restaurant, a just completed modern hotel, a few statues on the waterfront of explorers including Magellan and, strange to me anyway, a Lions Club. That's it for Ushuaia. If you're interested, go have a look, but it's a bit of a drive.

The next morning, we continued south on Ruta 3 through a forest of beech trees, and twenty kilometres south of Ushuaia we reached Lapataia Bay. It was here that the so-called Pan-American Highway came to an abrupt halt. South of here was Navarino Island, then the little Ramírez Islands, and finally Hornos Island with its well-known Cape Horn. Another thousand kilometres farther south lay Antarctica. Trees with their branches deformed by the strong westerly winds lined the forest edges. Locals called them flag trees because that's what they looked like. Waves crashed into the shoreline. It was windy and wet and foggy and bloody well freezing.

We had started from Circle City, Alaska, the farthest north one could drive in North America. We were now the farthest south a person could drive in South America. We had logged over thirty-two thousand kilometres. The only thing of interest at the bottom was the bottom. It was over. (Well, sort of over. There was still the small matter of getting home.)

Postscript

In 1974, the North Slope Haul Road (Dalton Highway) extended the Pan-American Highway system a further 725 kilometres north to Prudhoe Bay. It was only opened to public vehicles in 1994.

Argentina: El Calafate – Perito Moreno Glacier

Argentina: Ushuaia – Southernmost town in the world

A LONG WAY HOME

The following morning we started the long journey north by retracing our path to the Puerto Espora ferry terminal. In mid-morning, and about forty kilometres north of where we had earlier seen George and his girlfriend, we drove past a small orange tent tucked against the fence alongside the gravel road. Two days' walk, forty kilometres covered, and about thirty thousand left to go. I thought of that old Camel cigarette ad, "I'd walk a mile for a camel." I wondered if George smoked.

Then with no warning and within twenty minutes of the ferry, the steering completely went. I had to turn the steering wheel a full 360 degrees before the wheels would turn either right or left. Now, even if we could somehow manage to reach the ferry, we would still be left with a 170-kilometre detour west to the Chilean city of Punta Arenas. I knew it had a Ford agency and our steering issue could hopefully be fixed. The problem was that Punta Arenas had a population of over eighty thousand and the road in would certainly have a flow of traffic we couldn't possibly manage with virtually no steering. This option was out. Reluctantly, we turned back south, and then very, very slowly headed west to Tierra del Fuego's other ferry terminal at Porvenir, Chile, about one hundred kilometres away. This proved manageable as the road was virtually free of vehicles other than the odd truck. We reached Porvenir, took the two-hour ferry across the straits to just outside Punta Arenas, and somehow negotiated the remaining seven kilometres to the local Ford agency without incident.

The foreman appeared with two others and tackled what was,

to me anyway, a strange steering problem. Was it because the load carried by the truck exceeded the recommended weight? Was it a manufacturing defect? Was it a steering fluid leak? This was not just an issue of no power steering. It was no steering, period. I never did find out the reason for the steering problem because no one spoke English, although an explanation in English wouldn't have helped me anyway. Suffice to say, some sort of part was needed and would apparently have to come from Ford in Buenos Aires. Its delivery would take a week. Or, said the foreman, they could fix the steering the very next day but would be left with no power steering. We went for the quick fix option. The next morning we dropped it off for repairs and, as promised, the steering was fixed in short order. Then off we headed towards Argentina's capital city of Buenos Aires, a nice little two thousand eight-hundred kilometre drive north.

Upon entering the Atlantic port town of Comodoro Rivadavia, we made a quick decision to detour northwest back to Bariloche for a final visit. This tacked on another 730 kilometres to reach Buenos Aires, but after what we had driven, that was a non-issue. It was a three-day uneventful drive until what I figured was the final two-hour stretch. Suddenly we heard a grinding noise in the left rear wheel area and I pulled off the road. Now we had seen few vehicles that day so what happened next is almost impossible to believe but is absolutely true. Five minutes after we stopped and now in the middle of nowhere, the very first vehicle to come along was a truck from the Argentine Automobile Club. The driver said he was heading to Bariloche but would return in about six hours to check out our problem. Margaret got out some cold chicken, we had dinner, then we sat and waited and waited. We were feeling like idiots. The chances of him returning today, or ever, were slim and none, and Slim had surely left town.

Then at 9 p.m., and long after we had given up, and just as he said he would, he returned. He removed the wheel, took out all the loose bits and pieces that had been bashing about and laid them on the ground. In Spanish, he then asked Margaret if we had any fourteen-gauge wire. Seriously? He's going to fix things with some wire and expects me to have a wire supply and fourteen-gauge at that. What does he think we've got here, a travelling hardware store? Then I remembered what my father-in-law had suggested taking, and which, as an afterthought, I had tossed into the tool kit. "Si, señor, catorce," I proudly said handing him the exact gauge he had requested. He then proceeded to wire together whatever was needed to be wired together so now we had brakes, but not power brakes. We paid him what was owed and drove the remaining two hours to Bariloche. We visited the Ford agency the next morning, the power brakes were fixed and new shoes put on, and now we were just left with no power steering.

Now as it turned out, the Canadian owners of that recently opened golf course on Lago Gutiérrez needed to promote the selling of the lots surrounding the course. They had convinced the Argentine Golf Association to hold one of its tournaments on the pro circuit at their club. The tournament was the following week. All the pros would be there, including 1967 Open champion Roberto de Vicenzo.

Through a connection of Margaret's, I managed an invite into the pro-am. As it turned out, the field was short one professional, and after a quick nine with the local pro to see if my game would be an embarrassment, I received an invitation into the actual tournament itself. (For my result and prize in the scratch-to-nine handicap section please see footnote.)[28] At the conclusion of the tournament, the awards dinner was held that evening at a nearby hotel. I drove up to the gates and Margaret jumped out to open up.

28 You actually thought I would give you my score and prize? When a golfer wants to tell another his score, he (or she) should always remember the old saying: "Nine out of ten golfers could care less what you shot and the tenth wishes you shot worse." Please remember that. I always forget.

Suddenly, a man appeared out of the darkness and nearby bushes brandishing a sub-machine gun.

"Alto o disparo!" he yelled.

"David, stop the car!" yelled Margaret, "He's going to shoot!"

After a tense conversation, Margaret learned that the governor of the Province of Rio Negro was in attendance for the closing ceremony. The hotel was surrounded by the military and it was apparently taking just 'normal' security measures.

With both children locked in and asleep and now protected by the full force of Argentina's military, we went inside to an evening of food and wine and television cameras and speeches. (Margaret popped outside regularly to make sure the children were safe, in case child neglect is leaping to your mind.) My new best friend (well, in my mind anyway) Roberto and I sat chatting at the bar. I asked about the '68 Masters. He said he was remembered more for that scorecard screw-up than the '67 Open he'd won at Hoylake against Nicklaus and Player and the rest. Only when the crowd was reduced to myself and a waiter who spoke no English, or perhaps more correctly, the crowd was reduced to a waiter and a person who spoke no Spanish, did I return to the camper. The evening was clearly over, and I didn't wish it to ever end.

The next morning, with Margaret off for a stroll with the children, I was approached by a reporter and a photographer from *Gente*, Argentina's equivalent to *Life* magazine in the U.S. at that time and a version of *People* magazine today. They were interested in a photo of the family and camper. The reporter's opening question, and in halting English, was if we'd driven down here with a maid. A maid? Seriously? An actual maid?

"Well, no," I replied, wondering what she would ask next. The interview went downhill from there. Well, that's actually incorrect. After that 'maid' question, there was no further 'downhill' for things to go. Surely, I thought, a dumber question couldn't possibly be asked by a human being on planet Earth. Five minutes later, Margaret returned. By then, the *Gente* staff had left with no family photo, a lousy interview, and us losing our fifteen minutes of fame.

Now it turns out that we had parked that previous night next to two tents occupied by a Brazilian family who had driven down from São Paulo. That's a nice thirty-seven-hundred-kilometre drive. Shortly after Margaret's return the Brazilians popped out of their two tents. The family of four came out of the large tent. And out of the small tent came a young woman in her mid-twenties. It was their maid.

After a final series of goodbyes, we were off across the Pampas to Buenos Aires. Its original name back in 1536 was 'Real de Nuestra Señora Santa Maria' or, in English, 'Our Lady St. Mary of the Good Air.' I guessed that, like Bolívar's full name, that was too long for road signs. The Pampas are referred to as the breadbasket of Argentina. They're flat, have topsoil two metres deep, and are covered by thousands of cattle on huge estancias. The cattle are grass-fed, giving the beef, insist all Argentines, a nicer flavour and less fat than those fed with corn.

On arrival, we headed for the office of Margaret's cousin, Jackie Greene. Margaret explained that Jack had gone to England decades ago as mechanic for legendary racing car driver Juan Fangio. Interesting, I thought, but more interesting to me was that he owned the local Peugeot agency. We dropped the camper off to have the power steering fixed, then jumped into Jack's grey Peugeot sports coupe for a lift downtown to our hotel. On the way, Jack took a long detour to the outskirts to pick up some car parts for a client.

Now long retired from his racing days, he appeared still the dashing, in control aficionado of the motor vehicle. With a forceful yet relaxed style, he deftly snaked through a maze of cars, trucks, and dozens of black and yellow taxis barrelling down the highway towards central Buenos Aires. His right hand smoothly pumped the stick shift. His left rested comfortably on the wheel, forefinger continuously flicking out to press the horn. Nobody here paid much attention to turn signals. What counted was aggression and the horn. Everybody was hurtling to somewhere.

It's a trait of Argentines that if getting from one place to another is to be undertaken at all, it's to be executed quickly and efficiently. The destination doesn't matter. Being on time doesn't matter. And it never does matter. To be an hour late for dinner is quite common and very acceptable. What matters to the Argentine is how he gets there. With speed, with style, and with a stick shift. Traffic got heavier and slower until finally it halted altogether. Huge produce trucks, dozens of them, straddled the highway, blocking traffic in both directions.

"My God," said Jackie, "It's another bloody strike. We've got a banana republic here. Just a bloody banana republic."

His eyes darted left and right searching for an opening. Suddenly we were off, the only moving vehicle of dozens. Off the highway we shot, down an embankment and on to an adjacent dirt track. Two mongrels frantically chased behind as we bounced along past a startled old man on his horse. Glancing back, I saw a string of taxis on our tail. After about three hundred metres we bypassed the blockade, Jackie popped up onto the highway as if he did this sort of thing all the time, and perhaps he did, and we continued towards the heart of Buenos Aires. Jackie dropped us off at the Hotel Carsson on Calle Viamonte, nudged into the one-way traffic, and disappeared from view.

After a short rest and shower, we strolled the fifty metres to traffic-free Calle Florida. Florida was eight solid blocks of haute couture. For men, there was James Smart near Plaza San Martin, and for the elegant women of Buenos Aires there were jewellery stores, clothing stores, endless shoe stores, and boutiques offering all the latest Paris fashions. It was, however, the sale of leather that dominated. You could literally smell it as you walked the street. And here was located Harrod's, the only branch of Harrod's outside

England. No fast-food outlets were in sight except two small kiosks offering choripan, Argentina's answer to the hot dog. It was a chorizo in a bun and topped with some chimichurri.

Night had descended by the time we turned up Calle Lavalle. Hundreds upon hundreds of Porteños, as the eleven million residents of B.A. refer to themselves, were roaming the next four-block stretch and slowly being absorbed by a solid wall of bars, movie theatres, coffee houses, and restaurants. We passed La Casa de la Papa Fritas, the House of the French Fries, and settled on La Estancia, with its restaurant window displaying five whole lambs, jerked and stretched on iron crosses and leaning in a semi-circle over a huge fire pit of coals of quebracho wood.

After dinner, we left Lavalle and in a leisurely manner worked our way back towards Plaza San Martin before turning for our hotel. B.A. was a city of sweeping tree-lined boulevards and narrow cobblestone streets, of bookstores and art galleries and antique shops and melancholy cafes. It was a city for walkers, day or night, and beggar-free. It remained a great city, known like New York and Los Angeles by its initials alone, a city flavoured with Paris and Madrid and built with English capital and Italian muscle. Where else could you find Hermès and Gucci and Louis Vuitton in one block and the smoke of a construction worker's afternoon asado in the next? It had been constructed long before Perón came to power in the forties, yet had aged well. Little seemed needed, perhaps some garbage cans and litter laws, perhaps some dog-waste regulations, maybe a little masonry and roadwork.

Buenos Aires reminded me of an elegant woman in her eighties, a woman possessed of great wealth throughout her life, but now with it all gone. Still proud and defiant, yet a shoe needing repair and some stitching required in the lining of her coat. Still stately and beautiful in a dim light, but now too destitute to pay for repairs.

Five days later, and now with power steering and power brakes and extra pep in our step, we toured Paraguay, Uruguay, and southern Brazil and then returned to B.A. to confront the problem we had avoided for months. Exactly how were we going to get the truck and camper home? Driving back was sheer insanity, so that was out. Option two was to sell the truck and camper in Argentina. A man offered us a good price until I factored in the $15,000 carnet penalty for failure to return with the vehicle and a properly stamped carnet. (The penalty was 150 per cent of the pickup's value when the carnet was purchased.) Option two was out.

Option three was to ship truck and camper home, so off we headed by taxi to the Canadian Embassy for help. Iron bars surrounded the building. A guard with a metal detector was patrolling the entrance. Inside, the receptionist was surrounded by bulletproof glass. They all seemed quite nervous.[29] The visit turned to be a complete waste of time.

Now as it turned out, in three days' time one of Margaret's cousins was getting married and we were invited. After the reception dinner and with whiskey and red wine flowing endlessly, I explained our problem to a man named George Robinson, who was seated on my right.

"No problema," he said. "I own a major shipping line. I'll make all the arrangements to ship it to New York. Here's my card. Come to my office late tomorrow morning and we'll settle the matter." Seriously, I thought? You own a shipping line? Perhaps, señor, have another drink!

The next morning, at Margaret's insistence, I reluctantly worked

29 The extent of what later became known as the Dirty War became clear only years later. By 1976, the military were torturing suspected 'terrorists' to reveal other 'terrorists' and any sympathizers. Then they simply disappeared. Some of the 'disappeared' were executed and buried. Others were taken for a plane ride, hopefully first drugged, and then tossed out alive into the River Plate. Estimates run to thirty thousand people who 'disappeared.' Newborn babies of executed female 'terrorists' often ended up, unknown to the families of these young executed women, as children of either military leaders or wealthy government supporters.

my way to numero 277 on Avenida 25 de Mayo and then up the elevator to the second floor. I mean, what were the odds of me being seated next to a shipping magnate. Apparently the odds were excellent, for right in front of me was a sign "Agencia Maritima Robinson." Problema solved. Señor Robinson completed all the paperwork and off we went to complete packing.

A few days later we drove to the port. Because the truck was being shipped on deck, I had followed Margaret's cousin Jackie's suggestion and purchased a large jar of Vaseline. At the port, I slopped it on all the truck's chrome to protect it from corrosion. I boarded up the camper windows from the inside and chained the camper door to the camper's table post. Truck and camper were then wrapped in heavy plastic by Robinson's port staff. By the time we left the port, the wind had blown the plastic covering half off. That was not encouraging. Two days later on May 24, 1977, we flew to New York to await its arrival.

The camper arrived thirteen days later, and off we went by cab from our hotel to the port. The rain was pounding down as the four of us plus a customs officer approached our camper. Then he announced he would have to bring the dog team out. I had no idea what he meant by the 'dog team' until he uttered the word "drugs." His concern was someone could have hidden drugs somewhere and they could be retrieved sometime later in the States by an associate. I showed him our hidden compartment and the fake wall. No, that's wrong. I remember now. I 'forgot' to show him that specially designed hidden compartment, the one I had long ago claimed could only be discovered by either 'a stroke of luck equal to winning the lottery or by a complete dismantling of the camper.' (And just to clear the air, whatever we had hidden in there wasn't drugs!) In any event, whether it was the pounding rain and our drenched children, or Margaret's charm, or the fact it was 10 a.m. and his coffee break time, our man from the aduana never called in the dog team. In short order we had cleared customs and immigration and started the final push.

We headed 5,140 kilometres across the U.S.A. and Canada and finally reached the Tsawwassen ferry terminal outside of Vancouver, B.C. The ferry ride to Swartz Bay on Vancouver Island was a shade under two hours, and after a final drive south of thirty-five kilometres, we were back in Victoria, B.C. We had left on June 2, 1976. It was now June 12, 1977. We were finally home.

In the end, the truck and camper (and our marriage) had survived a journey of over fifty thousand kilometres, a distance equal to the circumference of the Earth plus a quarter more. The truck and camper were sold. Inside of three months, Lisa had started first grade, I had opened up another one-man law office, and life's normal routines began all over again. The years slowly passed by and the name George Meegan was soon forgotten. After all, how ridiculous had been his fantasy.

32

THE RETURN OF THE WALKERMAN

One day in 1981, so now four years after returning home, I was glancing through a copy of *People* magazine at the YMCA after a workout. And there he was. Bloody hell! There was the Walkerman! We had long forgotten the name George Meegan. If our trip ever came up in a conversation, he was referred to as the Walkerman, the strange guy attempting to walk what we'd done by vehicle.

George and Yoshiko had walked the Island of Tierra del Fuego in three weeks. After crossing the Straits of Magellan, Yoshiko had abandoned the walk. George had then continued to walk the entire length of Argentina. It's a long walk to cross Argentina, comparable to walking from L.A. to New York. He crossed it in a year. Then he had crossed Bolivia, Peru, Ecuador, and Colombia, and finally crossed the Darién Gap, the impassable stretch of jungle between Colombia and Panama. He had then crossed Central America, Texas, and then up to Plains, Georgia. And here was George in *People* magazine in a photo alongside President Jimmy Carter at Jimmy's peanut farm. Yoshiko had abandoned the walk but hadn't abandoned George. They'd been married in Mendoza, Argentina and now had two children. George was still on the move north. Unbelievable!

And Again

Another year went by. It was now November 2, 1982. I was having my morning coffee and reading the local newspaper when I saw a headline: 'Marching Dream Ends in Alaska.' And there he

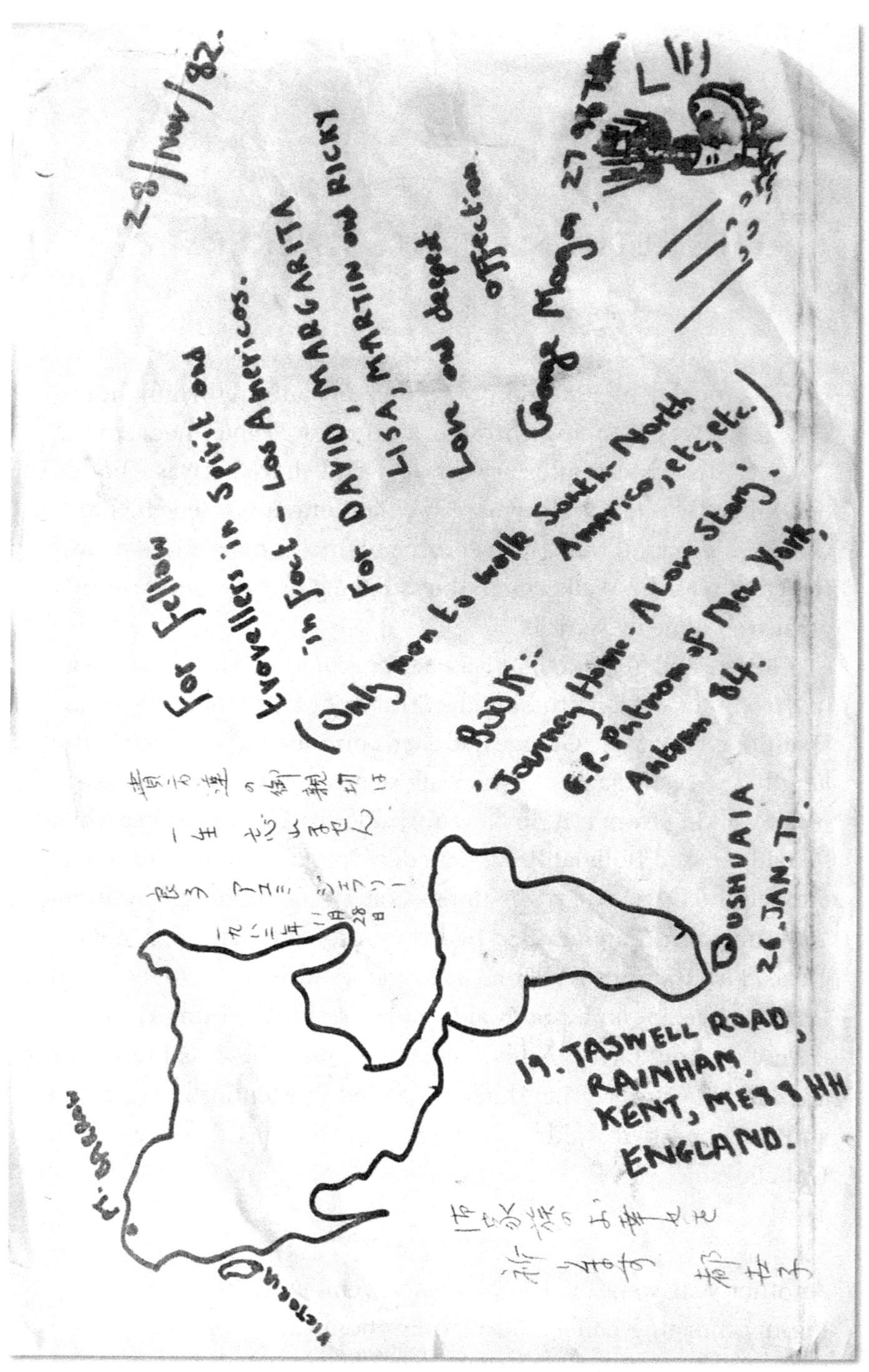

Presented by George Meegan to the author and family during his November 28th, 1982 overnight stay at their home in Victoria, B.C. and prior to his final push to Point Barrow, Alaska.

was again! Now twenty-nine, George was wintering in Vancouver and in the spring was heading up to Fort Nelson to start up once again going north. Now his original destination of Prudhoe Bay, Alaska, was no longer his goal. His goal was now Point Barrow, 414 kilometres farther north and the northernmost point of the U.S.A.

With the assistance of local newspaper staff, I tracked George down in Vancouver and invited him to come over for the night. George arrived with Yoshiko, their two children, and his mother-in-law.

"George," I asked, "I gather this hasn't really been a continuous walk because you're wintering in Vancouver. So is this really going to be the longest walk in recorded history? I mean you tell me you've stopped many times, and for months at a time, during your trek."

"Well, David," he replied, "there really are no rules to this journey. I guess I set the rules."

The next morning I gave George a copy of the movie footage I had taken of them just outside of Ushuaia. They left that morning and returned to Vancouver. We never saw him again.

On September 18, 1983, George reached the unincorporated community of Deadhorse at Prudhoe Bay, Alaska. He'd walked 30,608 kilometres in 2,425 days, and had worn out twelve pairs of shoes. He'd also perhaps worn out his welcome in various places throughout his journey, for in his book, *The Longest Walk,* he seems to pride himself on not paying a nickel of his own money for years on end. Just like young Ernesto Guevara had prided himself in his diary on surviving on the backs of others. Punch in "George Meegan, Guinness World Records." George is everywhere. He apparently holds eight Guinness World Records, the most official world records for any European. (I guess you could say he also holds the record for the most official world records, so George, there's your ninth!)

George never reached his newly revised goal of Point Barrow, Alaska. There was no road.

. . . .

Excuse me, and I really do apologize, but I simply am forced to digress here. This *Guinness World Records* book makes for some strange reading. How about Bob Hanley of Australia? He pushed a wheelbarrow 14,500 kilometres from April 1975 to May 1978. Then there's Burnaby Q. Orbax of Canada, who holds the record for the most nails inserted into a nose in thirty seconds. (Warning: kids, don't try that at home.) And Arvind Pandya, who ran backward from L.A. to New York City in 107 days, covering 3,100 miles. And let's not forget retired headmaster Anthony Victor. He holds the record for the longest ear hair at 7.12 inches. And finally we come to Bernard Clemmens of London, who holds a record that will surely never be broken because no one will ever be interested in giving it a go. Bernard holds the record for the longest official fart, at two minutes forty-two seconds. I mean, you really have to worry about some people. I, however, do have a question. Just who was the idiot that agreed to time that beauty?

. . . .

And Yet Again

Seventeen more years passed by. Little Lisa was now twenty-seven and baby Martin twenty-four. George had planned to reach Point Barrow back in 1983 but only been able to reach Prudhoe Bay. He was now getting concerned that some of his records could someday be broken by a walker covering that extra 414 kilometres from Prudhoe Bay to Point Barrow he hadn't been able to walk.

Then in April of 1999, and with no communication whatsoever since he had stayed with us that one night back in 1982, I received a letter from Japan from the Walkerman. George had kept my address all those years and was inviting me to meet him in Barrow, Alaska. George wrote he planned to first walk the four hundred kilometres from Prudhoe Bay, Alaska, to Barrow.

The plan was for me to join him, a few local Eskimos and a couple of others in Barrow. George wrote, and I quote his letter exactly, "the very last community in the world to be lit by the sun in the new millennium will be on January 23, 2000 at 1:04 P.M. in Barrow. Walk with George on the last 14km of The Longest Walk in all of mankind's history." (I don't understand it either.) This small group would then walk the remaining fourteen kilometres from Barrow to Point Barrow, the northernmost point in the U.S.A. I wrote George back. I explained I wouldn't be able to meet him in Barrow but stated that I "will certainly be with him in spirit." Writing back on June 21st, George thanked me for my wishes. That was the last I heard of him. (Then again, that's what I thought back in 1982.)

On January 23, 2000, George reached Point Barrow alongside a few villagers from Barrow. The walk of George Meegan was finally over, more than twenty-three years after he had left Ushuaia. The temperature with wind chill figured in during that fourteen-kilometre final push reached, according to George on Wikipedia, was minus sixty-three degrees Celsius. Gosh, George, I'm just so upset I missed the finish.

Now just why would he return seventeen years later to tackle this final stretch? Well, the reason was clearly to make sure his various walking records remained his forever. Today, however, on Wikipedia and decades after he started his walk, he gives another reason. It was, and I quote him here, "to bring hope to the indigenous world by developing an alternative educational route whereby they could maintain their endangered culture, and yet be a part of the 21st century, and to appeal to Uncle Sam not to block the option." Say what?

How this second grandiose reason has anything to do with him returning seventeen years later to walk to Point Barrow is beyond me. I can't find the words "indigenous people" and "alternative education" anywhere in his book. George, if you ever read this, the meaning of your journey is simple, really. Veni, vidi, vici: I came, I saw, I conquered. Challenge met, job done. Very English. That's it, George, and good on you. Let me put it this way. I doubt Sir Edmund Hillary ever claimed his ascent of Mt. Everest in 1953 had any particular value to mankind.

. . . .

NOTE: To all travellers: First of all, George mentions in his book he started from Ushuaia. The road, however, ended twenty kilometres farther south at Lapataia Bay, where we had driven, so George never actually started from the most southerly point of the Americas. And secondly, the Murchison Promontory in Canada is sixty-four kilometres north of Point Barrow, so he never actually reached the most northerly point of the Americas. As such, George's record for the Longest Walk in the Western Hemisphere is still seemingly up for grabs at either end.

As I write this, George is fast approaching seventy. But would I ever count him out nipping down south to knock off those twenty klicks and then heading north to walk that other sixty-four to preserve his records for all time, even if he was reduced to using a walker? What do you think?

Victoria, B.C., 1977 – back home

So there you have it. It was quite a journey! And not a journey away from anywhere or away from any thing. Nor a journey to somewhere or to some thing. Just a journey by a man and his family who for a brief moment stepped off the well-trodden path of life.

Just a brief step off the curb. Quite easy to do, really. And once you take that first step, then away you go. At first you may stumble a bit, but you will survive to see the sunrise of another day, and who knows, perhaps a more beautiful sunrise than you have ever seen before.

My past is secure,
My future, unsure.
Behind me are memories.
Before me are dreams.
—D.A.H., AGE 17

WE DREAMED IT. WE PLANNED IT. WE DID IT.
WHAT'S YOUR DREAM?

The Dalton to Deadhorse: The loneliest road on the planet

PART VII

EPILOGUE: DEADHORSE

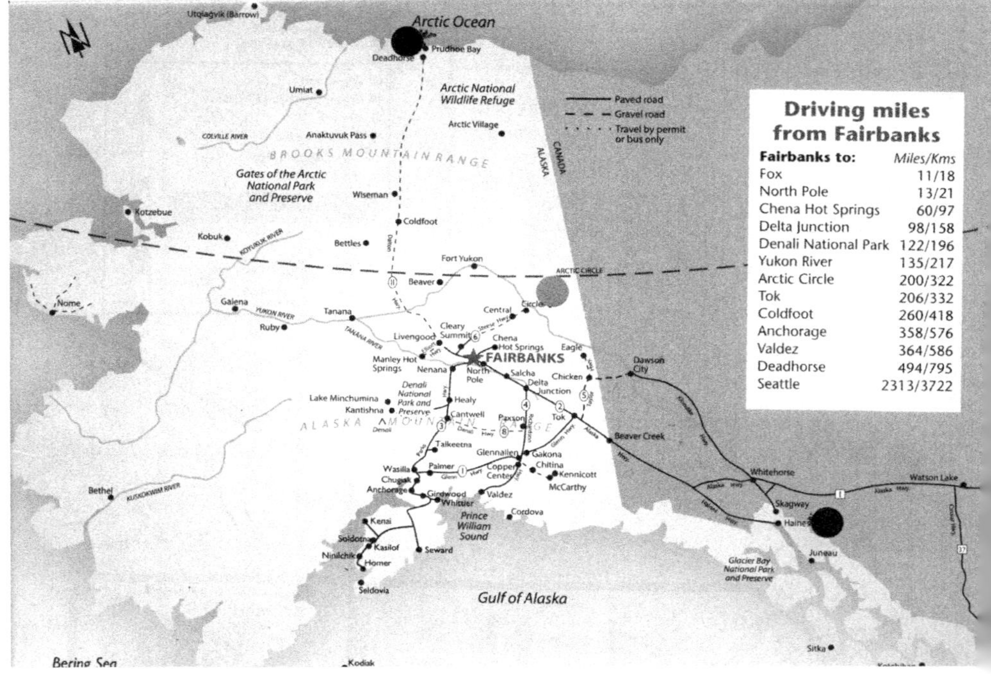

Haines, AK, to Beaver Creek, YT, to Fairbanks, to Livengood, to Deadhorse/Prudhoe Bay: 1,135 miles/1,826 kms

How far will mankind go:
To satisfy a hunger, or a desire?
To achieve a goal, or a dream?
To conquer a doubt, or a fear?
Oftentimes, a person will go
to the 'ends of the Earth.'

—The Author

Do not go gentle into that good night,
Old age should burn and rave at close of day;
Rage, rage against the dying of the light.[30]

—Dylan Thomas

In 1976, we had driven from Circle, Alaska, to Ushuaia, Argentina, at that time the longest north-to-south drive through the Americas by a family in recorded history. Then things changed in 1994. I will explain.

In 1968, the largest oil strike in U.S. history was made under the Arctic Ocean at Prudhoe Bay. To harvest that find, a pipeline was needed to carry the crude oil to the ice-free port of Valdez in southern Alaska, and pipeline construction required a nearby road to deliver all the necessary pipeline components. A road would also be needed for the eventual delivery to Prudhoe Bay of all drilling equipment and the modular housing and supplies required for the oil workers. Unfortunately, back in 1968, the only existing road heading from Fairbanks in the general direction of Prudhoe Bay ended after just eighty miles and at a cluster of buildings named Livengood, 414 miles short of that oil strike.

The necessary 414-mile road extension to Prudhoe Bay, originally called the North Slope Haul Road, and today the Dalton Highway, was completed in 1974. However, it only opened to the public in 1994, so was unavailable to us back in 1976. As Prudhoe Bay is located considerably farther north than Circle, Circle's claim as the northernmost point on America's highway system was, effective 1994, lost forever. The northernmost point on America's highway system was now an oil workers' camp at Prudhoe Bay called Deadhorse.

30 A promising young American singer-songwriter named Robert Zimmerman wanted a change of surname. Some suggest that Welsh poet Dylan Thomas provided him with that surname.

Life slowly unfolded as it should and soon it was 2021. Now, since long ago learning the Dalton Highway was accessible to the public, the thought of tackling this final leg to what had now become the northernmost point on America's highway system kept creeping into our thoughts. Somehow, we felt a sense of incompleteness to our journey back in the seventies. So what to do? Well, to do nothing was certainly the logical option. After all, a person can only achieve what's achievable at any moment in time and with those two young children, what we had long ago achieved, we had achieved in spades. And besides, I was now eighty and Margaret had just turned seventy-three. Yet we did have a new 2021 Bronco Sport with 4-wheel drive.... And we did have the time.... And it would be nice to tackle something challenging at our age.... And we did wish to complete—even if completed in two stages and over a span of forty-six years—what had, since 1994, become the longest north-to-south drive possible through the Americas....

So in early 2022, plans began to drive the Dalton. I obtained a copy of *The Milepost*, the bible for anyone heading to Alaska, and flipped to page 469. I read the Dalton had steep hills and dangerous curves and soft shoulders and embankments five to fifteen feet above ground level and tire-puncturing rocks and teeth-rattling washboard and enormous potholes, and, at spring thaw, portions of the road sagged and collapsed. And driving conditions would generally be cold, windy, and foggy, and the road itself slick and muddy. And snow could occur at any time of the year, especially from the Brooks Range north. And if you were tackling it in dry weather, monstrous tractor-trailer rigs would often send up huge clouds of dust, reducing visibility to zero.

There were warnings to watch for flash floods washing out culverts and bridges, for out-of-control wildfires leaving drivers trapped, and for those tractor-trailers barrelling along flinging rocks and gravel at tourists who hadn't grasped that the Dalton was just a rough industrial supply road servicing an oil camp.

There was a final warning to watch for wandering animals foraging at roadside including wolves, moose, muskox, caribou, Dall sheep, and grizzlies. It's a thousand-mile round trip from Fairbanks to Deadhorse. If an accident happened and a call was made to Fairbanks for a tow truck or ambulance, help would be a long time arriving and at quite a cost. Let me summarize the Dalton Highway this way. If your plans include tackling this supply road, all major car rental companies in Fairbanks will absolutely refuse to rent you a vehicle.

We loaded some camping gear on the off chance we became stranded by an accident or trapped by a snowstorm, forest fire, or landslide. We packed away sundry spare car parts along with the recommended two full-sized mounted spares. Not forgotten were head nets and bug spray to ward off the hordes of mosquitoes and gnats and biting flies that emerge from mid-June into August. Finally, I grabbed a can of bear spray with a spray range of thirty feet. To use it, you're to 'simply' stand your ground until a charging bear has reached those thirty feet, then to immediately hit the spray button. (Note to user: If it's windy, that can is now completely useless.)

In my research, I came across three tips to deal with a bear attack and written by an experienced Alaskan. If it's a black bear that's charging, you're to fight back. And if a grizzly (and hopefully you can recognize the difference), he wrote to play dead. And his final 'tip'? If Mr. Grizzly starts eating you, he suggested you fight back. Seriously? That's a 'tip'? On the other hand, maybe there actually are a few tourists out there who, without the benefit of reading his 'tip', might incredibly choose option number two. That would of course be to simply let Mr. Grizzly happily munch away until full, then trust he'll just stagger off for a snooze.

We left Victoria on July 27th, 2022. Three nights on a ferry from Bellingham, Washington, brought us to Haines, Alaska, and two days of easy driving later we reached Fairbanks. With cell phone service virtually nonexistent on the Dalton, we rented a satellite phone for emergencies plus a CB radio to communicate with truckers and with the flaggers and pilot cars of the maintenance crews servicing the Dalton. We stocked up on food and potable water because, other than Coldfoot, population thirty-eight, and located 240 miles south of Deadhorse, there's nothing on that 414-mile stretch between Livengood and Deadhorse. That's no grocery stores, no State Troopers, no medical facilities, no motels, no ATMs, no tow trucks, and no service stations. Absolutely nothing.

Early on August 2nd, we pulled out of Fairbanks and an hour later reached the Dalton. I reread the rules of the road in *The Milepost*. It stated that big trucks have the right of way, to keep your CB radio tuned to Channel 19 to monitor road conditions and oncoming traffic, to never stop on bridges, curves, or hills, to flash lights if passing, to keep lights on at all times, to lift hood and use flares if a vehicle breakdown, to keep headlights and tail lights clean, and to slow down and pull over if oncoming trucks. I read to watch for those road crews, wandering animals, falling rocks, slick metal bridge decking, handy turnout areas, and for any stretches with no shoulders and those five-to-fifteen-foot drop-offs to the tundra. I read to use the rear-view mirror continuously, shift to low on descents, not to block access roads for crews servicing the pipeline, and to monitor *The Milepost* for approaching dangerous road sections. Quite clearly, the driver had it far easier than the person riding shotgun.

At Mile 56, we crossed the half-mile-wide Yukon River, then continued north through the taiga, the name given to the strip of land just below the Arctic Circle. The stubby little evergreen trees of the taiga soon vanished and were replaced by large swaths of charred trees and fireweed, the remnants of the wildfires that had ravaged the area back in 2004 and 2005.

At Mile 115, we crossed the Arctic Circle and fifty-nine miles later reached Coldfoot, which consisted of The Truckers Cafe,

The beginning of the end

414–115 = 299 miles (481 km) to Deadhorse

Coldfoot: The point of no return
254 miles (409 km) to Fairbanks; 240 miles (386 km) to Deadhorse

Wiseman: Trading post, early 20th-century mining camp

Wiseman: U.S. Post Office, opened 1909; closed 1956

Leaving Wiseman: Pipeline snaking north

Your '5-Star' hotel in Deadhorse

two gas pumps, and a couple of dilapidated buildings. Coldfoot was the only place on the Dalton with cell phone service, the only place for a bite to eat, the only gas pumps, and, other than a couple of cabins fourteen miles further north in Wiseman, the only place to sleep, assuming, of course, you don't mind sleeping in a leftover road construction camp module. Coldfoot was a mining camp at the beginning of the twentieth century and apparently given that name because when prospectors reached this far north they would get "cold feet" and head back. We filled up, drove the fourteen miles north to our rented cabin for the night in the gold rush boom town of Wiseman, founded in 1908 and with a current population of twelve, then early the next morning headed out for Deadhorse.

An hour later, the Brooks Range appeared in view and shortly thereafter, we entered the Atigun Pass. At 4,739 feet, it's the highest pass in Alaska, but far less impressive than the pass we'd tackled when exiting Bolivia for Chile that had topped out at 15,000 feet, about half the height of Mt. Everest. Here was the Continental Divide, where rivers to the south flowed to the Pacific or Bering Sea and where rivers to the north flowed into the Arctic Ocean. Here was also the most dangerous stretch on the Dalton, so not a place to meet one of those gigantic trucks hurtling south with its brakes firing off streams of sparks and its driver attempting to reach the runaway truck ramp looming up ahead on our left before we either received our free ticket to heaven or that truck shot off into space. I figured that this was a good time to try out our rented CB radio. I gave it a go.

"Four-wheeler heading north and approaching the top of Atigun Pass," I announced in a commanding voice. "Any traffic coming south? Over."

Dead silence! Nothing! Not even static. God, I thought. Hope I'm working this CB gadget correctly. Anyway, as luck would have it, no hurtling truck appeared. (I must admit that, to this very day, I still wonder if I had even properly turned it on!)

Trees were gone now. We had left the taiga and were now well into the treeless landscape of the North Slope known as the tundra. (That's the other word along with 'taiga' you vaguely recall from grade school and the meaning of which has also long ago faded from your memory.)

In our 240-mile journey from Coldfoot, no vehicle ever appeared in our rear-view mirror, clear evidence supporting the Dalton's reputation as the loneliest road on Earth. We did, however, have one constant companion, the Trans-Alaska Pipeline. It took eight billion dollars, just over three years, and 20,000 workers working twelve-hour days to build this four-foot-in-diameter silver pipeline. It consists of 70,000 pipe sections coupled together, crosses three mountain ranges, and traverses 800 rivers and streams. If permafrost exists, and it exists north of the Brooks Range where it's up to 2,000 feet thick, the pipeline rests on 78,000 pipeline supports so animals can pass underneath. And if farther south and no permafrost, it disappears underground. It crosses the breadth of Alaska, so a total of 789 miles, before reaching the port of Valdez and was completed in June 1977.

In the end, the road was good, the Bronco well behaved, the planning flawless, the weather terrific, and the scenery spectacular, and on August 3rd, so on day two out of Fairbanks, we pulled into the parking lot of the Aurora 'Hotel' in Deadhorse. Sorry about that. No collision with a wandering grizzly or muskox, perhaps the hairiest four-legged creature on Planet Earth. And no empty gas tank, no forest fire, no sudden snowstorm, no use of bear spray, and no flat tire and need to install a spare while trucks came barrelling past spewing a shower of gravel at our new Bronco Sport. It was just a long, lonely, and very lovely drive to our final goal of Deadhorse.

In the 1970 Alaska Census and referred to as an unincorporated village, the name 'Deadhorse' made its first appearance. No one really knows why it's called Deadhorse. The unofficial explanation is that the area got its name from a company called 'Deadhorse Haulers' which was hired on a seasonal contract to haul away all the dead feral horses in the Fairbanks/North Slope area. Today, Deadhorse doesn't have any horses, feral or domesticated.

What it does have, however, are caribou. They roam the streets during the day and huddle at night underneath the raised equipment sheds. It's a godforsaken 'community' with a permanent population of about twenty-five and a non-permanent population of 2,000 to 3,000 oil workers employed by the various oil companies operating what has become North America's largest oil field. There's no bank, no restaurant, no pub, no police, no hospital, no movie theatre, no coffee shop, no bowling alley, no golf course (That's a joke!), and other than maybe a dozen women working as cleaners or cooks, no women. This is a dry 'town.' If caught with booze, you're fired and kicked out.

Our three choices for accommodation were Deadhorse Camp, Brooks Camp, both constructed on pilings embedded in the 2,000-foot-thick permafrost and with shared bathrooms down the hall, and the Aurora 'Hotel.' All three were essentially modular prefab sections attached and stacked to form a 'camp' or 'hotel' and brought to Deadhorse on either the Dalton or by barge. We had reserved at the Aurora with its price including three buffet style meals a day and a private bathroom. When entering, it was mandatory to slip on plastic blue throwaway booties to keep mud out of the building. When exiting, we were warned to watch for the odd wandering polar bear or grizzly.

Now, if working in Deadhorse, you're left with life's big three: eating, working, and sleeping. Working means twelve-hour shifts a day for two or three weeks and then hopefully a quick escape

The only 'Deadhorse' sign in 'town'

The end of the end

Deadhorse: Oil drilling rig

The oil industry v. the environment

on Alaska Airlines on your two or three weeks off to Fairbanks or wherever else you care to visit to regain your sanity. And if you're a tourist, there're only three possible places to visit. First, if you drove here, would be the Colville Retail Fuel Station. Second would be to the Prudhoe Bay General Store, found upstairs in the Brooks Range Supply Facility and offering a selection of vehicle parts, basic worker's clothing, first aid items, a few snack items, stickers to attach to your vehicle as evidence you actually were here, and little else.

Now visit number three for the handful of tourists that make it here. When a person punches the name of a town into a computer, a list often pops up of perhaps the top ten or so things to do. Punch in 'Deadhorse.' There's one entry. (The visit to the gas pump and that store never made the cut.) It's the 'Arctic Ocean Shuttle.' Now to reach the Arctic Ocean from Deadhorse, it's a further seven miles north through the oil company facilities and where wandering tourists are barred from entering. What aren't barred, however, to pass through the security gates and drive those remaining seven miles are two eight-person shuttle vans per day. Here's a tourist's big chance to go for a dip in the frigid Arctic Ocean. Arrive between July and October when the ocean is ice free. Bring $69.00 U.S., your passport, and a bathing suit. Have a wee dip. Your van's driver will then present you with a certificate stating you're now an official member of the Arctic Ocean Polar Bear Club. So that's the biggest thrill in Deadhorse. (Well, the only 'thrill,' actually.)

We bought our souvenir stickers, filled the gas tank, and then went for the obligatory dip in the frigid Arctic Ocean. While drying off, I watched a man about age seventy-five take off his shoes and socks and then bravely stick his toes in the water. All that way from his hometown in California to the Arctic Ocean and all he was able to manage was the smallest of nibbles out of the apple. His wife swam out fifty or so yards, treaded water for a spell, and then thrust up her right arm. Clutched in her fist was her bathing suit! A naked swim in the Arctic Ocean! Now that's taking a real bite out of the apple! In fact, it's eating the entire apple, core and all. It's an easy guess who returned home with the biggest smile, the best story, and the best memory.

Well, that's the Epilogue! For what it's worth (and in the grand scheme of things it's worth nothing, really), unless a road is ever punched through from Deadhorse to Barrow, Alaska, our two-part journey will stand forever, alongside countless others, as the longest north-to-south drive through the Americas in recorded history.

I started this book with a quote from Tennyson's "Ulysses" which posed a challenge to the reader. I have ended it by quoting the first stanza from Dylan Thomas' best-known poem which poses that challenge once again. So which will it be? When you enter the 'winter' of your life, will you 'go gentle into that good night,' muttering "I could have, but…," "I would have, but…," "I should have, but…," or will you 'Rage, rage, against the dying of the light?' Over to you, and out.

In the Arctic Ocean: The big chill for the 'biggest thrill'

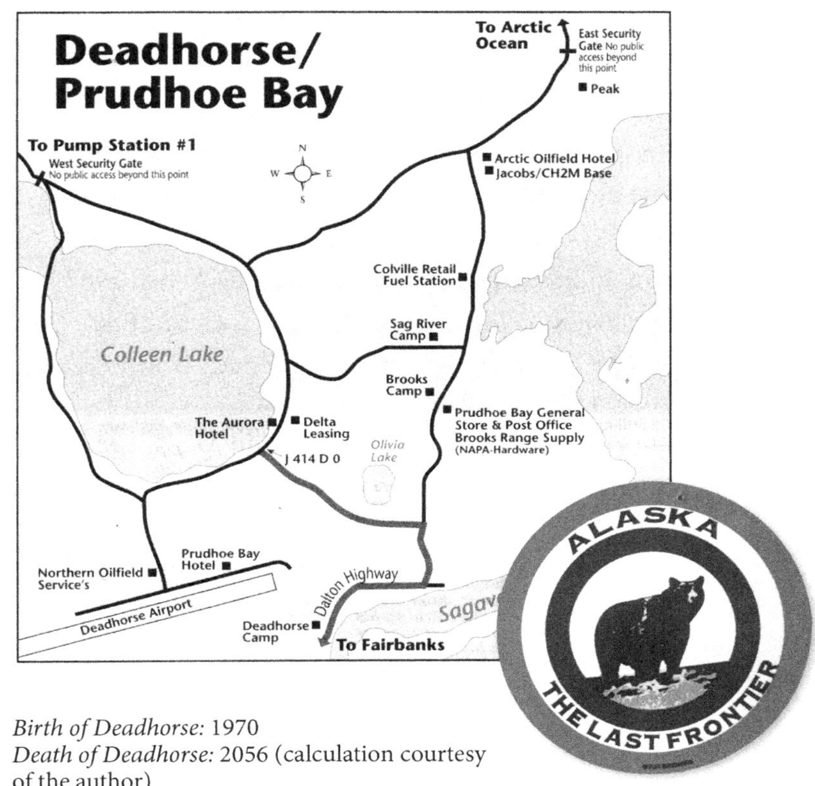

Birth of Deadhorse: 1970
Death of Deadhorse: 2056 (calculation courtesy of the author)

Prudhoe Bay Oil Field:
4 billion remaining recoverable barrels of oil estimated as of 2022, divided by 320,000 barrels recovered per day (in 2022)=12,500 days=34 years. (2022+34=2056)

Author's prediction:
As the year 2056 approaches, a businessman in Fairbanks will start cranking out a batch of stickers reading: "You can't flog a Deadhorse!"

Author's free financial advice:
Be prepared to start adjusting your stock portfolio well in advance of 2056.

SOURCES

Bracken, James, *Che Boludo*, Ediciones Continente, 2005

Brooks, John, *The South American Handbook*, The Mendip Press, 1954

Coleman, John, *Coleman's Drive*, Faber and Faber, 1962

Guevara, Ernesto, *The Motorcycle Diaries*, Ocean Press, 2003

Guinness World Records (author), *Guinness World Records*, Jim Pattison Group, 2019

Meegan, George, *The Longest Walk*, Dodd Mead, 1988

Moreno, Francisco P., *Perito Moreno's Travel Journal, A Personal Reminiscence*, El Elefante Blanco, 2002

Snow, S., *The Rucksack Man*, Hodder & Stoughton Limited, 1977

Tschiffely, A.F., *Southern Cross to Pole Star*, Windmill Press, Surrey, 1933

Von Däniken, Erich, *Chariots of the Gods*, Bantam Books Inc., 1972

Made in the USA
Columbia, SC
05 June 2025